The Idea of English Ethnicity

N
1
=

D1323372

Blackwell Manifestos

In this new series major critics make timely interventions to address important concepts and subjects, including topics as diverse as, for example: Culture, Race, Religion, History, Society, Geography, Literature, Literary Theory, Shakespeare, Cinema, and Modernism. Written accessibly and with verve and spirit, these books follow no uniform prescription but set out to engage and challenge the broadest range of readers, from undergraduates to postgraduates, university teachers and general readers – all those, in short, interested in on-going debates and controversies in the humanities and social sciences.

Already Published

The Idea of English Ethnicity

Robert J. C. Young

Blackwell
Publishing

BLACKWELL PUBLISHING
350 Main Street, Malden, MA 02148–5020, USA
9600 Garsington Road, Oxford OX4 2DQ, UK
550 Swanston Street, Carlton, Victoria 3053, Australia

First published 2008 by Blackwell Publishing Ltd

1   2008

Library of Congress Cataloging-in-Publication Data

Young, Robert, 1950–
    The idea of English ethnicity / Robert J.C. Young.
        p. cm.—(Blackwell manifestos)
    Includes bibliographical references (p.) and index.
    ISBN 978-1-4051-0128-8 (hardcover : alk. paper)—ISBN 978-1-4051-0129-5 (pbk. : alk. paper) 1.
National characteristics, English. 2. Ethnology—Great Britain. 3. Group identity—Great Britain. 4. Great Britain—Civilization. I. Title.
    DA118.Y67 2007
    305.82′1—dc22

                                                  2007008016

A catalogue record for this title is available from the British Library.

Set in 11.5/13.5pt Bembo
by SPi Publisher Services, Pondicherry, India.
Printed and bound in Singapore
by C.O.S Printers Pte Ltd

For further information on
Blackwell Publishing, visit our website at
www.blackwellpublishing.com

For Isaac

Contents

Figures

Preface

The title of this book, *The Idea of English Ethnicity*, addresses something which many people would say doesn't exist. English ethnicity? Irish, Welsh, Scottish, yes, but English? People don't regard 'English' as an ethnicity. Why is this the case?

The answer which I offer here involves a deliberate anachronism: through a return to the past, to the days before the concept of 'ethnicity' was invented. 'Ethnicity' was first differentiated from 'race' in 1941.[1] 'Ethnic' was used in the nineteenth century, but either in its original meaning of 'pagan' (as in 'ethnic civilization') or as yet another synonym for race or nation ('Pertaining to race; peculiar to a race or nation; ethnological', OED). Ethnic in the modern sense of an ethnic group was suggested by Julian Huxley and A. C. Haddon in 1936 as a replacement for the term 'race'. This was taken up by UNESCO (of which Huxley was the first Director-General) in 1945, as part of the post-Nazi assault on ideas of 'race', a successful strategy in which an idea founded on biological science was turned into a question of culture. The simple difference between race and ethnicity is that if race emphasizes nature rather than nurture, ethnicity emphasizes nurture rather than nature. This makes it just a bit too simple, however, for neither occupies exclusive ends of the spectrum. Could a blond Anglo-Saxon plausibly claim to be a Bengali? There is always a little bit of nature left within ethnicity.[2]

One problem with replacing 'race' by 'ethnicity' is that race meant so many things in the past. Ideas about 'race' did not always depend on the new science of biology. If Huxley's idea was to replace nature with culture, what do we do with those accounts of race in the past that were primarily cultural? It could be argued that if race as it is defined today must always involve biology, then those ideas of 'race' that antedated biology should be considered forms of ethnicity. So it was originally with English 'Saxonism'. Since English ideas of 'race' preceded biology, and biological racial science, you could say that what got racialized was an earlier idea of an ethnicity, a new version of which without biology has now reasserted itself back into an ethnicity. Because 'race' is defined by reference to biology, I shall at times use the term 'ethnicity' primarily to emphasize the extent to which many versions of the biologistic racial science of the nineteenth century remained decisively cultural. As ideas of nation, race and racial identity developed in the nineteenth century, it was probably inevitable that the mixed peoples of the British Isles, along with the rest of Europe, began to be characterized in racial terms. When racial science was deployed in the case of the English, however, it was used to challenge the exclusive claims of Saxonism, the ideology that had made the strongest racial claims for the English. This book tells that story. It is a story not of the elaboration of English racial identity as national character – but of its progressive diffusion.

For the end of Saxonism led to the adoption of a new identity, in which Englishness was an attribute of the English, but no longer directly connected to England as such, rather taking the form of a global racial and cultural identity – of 'Anglo-Saxons'. Though it is easy to assume that they mean the same thing, Anglo-Saxons were not just Saxon, that is, were not just English – they included Americans, and the English everywhere. The racial status of this new identity was deliberately left vague; certainly there were no attempts to give it the standing of hard science – in practice individuals or groups emphasized a racial component or not according to their prejudices and political needs. Most writers were fairly cavalier about the details, certainly with regard to any 'scientific' basis, which they tended to assume but not want to enquire into too deeply. It was the historian E. A. Freeman who saw most clearly that the idea of race at this level had developed its own popular political trajectory that was not necessarily consonant with what the philologists and scientists were saying. Though often projected in racial terms, the primary identity of this international English character was cultural and linguistic, and for this reason it seems not grossly illegitimate to characterize it as a form of soft racialism, or even anachronistically as an early kind of ethnicity. There was, after all, no other word for it at that time. The global identity created for the ethnic English may account for why, with the resurgence of minor nationalism in the UK since the 1980s, there was no specific language of English identity available for the people of England. Yet the way that English ethnicity was developed, I argue, has persisted in other ways – above all, that its development as a liberal form of 'soft racialism' was inclusive rather than exclusive.

Though it is anachronistic to use the term 'ethnicity', therefore, the English definition of themselves in terms of an English race was so elastic as only to have a tangential relation to biological racial science. This is not to say that English ethnic or racial identity did not involve forms of racism, racist assumptions of superiority, both of which increased in the later nineteenth century. To affirm the liberal tradition does not require the denial of its residual racialism. It does help to explain, however, why, in the second half of the twentieth century, it was comparatively easy to transform it in a positive way.

I am very grateful to the British Academy for giving me research leave which allowed me to begin this project, and to New York University for leave which enabled me to finish it. In many ways, it has developed out of the domestic part of a previous book, *Colonial Desire: Hybridity in Theory, Culture and Race* (Routledge, 1995); an early version of some of the material presented here was published then as "Hybridism and the Ethnicity of the English', in *Reflections on the Work of Edward W. Said: Cultural Identity and the Gravity of History,* ed. Benita Parry and Judith Squires (London: Lawrence and Wishart, 1996), 127–50.

I would like to thank the many people who have talked to me over the years about the ideas of this book, particularly those who have responded to lectures that I have given, suitably enough, in view of the story told here, in many places around the world, though not always Anglo-Saxon ones. A special thank you is owed to to Isobel Armstrong, Derek Attridge, Homi K. Bhabha, Maud Ellmann, Leela Gandhi, Paul Gilroy, Jo McDonagh, Matthew Meadows, Parvati Nair and Vron Ware. I am really grateful to Heather Zuber for volunteering assistance at a late moment and helping me to find elusive material and references with superb efficiency, to say nothing of correcting my own bibliographical eccentricities. I should also like to thank my dear former colleagues at Wadham College: the late, and lamented, Tim Binyon, Robin Fiddian, John Gurney, Christina Howells, Ankhi Mukherjee, Bernard O'Donoghue, Robin Robbins and Reza Sheikoleslami; at NYU, Emily Apter, Patrick Deer, Elaine Freedgood, Dick Foley, Toral Gajarawala, John Guillory, Hal Momma, Mary Poovey, Rajeswari Sunder Rajan, Cliff Siskin, John Waters and Jini Watson; and also Gillian Beer, Elleke Boehmer, Peter Burke, Allison Donnell, Rita Kothari, Peter McDonald, the late Colin Matthew, Bryan Sykes and Megan Vaughan. Andrew McNeillie and then Emma Bennett at Blackwell showed both exemplary support and patience. I am very grateful once again to Jack Messenger for painstaking copy-editing and guidance through the proofs. My father and mother both taught me much if not most of what I know about Englishness, and everything here is in some sense an appreciative filial response to their benign influence. My own family have taught me about a different Englishness, and I am grateful to Badral, and to Maryam, Yasi and Isaac for their love for their English (that is English, Irish and Scottish) father, and for their boundless enthusiasm for English cricket and football. This book is dedicated to Isaac, footballer *extraordinaire*, and best of sons.

Introduction: Exodus

Diaspora

In recent years, particularly since devolution in the UK, the question of what exactly constitutes the identity of England and of Englishness has exercised a whole range of cultural commentators.[1] This uncertainty about Englishness arises from more than just the challenges of devolution, or even the end of empire. It is also the long-term result of the ways in which, going back to the nineteenth and early twentieth centuries, Englishness was never really about England, its cultural essence or national character, at all.

The concept of Englishness in the nineteenth century was not so much developed as a self-definition of the English themselves, as a way of characterizing the essence of their national identity – after all, being English already, they hardly needed it. It was rather elaborated as a variety of what Benedict Anderson has called 'long-distance nationalism', though of a distinct kind.[2] Rather than being the creation of the far-off diasporic community, as Anderson describes, Englishness was created for the diaspora – an ethnic identity designed for those who were precisely not English, but rather of English descent – the peoples of the English diaspora moving around the world: Americans, Canadians, Australians, New Zealanders, South Africans, even, at a pinch, the English working class. Englishness was constructed as a translatable identity that could be adopted or appropriated anywhere by anyone who cultivated the right language, looks, and culture. It then allowed a common identification with a homeland that had often never been seen. Englishness paradoxically became most itself when it was far off.

In 1914, this paradoxical identity of Englishness was formulated forever in a poem that was taken to represent the highest expression of patriotism. Great Britain was at war with Germany, but the poem which in its moment caught the emotion and imagination of the entire nation was a poem about England. While commentators today spend much time trying to distinguish them, the fact remains that until the last decades of the twentieth century, England was commonly used as a synonym for Britain, and indeed was used far more often. 'Britishness' is a recent invention. In this poem, in the space of a fourteen-line sonnet, England or the English are evoked six times. What is noticeable is that this classic poem of Englishness is about not being in England:

> If I should die, think only this of me:
> That there's some corner of a foreign field
> That is for ever England.[3]

The soldier is most English when he envisages his death abroad. Here, Rupert Brooke unnervingly put his finger on the paradox of Englishness as it had come to be understood at that moment – whereby his dying body could extend its Englishness into the material soil of a far-off foreign place. In the poem that came to define national sentiment during the First World War, the poem that generated an overwhelming popular response across the country, the inextricable mix of Englishness with foreignness staged the paradox whereby Englishness was best defined, produced, created when the English body was dissolved into the soil of the foreign. The enriching dust of 'A body of England's' is in turn made rich in its Englishness by its distance from home. The Englishman is most English when he creates a new England far away, in the corner of a foreign field. As with Brooke, it is when he is away from home that the

Englishman becomes most English. It is distance itself that enables the identification with Englishness: 'Oh to be in England / Now that April's here...'. Which is perhaps why, even today, when you encounter someone who presents the appearance of being most authentically English, you inevitably discover that they were born in the USA, Canada, Australia, South Africa, or even Germany. The history of English writers and intellectuals is full of such Anglophile characters masquerading as Englishmen: Friedrich Max Müller, Henry James, Joseph Conrad and T. S. Eliot, for example, or, more interestingly, V. S. Naipaul. To say nothing of Sir Lewis Namier, Sir Karl Popper, Sir Isaiah Berlin, Sir Nicolaus Pevsner, and many others. The point, though, is not that they were inauthentic Englishmen masquerading as authentic ones: rather, that in their time authentic Englishness was itself transformed into a mode of masquerade that was best performed far from home, a global identity into which others could always translate themselves, however distant from England their place of birth. Ask Oscar Wilde – as an Irishman, he knew. 'Most people are other people', he observed, 'their lives a mimicry'.[4]

London

LADY BRACKNELL. *With a shiver, crossing to the sofa and sitting down.* I think some preliminary inquiry on my part would not be out of place. Mr. Worthing, is Miss Cardew at all connected with any of the larger railway stations in London? I merely desire information. Until yesterday I had no idea that there were any families or persons whose origin was a Terminus.[5]

It has become common to claim that 'Englishness' is in a state of terminal decline. At first, therefore, it's somewhat alarming to discover even Henry James, at the beginning of *English Hours* (1888–1905), writing of his enormous enthusiasm for the larger railway stations of London. For James, needless to say, London is hardly in

3

a state of terminal decomposition, but it does turn out that its pleasures are as much about leaving as arriving:

> Of course it is too much to say that all the satisfaction of life in London comes from literally living there, for it is not a paradox that a great deal of it consists in getting away. It is almost easier to leave it than not to, and much of its richness and interest proceeds from its ramifications, the fact that all England is in a suburban relation to it.[6]

As 'an adoptive son' of England (a claim he quickly proves by using the terms English and British as synonyms), James freely admits that he has submitted to what he calls 'Londonisation', adding, 'it is a real stroke of luck ... that the capital of the human race happens to be British'.[7] In fact, James adds enthusiastically, for the London-lover,

> It is perfectly open to him to consider the remainder of the United Kingdom, or the British empire in general, or even, if he be an American, the total of the English-speaking territories of the globe, as the mere margin, the fitted girdle.[8]

Not only Britain itself, therefore, but the entire English-speaking world exists, according to James, in a suburban relation to the capital: on the one hand its 'mere margin', but on the other, a girdle, centred in the capital, that has been fitted around the globe.[9] London becomes the navel of the world, the terminus from which all English people originate, and to which, in spirit if not in body, they return. And yet while they perform such dreams of homecoming, the paradox is that this can only occur in so far as much of the satisfaction of London 'consists in getting away': London may be 'the heart of the world', as Carlyle told an Emerson who had been drawn from the far-off hamlet of Concord to visit it ('he liked the huge machine', Emerson reported), but the dynamic role of London is also to be the place of exodus, of migration and renewed departures.[10] The moving machinery of London creates a strange economy of alienation and estrangement from the centre, repeatedly translating the English around the world to haunt its furthest borders where they become at once other and by the same token, more English, in a distant, uncanny doubling of the origin.

The fascination of the capital is thus counter-intuitive, for going there continually encourages you to leave for the broad girth of the other English world beyond: hence the importance of its railway terminals, which operate literally as the hub and symbolically as the nub of these comings and goings. London evokes this sense of attachment and yet detachment, so that it is at once the centre and yet its qualities as centre point to its links to the furthest margins of the English-speaking world. The greatest satisfactions of London come from the enigma of arrival, about which James himself wrote with zest and enthusiasm many times, and the allure of departure. London, 'that mighty heart' of the human race pumping blood in and out through its arteries, catches you in its pulsing systolic rhythms of perpetual motion, continually drawing in and then as quickly running out from itself. It repeatedly entices you inwards, but at the very moment you arrive to enjoy its domestic comforts, the city irresistibly expels you out away towards the 'fitted girdle' of its furthest provinces:

> It is for this reason – because I like to think how great we all are together in the light of heaven and the face of the rest of the world, with the bond of our glorious tongue, in which we labour to write articles and our books for each other's candid perusal, how great we all are and how great is the great city which we may unite fraternally to regard as the capital of our race – is it for this reason that I have a singular kindness for the London railway-stations, that I like them aesthetically, that they interest me and fascinate me, and that I view them with complacency even when I wish neither to depart nor to arrive? They remind me of all our reciprocities and activities, our energies and curiosities, and our being all distinguished together from other people by our great common stamp of perpetual motion, our passion for seas and deserts and the other side of the globe, the secret of the impression of strength – I don't say of social roundness and finish – that we produce in any collection of Anglo-Saxon types.[11]

The real interest of London for James rests on its role not so much as the capital of the human race as the capital of 'our race': its terminals perform and enact the 'great common stamp' of the perpetual motion and bustling energy of the Anglo-Saxon, whose 'types' can be found around the globe. London is not the capital of England, nor of Great Britain, nor even of the Empire, but of the whole Anglo-Saxon world. This world, peopled with varieties of Anglo-Saxons, is, according to James, drawn together 'with the bond of our glorious tongue, in which we labour to write articles and our books for each other's candid perusal'. It is, finally, English itself, at once spoken in intimate exchanges and written for reading from afar, whether in letters, telegrams, newspapers, magazines or books, which holds the Anglo-Saxon world together fraternally in its impatient, perpetual circulations.

In suggesting that English identity is actually 'our great common stamp of perpetual motion', James' image collates an image of violent stasis – the stamp – with the movement of diaspora, so that his enduring racial type is combined with dispersal to form English identity; a nomadic movement of sameness around the globe, of migrants who refuse to stop, to be rooted elsewhere. These journeys of identification and estrangement at the centre of English life which James evokes so intoxicatingly, tell us something of the dynamic identity of Englishness, in its literary, popular and political forms, as they developed in the nineteenth century. By 1888, the year of James' original essay, this restless sense of affectionate, emotional connection to England, yet detachment from it, a perpetual leaving, had becam a distinctive characteristic. For its adoptive, fugitive or questing subjects around the world, being English involved an ungovernable ambivalence of distance and desire, of attachment to England, yet remoteness from it – of being drawn in to identify with it most of all when you found yourself on the seas and deserts at the edges of the English-speaking world. The more that Englishness found itself emptied out, a kind of absent centre moving westwards, the more it operated by a structure of desire, whereby the taking on of Englishness was structured as a diasporic return if not to England, then to an English heaven. This dialectic of attachment to England, yet distance from it, of continuity and rupture, similarity and difference, became the dominant characteristic of Englishness itself – not Englishness in the sense of the local identity of the English, but Englishness as a diasporic identity around the world which simultaneously asserted a grounding in the past and continuity with the centre, and the distance of rupture, displacement, migration, colonization. The origins of Englishness indeed, in some sense, as Lady Bracknell suggests, rested in a terminus, a place of departure, in the energy 'of perpetual motion', of 'passion for seas and deserts and the other side of the globe', of Anglo-Saxon types held together in continuity and difference in the last instance by nothing more than type, language, manners and culture. London itself, unlike Paris for the French, has never functioned as a token of Englishness, only as the imperial capital, 'that compound of all the earth', as Robert Knox put it in 1850, bristling with the people and the goods of empire.

The Country

A telling anticipation of this combination of sameness and difference, of identification and estrangement at the centre of English culture which James evokes so powerfully can be found in one of the most famous books of the nineteenth century, Thomas Hughes' *Tom Brown's Schooldays*, published thirty odd years earlier in 1857, the year of the Indian Mutiny, and nine years after the moment in 1848 when Hughes, Charles Kingsley, F. D. Maurice and J. M. Ludlow had met to form the Christian Socialists, a group whose aim was to resolve the revolutionary class war that seemed about to break out.[12] The popularity of the book was such that it went into at least seventy editions while it remained in copyright. The book combines two apparently contradictory but intimate moments in the formation of a harmonious English identity, here centred around the relation to the countryside.

7

Self-consciously addressing an English audience, Hughes berates his boy readers for not developing a greater sense of national affiliation to their English inheritance – 'Oh, young England! Young England!' he exclaims, invoking a conservative vision of a return to a feudal social fabric in which aristocrat and peasant bond together once more, 'Why don't you know more of your own birthplaces?' Hughes invokes in particular the Saxon inheritance of their local landscapes, such as he himself finds in his native Uffington:

> And these are the sort of things you may find, I believe, every one of you, in any common English country neighbourhood.
>
> Will you look for them under your own noses, or will you not? Well, well; I've done what I can to make you, and if you will go gadding over half Europe now every holidays, I can't help it. I was born and bred a west-country man, thank God! A Wessex man, a citizen of the noblest Saxon kingdom of Wessex, a regular 'Angular Saxon', the very soul of me *adscriptus glebae* [attached to the soil]. There's nothing like the old country-side for me, and no music like the twang of the real old Saxon tongue.[13]

We learn, here, that the reader to whom this book is addressed is implicitly middle class, able to go off gadding about Europe in the holidays. Hughes, though, wants him to translate himself in class terms and bond together with the rural sons of the soil, who are in turn themselves bonded to the soil (*adscriptus glebae*), like the serfs of old. To do this, the young man must free himself not so much from his own class as such, but from the women of his class.

While stressing an attachment to things English and Saxon, to home and to the land, the 'robust and combative' Tom Brown fights his 'first war of independence' against the women of the family (20–2). Rejecting the attentions of his mother, Tom is effectively brought up by local men, particularly the rustic 'Old Benjy' who initiates him into the traditional games of back-swording and wrestling, and other boyish village pursuits. At the age of eleven, however, he leaves his local milieu for Rugby and the brotherhood of his peers – the account of which forms the major part of the book, consisting largely of stories of games, more fighting, and other boyish outdoor activities. The boys seem to do very little academic work, and repress all thoughts of family, lest they become 'softened and less manly for thinking of home' (204). Symptomatically, before he leaves for Rugby, Tom himself stipulates that any hugging or kissing between father and son must now stop, and they part on a reserved shake of the hand. The detachment is complete and completed.

This paradox, of a deep, primary affection for the English countryside at the same moment as the young Saxon Englishmen severs his relations with his family and sets out, off into the wider world beyond, speaks volumes about how being English was imagined in the mid-nineteenth century. It involves an attachment to the landscape, enforced through a detachment and displacement from the maternal home environment, together with a certain class mobility whereby the middle-class youngster is brought up as one of the village folk, Saxons all. He then reasserts himself, however, as a member of the privileged elite who goes far away to board at a 'public' school. Tom's journey to Rugby anticipates voyages further afield (Hughes himself would found a new Rugby in Tennessee in 1880): as he later watches a cricket match, a master remarks approvingly of the headmaster, a portrait of Thomas Arnold: 'Perhaps ours is the only little corner of the British Empire which is thoroughly, wisely, and strongly ruled just now' (304).

The Brown family is, as the common surname suggests, a deliberately ordinary 'middle England' family. It is not by chance that the most ordinary English surname is not White but Brown. Whiteness, even in England, is not an undifferentiated attribute. The Browns are those who bear the 'manly' ruddy complexion of work out of doors rather than the pale whiteness of aristocrats who do not work, or, for Kingsley, of unmanly intellectuals who linger inside with their books. These are the yeoman English whose end D. H. Lawrence announces with unabashed ambivalence in his short story, 'England, My England'. Tom Brown's face is as brown as his name, contrasted alike to any over-civilized 'whiteness', as well as to those who are unembarrassedly called 'wild niggers' (59, 265). Local folk as they are, the Browns are characterized as having developed a global reach: they are those who populate the fitted girdle of the global Anglo-Saxon world, working as the yeomen foot soldiers of the domestic and wider landscapes of the British Empire, even if the British nation remains unaware of how much of its greatness it owes to the Browns:

> For centuries, in their quiet, dogged, homespun way, they have been subduing the earth in most English counties, and leaving their marks in the American forests and Australian uplands. Wherever the fleets and armies of England have won renown, there stalwart sons of the Browns have done yeoman's work. (3)

The translation of this local Saxon ethnicity to James' global English-speaking fraternity of Saxon types also forms the story of Englishness in the nineteenth century. These are the yeoman stock of England, not those celebrated as the great generals or admirals who have won the empire in moments of victory, nor the aristocratic rulers, governor generals and Viceroys who rule India and other flagship colonies in pomp and ceremony, but rather the diasporic millions who have populated the English settlements. The Browns are the ordinary English colonizers of whom, by the end of the nineteenth century, there would be well over twenty million, one of the largest diasporas the world has ever seen.[14]

So the English performed a counterpoint to their own economic system of global circulation: whereas commodities and raw materials, such as cotton, flowed into London from all over the world, to be then re-exported back to their countries of origin as manufactured goods, so raw English people from abroad came to London for finishing before they returned to their point of origin as more wholly English, while the over-civilized city dwellers of England flowed abroad to take up the life of yeoman farmers in the great open spaces of the colonies, and so restored themselves, and their country, to a rude health by attaching themselves to the soil of foreign fields. 'Everything English', Emerson remarked in 1856, 'is a fusion of distant and antagonistic elements'.[15]

Chapter 1

Saxonism

> Every Englishman dislikes being lumped along with Scots, Irish,
> Welsh . . . as British
>
> Ford Madox Ford[1]

Some time ago, my employer asked me to complete an 'Equal
Opportunity Monitoring Form', based, it was said, on the categories
used for the 2001 Census of the United Kingdom. Part of it read as
follows:

> Please describe your ethnic origin: (*please tick one box only*)
> (*Ethnic origin questions are not about nationality, place of birth, or citizenship.
> They are about colour and ethnic group. Citizens of any country may belong to
> any of the groups indicated . . .*)
> WHITE
> British
> Irish
> Any other White background

Officially, therefore, 'White British' describes your ethnic group if
you are . . . white British. Yet who, in Britain, thinks of 'Britishness'
as an ethnicity? Being 'British' is not an ethnicity, it describes citizenship of the United Kingdom, a term cooked up in 1603 by the
Scottish King James I, after he had ascended to the English throne on
the death of Elizabeth I, as a way of pulling together the parts of his
new kingdom of South and North Britain, which together would

make up 'Great Britain', or more grandly, as he called it, the 'British Empire'. As Linda Colley has shown, 'British' has always been a particularly Scottish thing, precisely designed to distinguish between citizenship, nationality and ethnicity.[2] Now extended to other ethnicities, the concept 'Britishness' was invented as a cultural identity corresponding to the political identity, British, only fairly recently. The OED records just two uses of the term 'Britishness' before 1904. In the nineteenth century, 'British' was as likely to be used to describe the ancient Britons who preceded the Saxons as the modern inhabitants of the British Isles – in a time when the English identified strongly with the Saxons, to call themselves British could give out the wrong connotations.[3] Moreover, Britain is not and never has been a nation, any more than it is an ethnicity: it is a confederation of nations. 'Great Britain' is made up of England, Wales and Scotland. The 'United Kingdom' includes one more (or rather part of one more), Northern Ireland. Officially, therefore, the 'United Kingdom of Great Britain and Northern Ireland' is a United Kingdom of three nations plus another bit which seems not to be another nation united with the rest, but one which finds its identity through another nation, which is not (now) part of the United Kingdom.

The United Kingdom of Great Britain and Northern Ireland is the only country on earth allowed to field four national teams in international football and rugby (cricket is more complicated: 'England' represents England and Wales, 'Ireland' a united Ireland, North and South, and Scotland itself). When you go on a plane to the USA, and are told how to fill in your US visa form, when it comes to the line where you have to state your nationality, you are given strict instructions not to say that you are British but to put 'UK'. The Department of Homeland Security will accept no alternatives – certainly not 'British'. Which only goes to prove that the term 'British' represents many things, often ambiguous, but never an ethnicity – unless, of course, it is attached to an ethnic marker, such as 'British Asian'. English, Scottish or Welsh are the only categories that white people would apply to themselves in Britain in the context of ethnicity – as is signalled in the monitoring form by the alternative possibility of being Irish. The Welsh and Scots would doubtless have preferred to have been allowed their own ethnicity and nationality in the census form (Northern Irish Protestants would no doubt tick 'British', Catholics 'Irish'). Presumably the Welsh and Scots were not differentiated because that would have meant offering a separate category for the English. And this poses the important question, can 'English' really be an ethnicity? Yet if being Scots, Welsh or Irish is by common assent regarded as an ethnicity, why should being English not be an ethnicity?

One of the most striking things about all the recent attempts to characterize Englishness is that it is rarely defined as an ethnicity. The English are neither an ethnic minority nor ethnic majority. Yet the attempt to characterize the English as an ethnic or racial group was in many ways the origin of modern accounts of Englishness itself. In today's terms, Englishness may not be an ethnicity, but English was certainly once used to describe a race, and a top one at that by all accounts that you read of 'this island race'. Today, it is customary to portray the racialism of the nineteenth century as 'pseudo-scientific', and to assume that it was mostly designed to denigrate non-European or colonized peoples. While such denigration was clearly central to racial theory, modern readers tend be so appalled by what was said about Africans and other non-Europeans that they do not notice that much of the research on race, certainly from the 1840s onwards, was devoted to analyses of European ethnicity, the culminating works of which were John Beddoe's *The Races of Britain* (1885) and William Ripley's *The Races of Europe* (1900).[4] Ripley's *Selected Bibliography of the Anthropology and Ethnography of Europe*, published in 1899, runs to 159 pages.[5] The Victorians themselves were in fact far more pre-occupied with a complex elaboration of European racial differences and alliances than with what they perceived to be the relatively straightforward task of distinguishing between European and non-European races. Of this European racial science, only anti-Semitism is widely known, but anti-Semitism was itself the product of a much wider project of analysing European races and scrutinizing European racial identity, for which anti-Semitism provided a foil. In the nine-teenth century, the differences between European races and their national characteristics were increasingly emphasized in response to growing imperial competitiveness.

Charting European ethnicity has recently returned to favour in the realm of anthropology and genetics. In 1994, a book called *The Times Guide to the Peoples of Europe*, which was capitalizing on the re-emergence of ethnic nationalism after the break up of the Soviet Union and Yugoslavia, offered itself as a piece of anthropology in which sophisticated modern Europe was represented as a collection of ethnic groups.[6] In 2005, David Miles followed this with the *The Tribes of Britain*, while the next year Brian Sykes published the startling results of his archaeological genetics of Britain in *The Blood of the Isles*.[7] This tracing of British and European ethnicity is part of a long tradition.

The Racial Past of England

> There are probably few educated Englishmen living who have not in their infancy been taught that the English nation is a nation of almost pure Teutonic blood, that its political constitution, its social customs, its internal prosperity, the success of its arms, and the number of its colonies have all followed necessarily upon the arrival, in three vessels, of certain German warriors under the command of Hengist and Horsa.
>
> Luke Owen Pike, *The English and Their Origin* (1866)[8]

While nineteenth-century anthropologists such as E. B. Tylor and James Frazer became obsessed with the question of how much the primitive past survived in European culture, British historians grew equally preoccupied with the survival of the national past, and the question of the origin of the English nation (only rarely did they think in terms of the origin of the British nation, still less of the origin of the United Kingdom. How many times do you see the title *History of the United Kingdom* or *Great Britain* compared to *History of England*?).[9]

For the historians, to ask who the English were inevitably moved to the question of where they came from. Broadly speaking, as Hugh MacDougal shows in *Racial Myth in English History* (1982), there have been two myths of racial origin developed for the English, which we may call the myth of Arthur versus the myth of Alfred.[10] To promote Arthur or Alfred in the nineteenth century was a highly political project.[11]

The first historical myth put forward by Geoffrey of Monmouth in the twelfth century, and subsequently elaborated by Malory in the fifteenth, was, as the story is generally told, that Britain had originally been peopled by what are now called Celts, and triumphally led by the heroic King Arthur. Eventually the conquering Arthur came to be seen as the hero of the whole population, uniting the Britons with the Angles and Saxons and drawing them together into a single British nation. The Arthurian myth was used actively by Plantagenet, Tudor and Stuart monarchs, to suggest that they were the legitimate heirs of the early British kings, and to link them to romantic British history. As the process of unifying the country developed after 1603, the Arthurian myth was invoked to symbolize the idea of a composite nation. The new nationality, in this inscription, was fundamentally identified as British (Old English *Bryttisc*), deliberately invoking the pre-Roman ancient Britons. The reference of the term was gradually broadened to include not only Saxons and Normans but any inhabitant of the British Empire, wherever they might be. In the seventeenth century, however, the figure of the inclusive Arthur was unable to resolve the growing religious division between Catholics and Protestants, and the Protestant fear of a Popish conspiracy to return the country to the ecclesiastical rule of Rome.

As religious anxiety increased in the sixteenth century, the power of the Arthurian myth began to wane and was effectively eliminated in the political sphere by the so-called Glorious Revolution of 1688. With the arrival of the Hanoverian King from Germany, the old

Arthurian narrative gave way to an alternative Whig history, which stressed the nation's English and Protestant identity and its Saxon constitutional freedoms. Protestantism was always (ahistorically) Saxon and English. The Arthur who had united the diverse inhabitants of Britain was replaced by an identification with the Saxon English Alfred, described in the *Proverbs of Alfred* as:

> Englene hurde,
> Englene durlyng;
> On Engle-londe he was kyng.
>
> guardian of the English,
> darling of the English,
> he was king in the land of the English.[12]

In the nineteenth century, Alfred effectively became the national patron saint – indeed it was suggested by some that he replace St George. The Victorians celebrated the millennium of the birth and death of 'England's darling' in novels, history books, children's books, plays, pageants and statues, produced from English-speaking countries all around the globe.[13] If Alfred began life as a Saxon, by 1901 he had become an Anglo-Saxon.[14] The use of the term 'Anglo-Saxon' to describe modern Saxons, that is English, rather than the historical Anglo-Saxon people and their language, came into favour in England in the mid-nineteenth century, as will be shown in chapter 6. This usage seems to have been invented around the time of the American Revolution for the (formerly) English colonists who adopted the name of the English ancestors with whom they most identified.

The new myth of English origins appropriate to and appropriated for the aftermath of the Glorious Revolution began by characterizing the English as Saxons, Teutons, Goths or Germans, all of which were in practice more or less synonymous, since the terms could never be defined precisely. This racial identification replaced the earlier historical myth in which the English had thought of themselves as a mix of Celts, Vikings, Angles, Saxons, Jutes and others. Now the

English were Saxons, pure and simple (the various Germanic and northern tribes all being assimilated to this one name, though some preferred more general alternatives, such as Teuton, or, simply, German). It was this ideology of Saxonist purity that prompted Defoe's famous poem 'The True Born Englishman' of 1701, in which he satirized the pretensions of the Englishman to have a pedigree as pure as his horse and cattle:

> Thus from a Mixture of all Kinds began,
> That Het'rogeneous Thing, *An Englishman*:
> In eager Rapes, and furious Lust begot,
> Betwixt a Painted *Britton* and a *Scot*:
> Whose gend'ring Offspring quickly learnt to bow,
> And yoke their Heifers to the *Roman* Plough:
> From whence a Mongrel half-bred Race there came,
> With neither Name nor Nation, Speech or Fame.
> In whose hot Veins new Mixtures quickly ran,
> Infus'd betwixt a *Saxon* and a *Dane*.
> While their Rank Daughters, to their Parents just,
> Receiv'd all Nations with Promiscuous Lust.
> This Nauseous Brood directly did contain
> The well-extracted Blood of *Englishmen*.[15]

The effective response to Defoe's argument from the 1840s onwards was to characterize all these groups in terms of 'race' – and according to racial theory, they were either all Teutons anyway (for example, Saxons and Danes), or trivial in terms of their input (Britons, Romans).

From the seventeenth century onwards, the English (and not just those we would now call English) began thinking of themselves as Saxon in a variety of ways: in terms of the lineage of their King, their church, their language, and in terms of where one particular set of the great variety of their ancestor invaders had come from (interest here focused on the various Saxons, who were then linked to the Danes, the Vikings, the Belgae, even at times the Normans). The Saxon set, as they might be called, though vaguely defined and linked to a host of successive invasions, could always be anchored in the reign, four centuries later, of King Alfred (c. 870), and before that in the documented arrival of the 'real' English with Hengist and Horsa and the Saxon invaders who landed at Ebbsfield, Kent, in 449, a historical narrative of 'our island story' that would be parodied mercilessly in Sellar and Yeatman's *1066 and All That* (1930):

> The brutal Saxon invaders drove the Britons westward into Wales and compelled them to become Welsh; it is now considered doubtful whether this was a Good Thing. Memorable among the Saxon warriors were Hengist and his wife (? or horse), Horsa.... The country was now almost entirely inhabited by Saxons and was therefore renamed England, and thus (naturally) soon became C. of E. This was a Good Thing.[16]

Saxon identity was fundamentally rooted in the national characteristics attributed to the Germans by Tacitus, and from that basis then demarcated by being contrasted with two other groups, the Celts, described as the ancient native Britons, surviving in the Scottish highlands, Wales, Ireland and parts of France, and associated with Roman Catholicism, and, to a much lesser extent, the Jews, the most substantial other presence throughout most of recorded English history whose identity and religion had remained distinct. Where the native Celtic Britons had not been pushed back to the Celtic fringes of Wales, Scotland and Ireland, they had been exterminated: as David Hume suggested without a trace of scepticism in his *History of England* (1754–62), the English nation was founded on genocide.[17] (Even today, this remains a matter of debate, mysteriously circulating around two absences: the virtual absence of Celtic words in the English language, which seems to prove it, as against the absence of masses of skeletal remains, which seems to disprove it.) Hume's *History of England*, suitably written by a Scot, was written to counter the Whig narrative which presented the Stuarts as attacking ancient Saxon freedoms. The Whigs responded to Hume by starting their English history either from the Saxons, or from their modern reincarnation in seventeenth-century Protestants, as it suited them. The spirit of the narrative remained the same.

With the Celts conveniently exterminated or pushed back to the westerly margins by the Saxons, disaster struck. In 1066, Harold, the hero of the Anglo-Saxon kingdom, was himself killed by victorious Norman invaders, an image of heroic failure that itself presented a form of narrative of which the English would become particularly fond, perversely preferring heroic defeat to success itself – endemic to a whole succession of English heroes – Gordon of Khartoum, Scott of the Antarctic, and a role now frequently taken over by the England team in the European and World Cups. The nation was not born with the arrival of the Normans, but paradoxically it came into being at that moment of defeat, when the first invaders, who were the 'real' English, were defeated by the second invaders, the French Normans, who would have to be made English. Notice that the 'original' English, the Britons, figure nowhere at all in this narrative. The Saxons, having become English, would then subsequently work to anglicize the Normans in turn. The assimilation of the Normans represents the first instance of the idea that being English is something that you do not have to be born into but that you can become. As the historian E. A. Freeman put it at the beginning of *William the Conqueror* (1888):

> Our history has been largely wrought for us by men who have come in from without, sometimes as conquerors, sometimes as the opposite of conquerors; but in whatever character they came, they had to put on the character of Englishmen, and to make their work an English work. From whatever land they came, on whatever mission they came, as statesmen they were English.[18]

The Norman invasion showed that being English is something that you can 'put on': it is a perpetual process of becoming, a pursuit of authenticity in which the copy is allowed to be as authentic as any original. Being English was always about being out of place, about displacement from an earlier point of origin – but its dynamics can only be understood by realizing that there was rarely a prior moment of being in place.[19] From the Normans onwards, to be English was, literally, to be eccentric. Or at least to feel yourself so, which was why the attractions of moving off to the periphery were always a part of being from the centre. So Thomas Lawrence of 2, Polstead Road, Oxford, became Lawrence of Arabia.

Whereas the nation had been founded through its first invasion, the second – the arrival of the Normans under William the Conqueror in 1066 – was widely regarded as an infringement of the true racial and cultural identity of the Saxon English. Historians identifying with the Saxons therefore drew on the thesis of 'the Norman yoke', which portrayed English history as the story of the struggle against the invaders, who were eventually successfully assimilated: the Saxons eventually conquered their conquerors.[20] The bovine metaphor of the yoke had become popular at the time of the English Revolution in the seventeenth century, during the conflict between the Commons and the King. It remained embodied in popular culture thereafter, the best-known example being the struggle of Robin Hood against the Sheriff of Nottingham. Robin Hood in fact became far more popular than either Alfred or Harold ever managed to be. The significance of Magna Carta was magnified to emphasize the political liberty supposed to be intrinsic to the Saxon race (though it was in fact Edward Coke who, in his reorganization of English common law in the seventeenth century, had extended the basis of Magna Carta beyond the nobility), and celebrated as the beginning of the process of the English freeing themselves from the shackles of the Norman yoke. In the nineteenth century, the apogee of this view was developed by Freeman, said never to have recovered from the happy accident of his name: it was Freeman who developed most fully the popular ideology that intrinsic to the Saxon character were the qualities of Protestantism, freedom and liberty.[21] Saxon boys' names such as Alfred, Archibald, Clifford, Dudley, Harold and Winston became popular. Though Queen Victoria is represented as a Saxon Queen, alongside Prince Albert as a Saxon chief, in William Theed's monument in Windsor Chapel, Saxonism rarely applied to girls. For there was always an implicit gender division in operation: to be Saxon was to be masculine. The feminine was Celtic.

The reasons for this dramatic reorientation of national history were largely religious and political: from the time of the Reformation, when England became Protestant, and even more from the time of the 'Glorious Revolution' of 1688 when, under threat from a Catholic-sympathizing King James II, Parliament had brought in the fiercely Protestant German William of Orange as King, the English had identified with the Protestant Germans as opposed to the Catholic Celtic French. The ideological design of this Saxon supremacist myth of English origin was to legitimate not only the Hanoverians, but also the Reformation, and to provide a historical genealogy for its national institution, the Church of England. Saxonism was always closely identified with English Protestant values, which accounts among other things for its popularity among white Protestants in the United States.[22] For the English, the Saxon affiliations with the Teutonic Germans perfectly encapsulated a Protestant solidarity against the wiles of Catholicism and the French. Decades of struggle against the French during the Napoleonic Wars with France only reinforced the desire to assume a Germanic identity, and it was above all from this time that the English increasingly claimed that they were Saxons rather than Celts. They did so for another reason, closer to home: after the Act of Union between Britain and Ireland of 1801, effected in the aftermath of the French-assisted Irish rebellion of 1798, the English had found themselves in the embarrassing position of being united with their rebellious Celtic, Catholic other. Their response was to emphasize their own stable Saxon identity.

'Our English Race is the German Race': Saxonism and 'Stock'

These two myths, Arthur and Alfred, one dominant, while the other faded away only to re-emerge, circulated in a dialectical economy with each other: the one a story of return to the centre, of origins, the

21

other a tale of dispersal, of scattered peoples girding the country, and then girdling the earth, trying to hold on to a collective identity, even if in the perpetual return to Camelot, the centre was lost, absent, wounded like Arthur himself, with a lack at the origin. The one ran as the negative inside the other like a mobius strip of alterity, poetry inside prose, prose lurking within poetry, propelling each other in a relay of restless goings forth and returns. Despite their differences, there were similarities. Both told the story of ancient arrivals, subsequent defeats, expulsions, moving onwards, of riding westward. The origin of English origins was never an originary source of nativism – it was always the appearance of those who came from an elsewhere, a beyond to which they would, in time, return. Nothing captures the formation of Englishness better than these restless circuits of arrivals and departures, comings and goings, immigration and emigration, mixtures and dispersals.

How do such myths of origin and identity get created, disseminate, become the object of belief? In particular, how do they become dominant in a culture in the face of alternative narratives and ideologies circulating in the collective memory? In the case of Arthur versus Alfred, in the literary domain the poets stayed largely loyal to Arthur and the Celts, and identified with their exalted bardic provenance. The writers of prose, the historians and historical novelists, essayists and historical philologists, the Cobbetts and Hazlitts of the world, by contrast, identified themselves with the plain-speaking Saxons, and it was they who were largely responsible for developing an exalted identity for the English as Saxon in language, culture and history.[23] While these identifications of the Saxons were always interlinked, they were developed across different disciplines which in certain respects remained relatively discrete from each other. There was nothing that quite brought the different interests together. Until the nineteenth century, when they were all linked up to the new ideas about race.

Although the golden age of Saxonism came in the nineteenth century, it drew on a long history: it was during the political upheavals of the seventeenth century that the radical parliamentarians and levellers first identified Anglo-Saxon culture with institutions of representative government and common law guaranteeing political freedom, and with a pure primitive form of English Christianity. This was the moment of the first scholarly interest in the Saxons, particularly their institutions and their language. By 1768 Stuart Gilbert, in his *An Historical Dissertation concerning the Antiquity of the English Constitution*, grounded his bald opening assertion that 'the foundation and principles of the Anglo-Saxon constitution, are to be found . . . in the institutions and manner of the ancient Germans', with an epigraph from Montesquieu:

> Si l'on veut lire l'admirable ouvrage de Tacite sur les moeurs des Germains, on verra que c'est d'eux que les Anglois ont tiré de leur gouvernement politique. Ce beau système a été trouvé dans les bois.[24]

The identification between the English and the qualities of the freedom-loving sylvan Germans, as described by Tacitus, led to many translations and editions of the *Germania* being published from 1755 onwards, including one by the ethnologist R. G. Latham in 1851.[25] Tacitus' brief characterization of the German character was central to Saxonism. By the eighteenth century, the identification had become strong enough for the American Revolutionists to see themselves as reasserting their ancient birthright of Anglo-Saxon freedom when they rebelled against the British King in 1776. Jefferson, who, like many of the founding fathers of the American republic, was particularly fond of the idea that Anglo-Saxon society embodied the original founding principles of American democracy, and even proposed putting Hengist and Horsa on the Great Seal of the United States.[26] None of these forms of identification were racial in the modern or even nineteenth-century sense.

The interest was extended to include ancient myths and legends, particularly in the work of the Scottish antiquarian Thomas Percy, who followed his celebrated *Reliques of Ancient English Poetry* (1765) with a translation of Paul-Henri Mallet's *Northern Antiquities* (1770), a work which extended the idealization of the Germans to

Scandinavians. The antiquarian interest in the Saxons was transformed at the beginning of the nineteenth century by the advent of German philology, which moved interest to questions of language and its origins. Dr Johnson's *Dictionary* of 1755 had included a chart showing the derivation of English from 'Gothick or Teutonick': it was well known therefore that English and German shared a common 'origin'. There was a tremendous growth in scholarly interest in the philological history of the language and its affiliations to other Northern languages. The discovery of the Indo-European origin of the Anglo-Saxon language led to an interest in the geographical origins of the distant originating fathers of the language – the Aryans, and this would later be linked to racial theory, particularly in Germany. In England, an identification of the linguistic origins of English led to a movement to restore it to its purer and plainer Anglo-Saxon forms, first waywardly proposed in the eccentric work of Horne Tooke, and then vigorously developed by many since, from Hazlitt to Hopkins, from Herbert Spencer to George Orwell. At the same time, this identification led to the establishment of the study of English literature with a strong emphasis on Anglo-Saxon, significantly identified as 'Old English' in order to emphasize that there 'has been but one speech spoken in England by the Teutonic tribes and their descendants from Caedmon to Tennyson'.[27] Only outside England was English Literature ever called 'British Literature'.

The first scholarly work based on Anglo-Saxon manuscripts was Sharon Turner's enormously popular *History of England from the Earliest Period to the Norman Conquest* (1799–1805), a book which gave the first comprehensive account not only of the history but also of the language and literature of the Anglo-Saxons.[28] It was Turner who could be said to have first created the modern myth of King Alfred, to whom he enthusiastically devotes over two hundred pages. Himself inspired by Percy, Turner's work in turn paved the way for more orthodox scholarly work by Benjamin Thorpe and John Mitchell Kemble who studied in Germany with Rasmus Kristian Rask and Jacob Grimm, two of the founders of the new German philology. Between them, Thorpe and Kemble introduced German philology into Britain and integrated British philology with the German school: Thorpe translated Rask's *Anglo-Saxon Grammar* in 1830, and for many years after he and Kemble prepared scholarly editions, based on manuscripts, and translations of Anglo-Saxon and Old-Norse texts, particularly 'national' works such as *Beowulf* and *The Anglo-Saxon Chronicle*.[29] Under their influence the Philological Society of London was formed in 1842; twenty years later its members initiated the greatest monument to English German philology, a record of the complete history of written English, now known as the OED, and recently named as one of the British government's 'icons of England'. More than any other element, English would remain thereafter the core component of . . . being English. This is less simple than it might seem. The initial enthusiasm, encouraged by James Cowles Prichard's linguistically based ethnology, was to identify the language with the people or the race: by the time Ferdinand de Saussure dismissed the idea in 1916, however, this idea had been regularly challenged for nearly fifty years by linguists and anthropologists alike. And yet, as Freeman suggested in 1879, though it might by that time be considered a mistake to identify the one with the other, there still seemed a common-sense link between the two that people found appealing.[30] In general, the English continued to identify the English people with their language. The very reason why language was dissociated from race – anyone can learn another language, whereas biology for the most part prevents racial migration – came to open up a very different avenue for ideas of Englishness. You could always learn to be English, in the same way as you could learn English itself. There was 'proper' English, but there were also many Englishes.

Teutonism

For the most part, however, it was the historians and essayists rather than the historical philologists who, from the late 1830s onwards, were the most up-front ideologues of Saxonism. To call Saxonism an ideology, however, should not be taken to imply that it was a single set of ideas. The challenge for anyone writing about it is that each individual writer characterized it according to his own preferences and preoccupations, within an overall paradigm in which Germanic ideas of 'race' and 'nation' were set against French values of 'civilization'. Overall, what emerges is a cluster of interrelated ideas which succeeded in establishing a range of possibilities that produced the flexibility and contradictory qualities necessary to every successful ideology.

This is clear if we look at one of the first historians who developed the strong identification of the English with the Goths, or as he preferred to say, the Teutons. Thomas Hughes' emphasis on English-as-Saxon which we encountered in *Tom Brown's Schooldays* was itself a reflection of the ideas of the real-life version of the headmaster portrayed in Hughes' book, Thomas Arnold, Matthew Arnold's father, famous founder of Rugby School and Regius Professor of History at Oxford. In his *Inaugural Lecture* delivered at Oxford in December 1841, Arnold made a double argument about Englishness, one that would in a certain sense determine the parameters of the debate thereafter: the English were culturally mixed, but what made them great was their ethnic purity. The variations on this that would follow were that the English were racially mixed, but culturally pure, or that they were both racially and culturally mixed.

Arnold argued that English culture was a synthesis of Roman, Greek and Hebrew, but claimed that its greatness derived from the fact that it was supplemented by something extra. That X factor was the English race, itself derived from German 'stock'. Arnold was not thinking in terms of what we would now call biological or scientific racism, for he was rather drawing on the romantic nationalism of the German historian Barthold Niebuhr. For popular purposes, his romantic notion of race conceived in terms of 'stock' and 'blood' was the more persuasive:

> Here then we have, if I may so speak, the ancient world still existing, but with a new element added, the element of our English race. And that this element is an important one, cannot be doubted for an

instant. Our English race is the German race; for though our Norman fathers had learnt to speak a stranger's language, yet in blood, as we know, they were the Saxons' brethren: both alike belong to the Teutonic or German stock. Now the importance of stock is plain from this, that its intermixture with the Keltic and Roman races at the fall of the western empire has changed the whole face of Europe.... What was not [in the Ancient world] was simply the German race, and the peculiar qualities which characterize it. This one addition was of such power, that it changed the character of the whole mass.... But that element still preserves its force, and is felt for good or for evil in almost every country of the civilized world.

We will pause for a moment to observe over how large a portion of the earth this influence is now extended. It affects more or less the whole west of Europe.... I say nothing of the prospects and influence of the German race in Africa and in India: it is enough to say that half of Europe, and all America and Australia, are German more or less completely, in race, in language, or in institutions, or in all.[31]

Arnold's expansive lecture to his appreciative Oxford undergraduate audience, which included the young E. A. Freeman and Goldwin Smith, brings together a number of elements that would be strategically developed over the century: first, that though absorbing the influence of many different cultures, the English, as Saxons, are fundamentally of German stock, which is characterized as the feature that defines modernity against ancient times; and second, that this race, inherently restless and subject to what Charles Kingsley would call 'migratory manias', now girdles the earth – in Africa, India, Europe, America, Australasia.

Thomas Carlyle

In stressing the importance of Germanic or Saxon 'stock', a term which conveniently was also used by historical philologists to describe affiliations within the 'families' of languages, Arnold was in complete accord with the sentiments of his famous contemporary

Thomas Carlyle, who also portrayed the English as exclusively Saxon, and was overtly hostile to the Celts of the British Isles, particularly in Ireland. He dismissed historical accounts sympathetic to the Celts, expelled from their lands in the face of the Saxon invasion, by asserting simply that in such matters, might is right: 'The strong thing is the just thing'.[32] Like Arnold, Carlyle was exclusively interested in promoting a Teutonic identification for the English. By 1841, however, while Arnold was giving his lectures envisioning the spread of emigrating Teutons round the world, a new antithetical political issue had emerged: the 'flooding' of England with destitute immigrant Celtic Irish. It was Carlyle who gave these issues a racialized inflection by invoking an irresolvable dichotomy between Saxons and the 'Celtiberian Irish'.

Carlyle's analysis of the 'condition of England' question in *Chartism* (1839) addressed the issues of unemployment and the new Poor Law legislation. In this context, he raised the fact that at that time, around a third of the working Irish population were unemployed – a situation for which in the first instance he blamed the government:

> Has Ireland been governed and guided in a 'wise and loving' manner? A government and guidance of white European men which has issued in perennial hunger of potatoes to the third man extant, – ought to drop a veil over its face, and walk out of court under conduct of proper officers. . . . We English pay, even now, the bitter smart of long centuries of injustice to our neighbour Island. Injustice, doubt it not, abounds; or Ireland would not be miserable. . . . England is guilty towards Ireland; and reaps at last, in full measure, the fruit of fifteen generations of wrong-doing. (16–18)

Even though Carlyle makes a careful declaration of universal humanity between all men – 'The Sanspotatoe [Carlyle's ironic name for the Irish] is of the selfsame stuff as the superfinest Lord Lieutenant' – and begins by blaming the problems of the Irish on oppressive English rule, he soon begins to blame the Irish themselves. It is the defects in their national character that have led them to famine:

28

the oppression has gone far farther than into the economics of Ireland; inwards to her very heart and soul. The Irish National character is degraded, disordered.... Immethodic, headlong, violent, mendacious: what can you make of the wretched Irishman? (17)

While invoking the older discourse of 'National Character', Carlyle constantly augments this with a racial typology (the remark that the Irish are ruled by white European men implies that they do not fall into that category, and this is reinforced in the following passage, which emphasizes their 'wild Milesian features' and 'squalid apehood'). As so often, from that day to this, issues of race go hand in hand together with immigration. The problem, according to Carlyle, is not only that the Irish are destitute, but that the development of steamships means that the passage from Ireland to England has become cheap and easy. As a result, Ireland, he proclaims, is 'pouring daily in on us...deluging us down to its own waste confusion, outward and inward' (21):

Crowds of miserable Irish darken all our towns. The wild Milesian features, looking false ingenuity, restlessness, unreason, misery and mockery, salute you on all highways and byways. The English coachman, as he whirls past, lashes the Milesian with his whip, curses him with his tongue; the Milesian is holding out his hat to beg. He is the sorest evil this country has to strive with. In his rags and laughing savagery, he is there to undertake all work that can be done by mere strength of hand and back; for wages that will purchase him potatoes. He needs only salt for condiment; he lodges to his mind in any pighutch or doghutch.... The Saxon man if he cannot work on these terms, finds no work. He too may be ignorant; but he has not sunk from decent manhood to squalid apehood: he cannot continue there. American forests lie untilled across the ocean; the uncivilised Irishman, not by strength but by the opposite of strength, drives out the Saxon native, takes possession in his room. There abides he, in his squalor and unreason, in his falsity and drunken violence, as the ready-made nucleus of degradation and disorder.... We have quarantines against pestilence; but there is no pestilence like that; and against it what quarantine is possible? (18–19)

According to Carlyle, the Irish are either driving out the Saxon natives, forcing them to emigrate to America, or, as Engels was also to argue five years later in *The Condition of the Working Class in England* (1844), they are bringing them down to their own degraded level. Carlyle's solution is a stark alternative:

> The time has come when the Irish population must either be improved a little, or else exterminated.... In a state of perennial ultra-savage famine, in the midst of civilisation, they cannot continue. (19)

Carlyle's call for extermination of the Irish, on what he presents as the humane grounds that their condition was so terrible, an 'ultra-savage famine' appropriate to their savage state, was to be partly realized during the years of the Great Famine that would shortly follow: during that time the Irish population was reduced by a half, from eight to four million.

For those who assume that Scottish nationalism has always existed in its present form, it might seem surprising that Carlyle, himself a Scot, should take so hard a line on his fellow Celts. In fact, after the 1745 Rebellion, a majority of Scottish Highlanders had themselves been cleared out of the Highlands and forced to emigrate, with scarcely more compassion offered than would be given to the Irish a hundred years later. In Carlyle's time, 'Scotland' was only at that moment being invented in the novels of the appropriately named Sir Walter Scott. After the Act of Union of 1707, and the creation of the 'United Kingdom', Scotland was often referred to as North Britain (the *North British Review* was founded in 1844). At this time many North British (that is, Scottish) intellectuals argued that Lowland Scots, that is those from Edinburgh, Glasgow, and the Lowlands of the South, were Saxons, and that only the Highlanders, whose origins, like the name Scotland itself, lay in Ireland, were Celts. In *The Highlands and Western Isles of Scotland, in Letters to Sir Walter Scott* (1824), the Scottish historian John Macculloch even argued that the Highlanders were not really Celts.[33] It is striking, in fact, how many of those who developed the racial romance of Saxonism were themselves Scottish – so much so that, taking Scott's *Ivanhoe* (1819) on board as well, you could plausibly claim not only English Literature but also racialized English Saxonism as a Scottish invention.[34] Though modern Scottish nationalism often presents an unbroken continuity of nationalist sentiment, at this time many Lowlanders did not describe themselves as Scots, identifying themselves rather as English.[35] So we find Carlyle, in his 'Occasional Discourse on the Negro Question' (1849), asking: 'What, then, is practically to be done by us poor English with our Demerara and other blacks?'[36] Carlyle clearly had no difficulty with describing himself as English and identifying himself with them.

As the topic of his essay also indicates (he later deliberately changed 'negro' to the more offensive 'nigger'), it was Carlyle who was among the first to reinterpret contemporary political issues according to the category of race. The new science of race, or ethnology as it was called, was being developed at that time in Edinburgh, the cutting edge of contemporary medical and zoological science (George Eliot's Lydgate, the new up-to-date doctor in *Middlemarch*, studied there). The new science of race was utilized as an important adjunct to the projection of the already fully formed view of England as culturally Saxon: Saxon in its history (yeoman Saxons throwing off the Norman yoke), Saxon in its language (Anglo-Saxon as the originary language and literature of England, the study of which was gradually institutionalized in universities), Saxon in its law (the Anglo-Saxon principle of precedence as opposed to Roman law, with Anglo-Saxon law being originally composed and written in English), and Saxon in its political institutions, which were identified with the idea of freedom (freedom and liberty, but not democracy, for at that time Britain was not a democracy), symbolized in Magna Carta of 1215, by which the King was brought within the rule of law and guaranteed the right of liberty to his subjects.

Saxonism was not invented by racial theorists but by historians: it was they who most comprehensively over many years developed the ideology of the English as Saxons, and of the continuing national Anglo-Saxon legacy.[37] Macaulay's hugely successful Whig,

Protestant and patriotic *History of England* (1848–61), with its Teutonic hero William of Orange and its Catholic villain James II, constantly analysed relations between England and Ireland in terms of the antipathy of Saxon and Celt. In different ways, Sir Francis Palgrave emphasized the foundational importance of England's Teutonic institutional heritage in his *History of England* (later renamed *History of the Anglo-Saxons*) (1831), *The Rise and Progress of the English Commonwealth: Anglo-Saxon Period* (1832), and *The History of Normandy and of England* (1851, 1857, 1861).[38] Palgrave's stress on the importance of the judicial institutions of the Germanic invaders in preventing constitutional absolutism throughout the history of conquests of England was accompanied by the claim that not only the Saxons but even the Southern Celts were Germanic (Belgic Kymrys) in origin. For him, nations were as individuals, inheriting in a Lamarkian way acquired characteristics that were then transmitted through the blood down the generations. It was for this reason that he was able to argue that 'the continuity of English national life never was broken by the Normans: hence the vigorous and uninterrupted progress of national power'.[39]

Saxonism and 1848

'But England flourishes. Is it what you call civilisation that makes England flourish? Is it the universal development of the faculties of man that has rendered an island, almost unknown to the ancients, the arbiter of the world? Clearly not. It is her inhabitants that have done this; it is an affair of race. A Saxon race, protected by an insular position, has stamped its diligent and methodic character on the century. And when a superior race, with a superior idea to work and order, advances, its state will be progressive, and we shall, perhaps, follow the example of the desolate countries. All is race; there is no other truth'.

'Because it includes all others?' said Lord Henry.

'You have said it.'

Benjamin Disraeli, *Tancred* (1847)[40]

At one level, Saxonism seems to have been precipitated into a full-scale political ideology by the revolutions of 1848. While the foundations of European nations were crumbling all around, the stable Saxon identity of England was increasingly stressed in political and cultural terms. Books on Saxons and Anglo-Saxons abound from this date. 1848 saw the appearance of Sir Edward Bulwer-Lytton's *Harold: The Last of the Saxon Kings*, in which Harold was represented as a staunch Saxon, a native patriot resisting foreign invasion.[41] In 1849, the eminent Anglo-Saxon philologist John Mitchell Kemble published *The Saxons in England*, a work which attributes the political stability of England to the permanence and power of endurance of its Saxon institutions, in particular its system of land laws, as well as its language, and its municipal, religious and social institutions. Like many other Anglo-Saxonists, Kemble justifies the importance of his investigations 'from their bearing upon the times in which we live', far more than from any mere antiquarian value. His dedication to the Queen describes *The Saxons in England* as a 'history of the principles which have given her empire its pre-eminence among the nations of Europe'.[42] The book, like many accounts of Englishness, was written abroad. Composed in Germany at the time of the 1848 revolutions, Kemble consistently suggests that England's (comparative) present political stability and prosperity are the direct effect of the Teutonic foundations of English society. The Saxon childhood, as described in Tacitus' *Germania*, produced a Saxon manhood in England. Kemble writes in the preface:

> The following pages contain an account of the principles upon which the public and political life of our Anglosaxon forefathers was based, and of the institutions in which those principles were most clearly manifested. The subject is a grave and solemn one: it is the history of the childhood of our own age, – the explanation of its manhood.
>
> On every side of us thrones totter, and the deep foundations of society are convulsed. Shot and shell sweep the streets of capitals which have long been pointed out as the chosen abodes of order: cavalry and bayonets cannot control populations whose loyalty has

become a proverb here, whose peace has been made a reproach to our own miscalled disquiet. Yet the exalted Lady who wields the sceptre of these realms, sits safe upon her throne, and fearless in the holy circle of her domestic happiness, secure in the affections of a people whose institutions have given to them all the blessings of an equal law. (v)

Kemble follows Burke in arguing that freedom in England is an inheritance, based on subservience to law rather than democracy or the rights of man. He argues that it was the Germans who developed the institutions that incorporated the essential qualities of individual freedom and equality, and regenerated the degenerate Roman civilization that they found around them:

> Throughout the latter day of ethnic civilization, when the idea of *state* had almost ceased to have power, and the idea of *family* did not exist, there was a complete destruction both of public and private morality; and the world, grown to be a sink of filth and vice, was tottering to the fall which Providence in mercy had decreed for its purification. The irruption of the German tribes breathed into the dead bones of heathen cultivation the breath of a new life. (231)

According to Kemble, the two principles on which Saxon society rested were the possession of land and the distinction of rank. Perhaps because of this need for land, Kemble characterizes the Saxons as naturally migratory, beginning with their emigration towards the coasts of Britain, and imagines their householders spreading across the English countryside, like 'the backwoodsman in America, or the settler in an Australian bush' who now continue the same process. This preference for the rural and the agricultural meant that after they had left, the old Roman towns became deserted and 'slowly crumbled to the soil' while England was transformed into a network of small village communities: 'the principle of whose being was separation, as regarded each other: the most intimate union, as respected the individual members of each' (67–70). In its foundation in the possession of land and distinction of rank, Germanic society was thus essentially rural, and antipathetic towards the city:

34

It is not the city, but the country, that regulates their form of life and social institutions: as Tacitus knew them, they bore in general the character of disliking cities: 'It is well enough known,' he says, 'that none of the German populations dwell in cities; nay that they will not even suffer continuous building, and house joined to house. They live apart, each by himself, as the woodside, the plain or the fresh spring attracted him'. Thus the German community is in some sense *adstricta glebae*, bound to the soil. (89)

The Germans live in detached houses, in a condition of *adstricta glebae*, bonded to the soil – here we find an anticipation of Hughes' cheerful claim to Anglo-Saxon heritage that would follow eight years later ('I was born and bred . . . a regular "Angular Saxon", the very soul of me *adscriptus glebae*'). Kemble and Hughes' characterization of the essential qualities of the Anglo-Saxon as a country-dweller, living alone with his family, physically apart from his neighbours, goes straight back to Tacitus' characterization of the Germans. The ideal of the house in the country, standing in its own grounds, remains to this day a constitutive characteristic of every idealized form of what it means to be English. In pursuit of this quintessential dream, the English at the turn of the twenty-first century have spread themselves once more, across the comparatively empty countryside of France, Italy and Spain.

Kemble's work in establishing the Anglo-Saxon provenance of English culture was subsequently augmented by many other eminent historians – by Bishop Stubbs in his *Constitutional History of England in its Origin and Development* (1874–8); by John Richard Green in his popular *A Short History of the English People* (1874) and *The Making of England* (1881); and above all by Edward Freeman, the most powerful figure in the Oxford school of Germanist historians, who in *The Norman Conquest* (1867) and many other books elaborated unwearyingly, in somewhat wearisome Teutonic prose, the thesis of the Germanic character of the nation that could be found embodied and expressed in the events of its history.[43] The Norman Conquest had not, according to Freeman, succeeded in perverting the essentials of the national character, which demonstrably remained fundamentally Saxon. It was in his researches for a university prize competition in 1845–6 on the effects of the Roman conquest that Freeman first read Amédée Thierry's *L'Histoire des Gaulois*, where Thierry projects a view of French history as the result of a historic struggle between the Gauls and the Cymris, a racial difference now subsumed into one of class.[44] Amédée Thierry's thesis of French history as the product of racial conflict was in turn a reworking of the main part of the thesis of his elder brother Augustin Thierry's influential *Histoire de la conquête de l'Angleterre* (1825, first translated into English in 1841, and retranslated by William Hazlitt in 1847), which portrayed English history as a story above all of colonizers and colonized, the Saxon people's struggle for liberty against the yoke of the aristocratic Norman conquerors. From this, Freeman drew the idea of national history as a struggle between different races, of the Saxon people against the aristocratic Norman conquerors (the Celts were largely ignored). For Freeman, however, the emphasis was always on the success of assimilation rather than continuing conflict. While William the Conqueror is presented as racially distinct from the Saxon people of England – 'William was the greatest of his race, but he was essentially of his race; he was Norman to the backbone' – Freeman presents William's political strategy as one of self-assimilation to the local culture:

> It was his policy to disguise the fact of conquest, to cause all the spoils of conquest to be held, in outward form, according to the ancient law of England. The fiction became a fact, and the fact greatly helped in the process of fusion between Normans and English. The conquering race could not keep itself distinct from the conquered, and the form which the fusion took was for the conquerors to be lost in the greater mass of the conquered.[45]

Freeman's emphasis on fusion between the Normans and Saxons represents a characteristic inflection and modification of the Thierrys' story of racial and class struggle. The Thierrys themselves derived this idea from Chateaubriand and from Arnold's hero, Barthold Niebuhr;

however, in a circular return of the flows of influence, they had, in turn, also been inspired by Edward Coke, Thomas Hobbes and Sir Walter Scott.

Scott

When Samuel Taylor Coleridge complained on reading (though not finishing) *Ivanhoe* (1819) of 'our utter indifference to the feuds of Normans and Saxons', he was showing how much he belonged to an earlier generation.[46] Scott's importance in the development of contemporary ideas of Saxonism can hardly be underestimated. He himself drew on the work of both Percy and Turner to create his romantic representation of Scottish history, but his imaginative re-creations of the medieval past were far more effective in charging the popular imagination than the books of any earlier writers, whether poetic (Percy) or scholarly (Turner). It was above all in *Ivanhoe* that Scott is commonly reckoned to have invented English national cultural identity.[47] It was Scott who brought the idea of the continuing division of England into Saxons and Normans, defined according to their differences of language, class and race, into an imaginative reality. The claim by Michael Banton, the sociologist of race, and John Sutherland, Scott's biographer, that it was Scott above all who was responsible for the popularization of the idea of race as such in England in the nineteenth century is probably a bit over the top.[48] What they are pointing to, however, was that unlike Percy, Turner or Freeman, or any of the contemporary anatomists or anthropologists who were developing ideas of race, Scott's popular novel, centred on the theme of race and racial antagonism, reached a very wide audience, comparable only to Macaulay's *History of England*. Like many writings on race, Scott's portrait of an England fundamentally Saxon in blood, manliness and freedom, ruled over by perfidious Norman aristocrats, allowed for two simultaneous interpretations. On the one hand, he emphasizes how an undying racial antagonism survives like an open wound: 'Four generations had not sufficed to blend the hostile blood of the Normans and Anglo-Saxons, or to unite, by common language and mutual interests, two hostile races, one of which still felt the elation of triumph, while the other groaned under all the consequences of defeat'. This is brought into the present through the emphasis on the continuing survival of the Jews as a separate race – in fact, as the novel proceeds, Scott naturalizes the Saxon racial identity of the English increasingly less by contrast with the Normans, than with the Jews, whose separate racial identity is emphasized throughout.

On the other hand, while enabling the idea of the English being residual Saxons, with the passing of generations unable to unite the two hostile races, Scott also at the same time allowed for the integration and assimilation of the foreign elements of the conquerors, in the first place through language:

> the necessary intercourse between the lords of the soil, and those oppressed inferior beings by whom that soil was cultivated, occasioned the gradual formation of a dialect, compounded betwixt the French and the Anglo-Saxon, in which they could render themselves mutually intelligible to each other; and from this necessity arose by degrees the structure of our present English language, in which the speech of the victors and the vanquished have been so happily blended together.[49]

To this degree, Scott also suggested that in time racial and cultural differences were resolved and reconciled, and that in the course of this process the hierarchy was gradually reversed, so that England eventually conquered its conquerors. To invoke race while simultaneously arguing for cultural assimilation was to be a widespread English response to racial theories in the nineteenth century.

For his part, Kemble, though stressing the enduring importance of Saxon legal and cultural institutions in English history, strikes a comparable note. Denying the theory that the Celts were exterminated, he freely concedes that the lower orders remained largely Celtic under German rule and suggests a novel sort of proof: 'we may very safely appeal even to the personal appearance of the peasantry in many parts of England, as evidence [of] how much Keltic blood was permitted to subsist and even to mingle with that of the ruling Germans'.[50] What is noticeable here is that for Kemble in 1849, the arguments about the survival or extermination of the Celts were not to be solved by recourse to the evidence of language, or of history, but to the physiognomy of the English peasant. This marks a decisive moment in the history of the formation of ideas about English identity. The claim for national origins and cultural identity through history, and the uses of historical sources such as Tacitus, were henceforth to be examined not only through the survival of institutions and language, but also through the human body. This possibility was the result not just of the new science of race that was being developed in contemporary anatomy, anthropology and zoology, but also of a second filiation which linked zoological ideas about race to human history. This articulation involved the connection between race as lineage over time, and ideas of pedigree and 'stock': concepts that were connected through the idea of 'blood' and the transmission of the 'blood line'. It only required a small conceptual adjustment to link these to the use of 'race' as a characteristic defined in anatomical and bodily terms in zoology – and with it, to produce a new, 'scientific' racialization of the English.

Chapter 2

'New Theory of Race: Saxon v. Celt'

The Discourse of Race

Until the eugenics movement got under way, 'race' was always in some sense a popular science. While many of the early writers on race were medical men, they were part of a company that included anthropologists, ethnologists, historians and essayists, very few of whom were 'scientists' – a word which itself was only invented in 1834. Arthur de Gobineau, one of the most notorious writers on race of the nineteenth century, was an Orientalist, a *feuilleton* writer for periodicals; Houston Stewart Chamberlain could be described as a cultural historian, in today's terminology.

Nineteenth-century racial science is commonly referred to as 'pseudo-science', a designation of contemporary superiority that would be more comforting if scientists today did not continue to argue about the existence of race, the importance of genes, even the question of correlations between brain size and intelligence.[1] The notion of a 'pseudo-science', a favourite of Mill's, was invented in the mid-nineteenth century to designate a pretended or spurious science. There was no pretence about racialism, however. It was deadly serious. It's easier with the hindsight of history to say that it was a spurious science, in the sense of a discredited science, a designation which can be applied most usefully to racial science of the 1920s and

1930s. If racial science was a pseudo-science, then it was really several different pseudo-sciences, in different epochs. The racial science of the nineteenth century was a pseudo-science in a different way to eugenics: it was rarely scientific at all in the modern sense, and spent much of its energy considering the role of race in history and society. Since no one had to have any qualifications to write on race (and no one did), those who wrote about it established their authority by allying their observations to an already established consensus, invoking a series of higher 'authorities'. They then made their mark by proposing a different argument, just as in modern literary criticism or history.

Very little nineteenth-century racial science can be described as offering a purely 'biological' account of race, that is, the exclusive use of biological principles for explaining human diversity and the diversity of human behaviour. Alongside its delineation of racial difference through definable physical features, what made racial theory so powerful was the combination of its scientific and cultural argument. Chronologically, the culture came first: the first forms of racialism were inspired less by biology (which did not then exist) than by history and philology and seemed to work perfectly well, as racialist discourses, without it. Although naturalists such as Linnaeus or Cuvier began to classify human beings along with plants and animals in the eighteenth century, this approach was largely of interest to those working in the area of comparative anatomy. The racialization of disease formed an early attempt to understand areas still being investigated in contemporary research on the relation of genes to health. Its immediate stimulus was the observed tendency of people to be more susceptible to diseases in foreign climates, whichever way they were transplanted, and for some peoples to be more vulnerable to particular illnesses. Why could Africans survive in West Africa but Europeans not? Were Europeans more susceptible to hernias than people from other continents, and if so why?

As we have seen, racialism as a cultural discourse was originally created by late eighteenth and early nineteenth-century historians as a principle of national history, the racial argument deriving from historical accounts of where the inhabitants of their respective countries had originated. More or less at the same time, but separately, different kinds of racialism were gradually developed out of linguistics, or historical philology as it was then called. It was only in the very late 1840s that these disciplines were brought together with physiology under the general concept of a principle of race, in a critical moment determined by the eruption of 'race' or 'nationality' as a new popular political principle in the widespread European revolutions of 1848. However, with at least three different criteria to choose from, writers on race could weight their arguments according to a wide range of rules and evidence and freely did so. So-called pure 'biological racialism' only emerged at the end of the century at the very time when race was already being challenged in the realm of anthropology, history and linguistics. It was at that point that a 'properly' scientific theory of race emerged in the sphere of eugenics, a discrete science unencumbered by other discourses, in a comparable move to Ferdinand de Saussure's transformation of historical philology into linguistics. Eugenics was pioneered by Darwin's cousin, Sir Francis Galton, polymathic traveller, anthropologist and scientist, the man who appropriately enough coined the phrase 'nature versus nurture'.[2] Although Galton first sketched out his ideas of a science for improving the inborn characteristics of a race in the 1860s, eugenics was not institutionalized as a practice until the last decade of the nineteenth century. From that time onwards its ideology and practice were institutionalized not only in Germany, but also in many other countries, including Australia, Canada, Norway, Sweden, Switzerland, the UK, and the USA.[3]

Racial theory did not simply emerge as an autonomous science: one of the limitations of modern accounts is that because race became a discrete discipline for study in the twentieth century, histories of race isolate it from other contemporary forms of thought. In the early nineteenth century, many now-distinct disciplines remained woven together and cannot be individually distinguished: as Stephen G. Alter comments, 'conceptually speaking, zoology, race, and language were all intertwined. Linguistic study did not yet stand as a separate field but was paired with ethnology and, through it, was linked to the biological domain'.[4] While these remained intimately connected at the level of their conceptual frameworks and objects of study, grouped around ideas that could be extended at will through language, history and anatomy, it could also be said more generally that racial thought involved the development of what could be called a *discourse* of race, an enmeshed language of race that permeated the culture as it developed across a whole range of different kinds of knowledge, from the scientific to the popular. It moved indiscriminately across anthropology, aesthetics, history, literature, medicine, philology and political thought, providing a common source of cultural capital that writers of all kinds were able to draw on. There were very few writers who did not at some level invoke issues of race, in doing so showing that they accepted the basic premises of racial thought, without for the most part being extremists in any sense. To read English Literature in its Victorian definition – as in Macaulay's famous 'shelf of English Literature', which for him would have included not just fiction and poetry but history and the social and natural sciences – is to discover a world in which though individuals might vary in how far they foregrounded it, there was a consensus that races existed, and, almost always, that there was a hierarchy of races – within the country, within Europe and across the world.

Within this discourse of the nineteenth century our modern distinction between ethnicity and race did not exist. For much of the nineteenth century the words 'race' and 'nation' were also used virtually interchangeably. In 1844, for example, the historian Sir Francis Palgrave complained of the popular French historian Augustin Thierry that: 'He speaks as if he wishes to identify himself with the Anglo-Saxon *nation*. Of the conquered *race*, he presents himself, not merely as the historian, but the earnest defender.'[5] When people used the term 'race', occasionally they meant something close to what we now think of as ethnicity, occasionally they meant something more like biological race, but most usually they used the term without it being anchored in any precise meaning at all.

It is frequently impossible to tell what exactly a particular writer may have meant by race, not only because the word is never defined (the writer assumes of course that it needs no definition), but also because it can be used in very contradictory ways. The discourse of race, like many successful ideologies, is itself paradoxical, which is why it is possible to find people making contradictory assertions about it, without this necessarily implying that they have changed in their views.[6] One cannot immediately assume that contradictory statements represent a change of opinion on a developmental principle ('he became more (or less) racist because later he said...') unless the individual says this very explicitly, since the language of race itself encompasses a heterogeneous range of positions, and what people say is always determined by the context in which the statement is being made, and the audience that is being addressed. What suits them on one occasion, may not on another.

The ambiguity surrounding the word race in the nineteenth century was compounded by the tendency of those working in one science to employ technical terms currently in fashion in other sciences, especially in this case, the fondness of historical philologists for using biological metaphors such as 'tree', 'stock' and 'stem', all of which encouraged an identification between language and race. The general public used these terms often at a metaphorical level as well, apparently assuming that they were validated somewhere by 'hard science'. So with race, the sight of the callipers had more effect in giving the aura of science than any proof provided by the statistics amassed by the measurement of countless heads.

What we can say certainly is that though most people did not read the more 'scientific' anthropological accounts of race (which themselves often contradicted each other), the knowledge that men of science wrote about race in a similar manner to the way that they wrote about, say, geology gave the idea a substance that allowed the simultaneous concreteness and vagueness of use of the term. In general, race was taken to involve a certain identifiable physical 'type', and a level of cultural achievement, which could be traced in the history of the race or nation and hence involved certain common institutions, such as language and religion. Along with the physical characteristics taken as a marker of race, certain 'moral and intellectual' qualities would be invoked, which were for the most part anecdotal, emphasizing particular traits according to an already established general consensus. Even J. S. Mill, when challenged in 1832 for insulting the Irish character, his correspondent demanding that he state his sources of authority, responded: 'As for our "sources of authority" in regard to the Irish character, we have none that are peculiar to ourselves: our evidence is public notoriety'.[7] The ideas about the nation or the race that are expressed in all of these contexts remain relatively stable and restricted. Particular debates go on, but within a common frame of reference. The differences between Saxons and Celts, for example, are almost always characterized in similar terms. The same kind of comments are repeated from one author to another whatever the individual context in which they are writing, and it is this common ground which allows such a practice to be characterized as a discourse. So the independent, energetic, self-reliant, masculine and liberty-loving Saxon can typically be found characterized against the emotional, imaginative, feminine and gregarious Celt in any number of different disciplinary definitions. This becomes part of a knowledge which has no distinct source or centre, but which a whole range of writings, from history to science, all repeat and reaffirm with an authority drawn from its very ubiquity. The science of race only added one more knowledge base to this established consensus. While it seemed to ground the ideas in a new way, more directly in the body than ever before, and thus to provide a centre for them, it took over a ready-made stock of ideas from elsewhere. This characteristic explains why, when challenged and disproved, race did not simply disappear from view as a discredited scientific theory, in the manner of Joseph Priestley's phlogiston.

Though weighted towards culture rather than biology, modern notions of ethnicity draw on much the same ideas about human identity that were developed in the nineteenth century – a sense of a common history, language, traditions, sometimes religion. Since the biological status of race was so vague and malleable, it was easy enough to drop that element, with the result that the same traditions have developed in notable continuity. The replacement of race by ethnicity did not lead to significant upheavals in forms of identification. While it was common to discuss Ireland in terms of Celtism in the nineteenth century, in a different way that identity remains strong today. But what about the English? Where is the discourse of their ethnic identity? Was it that the English never really had a racial identity, or never thought of themselves in racial terms?

Such is the argument of Peter Mandler's recent book, *The English National Character.*[8] Mandler suggests that the notion of 'national character' was proposed by Mill as an alternative to a racialized identity for the English. In 1843, the year of the founding of the Ethnological Society of London, Mill gave the name 'ethology' to the study of character, implicitly opposing it to ethnology.[9] In this context it was unfortunate for Mill that the zoological meaning of ethology, the study of instinctive animal behaviour, would soon surpass it in a linguistic version of the survival of the fittest, and become the predominant usage. Mandler's project, in the spirit of Mill, is to show that the English never really defined themselves in racial terms at all. His playing down of race is in many ways a welcome antidote to many recent accounts of the nineteenth century which foreground racist statements by particular individuals as if they were typical, without mentioning the large middle ground of liberal opinion. However, it hardly helps the defence of English liberalism to go to the other extreme and suggest that race was never really there at all. Mandler, to use his own language, 'rather overeggs the pudding'.

Mandler's argument is that the English never really defined themselves in racial terms – if, and this is the big if, by race is meant what he calls 'real biological racism' (89). The only person in his account who qualifies as a real biological racialist (or racist) is the anatomist Robert Knox, whose influence Mandler claims was minimal anyway (though if so, why recur to him so frequently?). Everyone else, though they may have used the term 'race' and its characteristic language, did not, it seems (in the spirit of the dairymaid in A. A. Milne's 'The King's Breakfast') really mean it. Walter Bagehot, for example, is said to abandon the language of race after the opening passages of *Physics and Politics* (1872) and spend 'the rest of the volume reverting to type, frankly acknowledging a traditional whiggish Englishman's difficulties with a biological understanding of national character; his preference for progress, individuality and diversity' (79). Mandler's evidence for Bagehot's 'reverting to type' (itself a biological concept) is that he spends the rest of the volume pursuing the issue of 'variability'. Technically, however, a race is a 'variety' of a species, a sub-species, so Bagehot's pursuit of the question of variety among nations hardly represents an abandonment of a racial discourse. Bagehot, it is true, says that his concern is with the making of nations rather than of races. But this does not mean that he abandons an overall perspective grounded in race, as is clear from the following statement which comes, well after the 'opening passages', halfway through the book:

> I assume a world of marked varieties of man, and only want to show how less marked contrasts would probably and naturally arise in each. Given large homogeneous populations, some Negro, some Mongolian, some Aryan, I have tried to prove how small contrasting groups would certainly spring up within each – some to last and some to perish. These are the eddies in each race-stream which vary its surface, and are sure to last till some new force changes the current. These minor varieties, too, would be infinitely compounded, not only with those of the same race, but with those of others.[10]

These are the words of a man who, we are told, abandons the language of physiology and race soon after the book's opening passages.

The problem, moreover, with characterizing Knox as the only real biological racialist is that, as we shall see, Knox's racialism was not simply a matter of biology: his philosophy of 'transcendental anatomy' was a good deal more complex and wide ranging than that. By contrasting Knox with everyone else, Mandler assumes that only the idea that races are permanent and unalterable constitutes 'real' biological racialism. Biological racialism, however, does not in itself mean that races are fixed; rather, it involves the use of biological principles for explaining the social behaviour of humans. Whether they believed races were fixed or evolving, ethnologists and anthropologists alike shared the same basic perspective according to which human behaviour was subject to natural law, race was a determining factor in the development of civilization, and Caucasians were superior to all other races. The relation of 'race' to 'civilization' also changed significantly – they were hardly oppositional, as Mandler suggests. As George Stocking observes, 'as it emerged in the later eighteenth century, the idea of civilization was seen as the destined goal of all mankind. But in the nineteenth century, more and more men saw it as the peculiar achievement of certain "races".'[11] Cuvier, for example, argued that some races were progressive, others stationary; Maine that societies could be divided between the progressive and the stationary; Kames and Pinkerton considered savages (which for Pinkerton included the Celts) fixed, while Europeans were progressing dynamically in historical time;[12] Robert Chambers argued simply that the different races had become arrested at particular points along the way: 'The leading characters . . . of the various races of mankind, are simply representations of particular stages in the development of the highest or Caucasian type.'[13] The idea that in time other races could 'catch up', though more liberal than the conviction that the hierarchy was fixed, was no less racial in its fundamental assumptions that a vast gulf lay between them. Moreover the time-scale on which the liberal progressive civilizational model was conceived was so large that in practice it made no difference – no one ever cared to give a date, or even a time-frame, for when the supposedly inferior races were going to catch up, though the historian J. A. Froude did concede that 'with a century or two of wise administration' the 'West Indian negro . . . might prove that his inferiority is not inherent'.[14]

In another sense, the very idea of a real or pure biological racism in the mid-nineteenth century suggests a twentieth-century understanding of the idea of race. Knox published his book in 1850. The OED records the first use of the term 'biological' in 1859, the phrase 'biological race' not before 1916. Race in the nineteenth century was always about more than just biology. Mandler seems to assume that any 'real' racialism must come pure, unmixed with any other elements, in the manner of modern science. So, for example, when he finds Teutonism mixed with the spirit of the Reformation, and ideas of 'a manly purity', then this is enough for him to discount, or bury, its implicit racial ideology: 'If this was Teutonism, it was Teutonism overlaid, often obscured, with many other things' (95). But race in the nineteenth century never came unalloyed, it always appeared dressed in full panoply, a *bricolage* of cultural, religious and historical values. Even the 'pure' racism of eugenics always carried its own ideological baggage – the only difference was that it was more deftly hidden behind the objectivity of 'science'.

Mandler concedes at times that individuals such as E. A. Freeman 'may have caught', as he puts it, 'a whiff of racial explanation' (89) from others such as Thomas Arnold, but always ends by reassuring the reader that the English felt much more comfortable without it: 'it was still easier for many Englishmen to think of themselves as the product of civilization . . . than as the ideal types of racial myth' (105). The English, according to Mandler, thus never really believed in the concept of race at all, largely preferring the Enlightenment notion of 'civilization' (as if that was somehow an ideology free of racial assumptions).[15] The logical corollary of Mandler's argument, however, is that if there was never more than a whiff of race with regard to English ideas about themselves, then neither could or would they have entertained more than just a *soupçon* of any racist ideas about anyone else. Unfortunately the histories of anti-Semitism or the British Empire, to say nothing of race relations in Britain in the twentieth century, provide (literally) volumes of evidence otherwise.

Race 1: Blood

Rather than attempting to claim that the English never seriously thought of themselves, and therefore of anyone else, in racial terms, the argument of this book is that early attempts to develop a singular racial identity for the English, derived loosely from history and philology, were in fact, paradoxical as it may seem, disproved by the emergence of a 'proper' racial science which argued that the English were irreducibly mixed, as some in fact had long thought. This then allowed a new, and in some ways unexpected, transformation.

When people used the term 'race', they could mean a lot of different things: ideas about 'race' did not depend on the new science of biology. From its early days, however, race, like ethnicity today, always involved some idea of physical ancestral descent. Starting with the family line, ancestors and descendants, by the eighteenth century the word 'race' was also being used to describe clans, tribes and nations. In all these contexts, race implied a bodily relation that was typically invoked by the word 'blood'. It was in these terms that Saxonism was originally conceived. Though sometimes emphasizing the traits of physiognomy, Scott's idea of race is generally projected in terms of blood, lineage and pedigree. He is as happy describing a race of horses as a race of Normans or Saxons. The idea of the English as a race began as a metaphorical transfer whereby they were projected as all being part of an extended family which together made up the nation: all 'men of one blood and one speech' as the Victorian historian of England J. R. Green liked to put it. 'Blood' is typical of the discourse of race: it sounds physical and corporeal. Blood suggests a notion of belonging, of one's 'own flesh and blood' (even if we now know that actually families may belong to different blood groups).[16] As E. A. Freeman remarked in 1879, 'our whole conception of race starts from the idea of community of blood. If the word "race" does not mean community of blood, it is hard to see what it does mean.'[17] But what does a 'community of blood' mean? It was Freeman's traditional concept of race, as families or nations, that led him to emphasize a commonalty of 'blood'. His idea of race as a blood line, and his stress on English history as a history of successive assimilations to English cultural norms, meant that he could be relatively relaxed about the actual racial identity of the English in what we would now call biological terms. A generic claim for 'blood' did it nicely. As a metaphor, the term 'blood' has a powerful emotive aura, fully extended in Thomas Arnold's redolent 'whiff of racial explanation' of 1841: 'Our English race is the German race; for though our Norman fathers had learnt to speak a stranger's language, yet in blood, as we know, they were the Saxons' brethren: both alike belong to the Teutonic or German stock'.[18] Blood, in this context, looks back to the traditional idea that the 'same' blood flows through the veins of the family, who are of 'the same flesh and blood', and hence race.[19] Blood and 'stock' here give race a strong link to the body, compared to which language is regarded as superficial, even if a distinguishing element of nationality. Among all possible factors, Arnold points to 'race' as the key element that has determined the difference of the English within a shared European culture.

Like Arnold, in his *History of England* of 1849, Macaulay also denies 'emnity of race' in England between 'the Great Teutonic family' of Normans and Saxons. He goes on, however, to portray English–Irish relations in terms of a simple racial antithesis. In the course of his account of the destruction of Derry and its reconstruction as Londonderry in the reign of James I, he remarks:

> The [new] inhabitants were Protestants of Anglosaxon blood. They were indeed not all of one country or of one church but Englishmen and Scotchmen, Episcopalians and Presbyterians, seem to have generally lived together in friendship, a friendship which is sufficiently explained by their common antipathy to the Irish race and to the Popish religion.[20]

Anglo-Saxon blood, Protestantism and hatred of the Irish race: so much did the colonial settlers in Northern Ireland have in common. So much did Saxonism in general often have in common.

Race 2: Stock

What is perhaps most extraordinary about the Teutonic Saxon model is the way that a single remark by the early historian Gildas – that the ancient Britons had been exterminated – allowed the

English to claim a pure Saxon lineage for themselves. In racial terms, the arrival of the Normans did not necessarily pose a problem for this since they were, both Arnold and Macaulay claim, themselves of Teutonic origin, so that the conquest involved no racial dilution: the Normans were of the same German 'stock'. Up to the mid-eighteenth century at least, race was still generally thought of in terms of stock, or lineage, of an aristocratic family line, encapsulated in the popular motif of the tragic aristocrat who lingers on as the last of his 'race' – as in Walpole's *Castle of Otranto* (1765), the first 'Gothic' novel in English.[21] In Britain, lineage was always associated with 'stock' and 'pedigree', and by analogy, with the breeding of domestic animals. Doubtless British pride in their racial stock connected for many with the idea of the thoroughbred animals that were the constant focus of attention in their day-to-day country life. This connection was foregrounded in 1868, when Thomas Nicholas published *The Pedigree of the English People: An Argument, Historical and Scientific, on the Formation and Growth of the Nation; tracing race-admixture in Britain from the earliest times, with especial reference to the incorporation of the Celtic aborigines*, a work that achieved some popularity.[22] In emphasizing mixture, however, Nicholas was really presenting a counter-argument to the idea of racial pedigree, since it usually implied purity of descent, as in 'blue blood', which referred to Spanish aristocrats whose families had not mixed with the Moors or the Jews.

Ideas about heredity and race were significantly influenced by the historical confluence of racial theory and the new science of the breeding of farm animals. The key figure here is Robert Bakewell (1725–95). The customary practice up to Bakewell's time had been to 'outbreed', that is to mate cattle or sheep with bulls and rams from different stock. Bakewell reversed this practice, rigorously isolating his sheep and cattle and then breeding them successively according to their characteristics as providers of wool or meat. As Arthur Young put it, 'he sets entirely at naught the old ideas of the necessity of variation from crosses; on the contrary, the sons cover the dams, and the sires their daughters with no attention whatever to vary the race.'[23] Through careful inbreeding, Bakewell developed the New Leicester sheep and Longhorn cattle as eugenically engineered domestic animals, and was able to charge enormous fees for hiring out his rams to other farmers – in 1789 he made 1200 guineas from three rams. This dramatic augmentation of the meat content of British livestock was one factor which enabled the British to escape the Malthusian trap of famine in the face of an expanding population in the nineteenth century.[24] Such was the prestige of Bakewell's experiments, and the widely accepted success of breeding remarkable specimens, that previous assumptions with respect to outbreeding were reversed to inbreeding – at the very time when theories of race were beginning to stress the maintenance of difference and isolation in order to preserve, or re-establish, racial purity. Outbreeding was denigrated through association with theories of hybridity as a degenerative process. Technically, this opened up a gap in the analogy between race as family and pedigree and race as nation, which no longer fitted exactly: whereas a family must continue to outbreed, a nation, according to racial theory, must inbreed. The desire for nations to inbreed rather than outbreed became the foundation of racial theory, which propagated notions of purity and pedigree. In the case of England in the early nineteenth century, this meant being of Saxon or Teutonic stock, the qualities of which were identified with 'British beef', or its personification in John Bull.

Later in the century, after Darwin, who was very interested in the links between the creation of new forms of domestic animals and the natural modification of races, devoting the first chapter of *Origin of Species*, 'Variation under Domestication', to the breeding of domestic animals, Bakewell's model of breeding would be adapted by Galton and others to the idea of the English as a developing, dynamic race.[25] Ideas of race at that point became more prospective than retrospective: instead of a view of human types as a static hierarchy, in which you claimed your race as a historical descendant of the highest, in a war of the fittest, you had to start looking forward, as races must either degenerate or evolve and improve.

Race 3: Language

While history, and the tracing of a particular genealogical line, was the oldest area of knowledge in which ideas of race were elaborated, with the rise of interest in the religious and political dimensions of the vernacular in the seventeenth century, a common 'mother tongue' was gradually added to the idea of a race or nation.[26] From the 1780s onwards, analysis of the nation conceived as being made up of one or more races was augmented through the historical study of language according to the new protocols of comparative philology. By Arnold and Macaulay's day, a benign alternative to the grim racialized histories of blood could be found in the philological emphasis on communities of language. Historical philology precipitated a new way of conceiving race.

In the earlier decades of the nineteenth century the word 'race' was already being used in a whole range of different, but interrelated contexts. The sense of race as an extended family line had already shifted towards the idea of race as the national family and at the same time as a form of classification of the families of man, usually on the Mosaic biblical model of the division of the families of man after Babel. Although this approach was dominant in Britain, a further discourse was already being developed in continental Europe – the anatomical and zoological. Since the eighteenth century, natural philosophers, beginning with the German physiologist and anthropologist Johann Friedrich Blumenbach, had begun to extend their work of classification of the natural world to the people who inhabited it. Just as animals were put into different species and varieties, so were humans. Measuring a hundred skulls from different nations all over the world, Blumenbach, in what became the most widely used classification, divided humans into five races.[27] Race, and racial division in its modern form, was ultimately the result of the scientific urge to classify and order the natural world. With respect to plants and animals, chemicals or stars, this was one innocuous aspect of what we call the formation of modern science. In the eighteenth

54

century, physical differences between humans, which at that time could be marked on a geographical basis, were generally ascribed to the effects of the different environments in which they lived. Environment was offered as the explanation for physical differences. The problem with this was that people in similar environments could evidently become culturally very different and look very different, and recent history showed that if people or animals were transported into different environments, they did not change physically. One answer to this was to explain the difference between races as one of the difference of species – a view that found favour with the Scottish Enlightenment philosopher Lord Kames in his *Sketches of the History of Man* (1774). Although this was acceptable for progressive anti-religious materialists of the Enlightenment, and became the dominant position in France and the United States, in England where radical scientists and philosophers were far more likely to be Unitarians or Evangelicals, or at least anti-slavery campaigners, an account so radically at odds with the Bible was unacceptable. This is why in early British ethnology, language was generally used as the basis for classifying ethnicities, and regarded as offering the true test of their kinship ('The use of languages really cognate must be allowed to furnish a proof, or at least a strong presumption, of kindred race').[28] This approach was pioneered in the work of the greatest British ethnologist of the early nineteenth century, James Cowles Prichard, who refused the zoological direction of Blumenbach in classifying races through a primary emphasis on skull shape, and used instead the taxonomies of the language families being developed in contemporary historical philology.[29] Language difference afforded a – relatively – value-free, non-hierarchical way of distinguishing between different groups of humans, and this was the dominant model used in England by Prichard and the members of the London Ethnological Society in the first half of the nineteenth century. Even language, however, was not necessarily always so innocuous.

'The study of the sacred languages of India', the comparative jurist and historian Sir Henry Sumner Maine noted succinctly in 1883, 'has given to the world the modern science of Philology and the modern theory of Race.'[30] As Maine went on to remark, the key moment in the formation of historical philology had occurred around 1785 when the British Orientalist scholar Sir William Jones realized that the ancient Indian language of Sanskrit shared a common origin with the European languages. From this he developed the idea of an Indo-European (the term is Thomas Young's) or Aryan (Friedrich Max Müller's) family of languages which linked all European languages back to Sanskrit. Jones' ideas were given wide circulation in Europe through Friedrich Schlegel's *Über die Sprache und Weisheit der Indier* (*On the Language and Wisdom of the Indians*) of 1808, a book which laid the foundation for the new comparative and historical study of languages initiated by Franz Bopp in his *Über das Conjugationssystem der Sanskritsprache* (*On the System of Conjugation in Sanskrit*, 1816).[31] Schlegel suggested that his new method for the historical study of languages through analysis of their genealogical pedigree was analogous to the methods of comparative anatomy, commenting:

> The structure or comparative grammar of the language furnishes as certain a key to their general analogy, as the study of comparative anatomy has done to the loftiest branch of natural science.[32]

The new philology was thus connected methodologically to anatomy from the first, while it gave a whole new range of possibilities for classifying humans, by the forms of their languages rather than the shapes and colours of their bodies. These were not kept separate, however. By the 1820s, scholars such as F. Augustus Pott and Jacob Grimm had linked the historical evolution of Indo-European languages to ideas of race by asserting a common genealogy for the speakers of Indo-European languages, tracing the origins of Sanskrit back to the Aryan peoples of Asia from whom it was claimed Europeans must be descended. They had then migrated westwards, and the different European languages that developed could be identified with the particular people, and nations, who spoke them.[33] With the work of August Schleicher, who developed the model of the *Stammbaum*, or the linguistic tree, the roots, trunks and branches

56

of lines of evolutionary descent of 'families' of languages and of races could be conveniently traced alongside each other.

The actual genealogies and divisions between languages or races, however, were by no means universally agreed. For example, while some argued that Celtic was not related to Sanskrit, others maintained that Hebrew was, and it was the latter linguistic theory of race that allowed Disraeli in the 1840s to claim racial superiority for the Jews, based on the argument that they were a pure, unmixed Aryan race. The Jews, according to Disraeli, were Aryans or Caucasians (according to Robert Knox, it was Disraeli who popularized Blumenbach's term 'Caucasian' in England), and like the Teutons their superiority rested on their racial purity, which he contrasted to other mixed and therefore degenerate races.[34] Disraeli's racialism is an early example of a phenomenon that in the context of anti-racism receives little attention today, that is someone from a racial minority actively invoking racial theory to promote his own status. While clearly part of the current of racialism that developed so markedly in the 1840s, Disraeli's racialism, particularly his assimilation of the Jews to Aryanism, remained idiosyncratic, even though as commentators have pointed out, in some ways it anticipated later notions both of Zionism and anti-Semitism. To that extent, as in the case of Sir Walter Scott, the cultural assimilation that Disraeli evoked through the plots of his novels was less influential that the discrete racial identities that he invoked for both Saxon and Jew.

As Disraeli's arguments suggest, the conceptual difference between ideas of race derived from history, 'blood' and 'stock', and those from philology was that while the first was based on some perceived connection (historical, regional, visual) between people, what was revolutionary about philology was that it established connections between peoples who might never before have considered themselves part of a group.[35] The effect of Jones' researches on Sanskrit was that scholars such as Grimm could claim a racial identity between the Europeans and the Indians, a blood bond that had doubtless occurred to neither previously. With racial identification resting on either (or both) visible and invisible bonds, its possibilities became almost limitless.

The historical and comparative philologists of the nineteenth century developed the links between Sanskrit and European languages into the story of the Aryan migration from India into Europe which, it was claimed, formed the basis of European languages and civilization, and which was used by some to justify the subsequent sweep of the Europeans westwards as they colonized much of the globe. Many commentators preferred the term 'Teuton' because it kept them separate from other races, particularly the Jews, with which the category of 'Caucasian' put them into contact. However, the links were in any case soon challenged: by the philologist Ernest Renan who in 1855 revised Blumenbach's original thesis to suggest that there were two significantly different branches within the Indo-European family: the Aryan and the Semitic.[36] Renan argued that whereas Hebrew, the language of the Bible, had formerly been assumed to be the most ancient language on earth, the discovery of Sanskrit and the Indo-European language family for the first time put European languages in opposition to Hebrew, which derived from a different language family – the 'Semitic'. This linguistic difference, already implied in Schlegel, was then developed in the nineteenth century into theories of racial difference and racial and cultural identity. So linguistic sameness became the basis of race, culture and nation, while on a larger scale the European and Asian worlds were divided into Indo-European or Aryan languages and Semitic ones. It was this linguistic division which became the basis of 'anti-Semitism', a word which did not appear until the 1880s, but whose emergence can be traced much earlier. Arnold's emphasis on Teutonism, for example, was based on the assumption that the Germanic languages and peoples had separate identities from those of the Celts (including the Gauls), as well as the Jews – Arnold was one of the first to find what may anachronistically be called his anti-Semitism justified by language theory and the racial identities that were derived from them.

By 1848, the tracing of ethnological kinship through comparison between languages was already being challenged. Up to this point, both ethnologists and philologists (including Prichard, Bopp, Renan,

Baron Bunsen and Müller) had affirmed that it was in the families and genealogy of languages, not in physical characteristics such as skin or eye colour, that evidence of racial kinship and common origins could be found. Physical differences could then be explained by the effects of different environments. In 1854, however, Müller, who had been largely responsible for popularizing the Aryan thesis of the new comparative philology in England, began to deny the link between race and language.[37] Language, he argued, should be studied as a separate category or discipline from ideas of race. There were also theoretical difficulties with the assumption that language was the best indication of the relation of one racial group to another. The problem with seeking for proof of racial identity through language was that the language had changed and mixed with other languages through time (in what sense is Anglo-Saxon really 'English'?). Above all, language could simply be acquired and learnt – as MacCulloch put it, 'Languages may be cast off and assumed; but the form and constitution, never'.[38] Both these factors were at odds with those who wished to assert the permanent bodily materiality of racial difference. From this time onwards it became increasingly common to deny any connection between language and race. The denial of the link did not mean, of course, that the writer was discounting the idea of race as such, only the connection between the two. One effect of this disciplinary separation was that the hitherto dominant linguistically based ethnology gave way to an anatomically based, racialized anthropology. This move was completed when Darwin's work made it clear that the chronologies of the evolution of languages and races were completely out of synch with each other in any case. The language-based ethnological work of R. G. Latham was the major academic casualty of this disciplinary parting of the ways.

However, the determined backtracking of the denial of the link between language and race (or nation) by philological scholars was made at a time that only marked the beginning of the idea's wider political life. Having created it, the philologists then began to deny it, but largely addressing only domestic academic audiences their protestations made little difference in the wider world.[39] Especially since there were still some, such as Adolphe Pictet or Léopold de Saussure in France, who continued to make the connection, the latter producing what might be called a biological theory of language difference.[40]

Race 4: Physiognomy, Phrenology

The idea that the English were a race certainly preceded the development of racial theory, and where it was theorized it was, as has been seen, originally primarily historical and linguistic. What changed in the mid-nineteenth century was that a physiological racial theory put the idea on a new foundation so that it took on the authority of science. This meant that, in a completely new way, the sense of a common culture could be tested against the identity of human bodies.

The sciences of phrenology and physiognomy were particularly important for the development of racial thought. Focus on anatomy was less significant in terms of defining racial difference than contemporary research on heads, faces and skulls. The idea of the face as the index of the soul was a discourse going back to Aristotle; by the sixteenth and seventeenth centuries, in the work of Giambattista della Porta and Sir Thomas Browne, physiognomy was often associated with other forms of reading signs for their hidden meanings – 'signatures' in nature, astrology and palmistry. Physiognomy, or 'the corresponding analogy between the conformation of the features, and the ruling passions of the mind', was first developed as a science in Germany by J. C. Lavater towards the end of the eighteenth century. In Britain, the work, as always, was pioneered in Edinburgh: Sir Charles Bell, physiologist and neurologist, Professor of Surgery at Edinburgh University, developed an early interest in the relation of anatomy to aesthetics in works such as the oft-reprinted *Essays on the Anatomy of Expression in Painting* (1806). Alexander Walker, lecturer on Anatomy and Physiology at Edinburgh and author of *Physiognomy*

Founded on Physiology, and Applied to Various Countries, Professions, and Individuals (1834), focused on the application of the principles of physiognomy to delineate the different racial characteristics of Celts and Goths across the English, Scottish and Irish, an approach that influenced the work of Robert Knox, who believed that 'the exterior must ever . . . translate the interior'.[41] By the time of Knox's own *A Manual of Artistic Anatomy* and *Great Artists and Great Anatomists* (both of 1852), physiognomy had become an accepted science, particularly popular with artists and writers in so far as it offered a visual instrument to augment their portrayal of characters, enabling, as was thought, an accurate depiction of a particular race or class.[42] Later in the century, in his *Inquiries into the Human Faculty* (1883), Francis Galton sought to redefine the physiognomical differences between races according to the principles of heredity and eugenics.[43]

The resemblance of physiognomy's illustrative sketches to the cartoon (the first use of the word 'caricature' is recorded in Browne) meant that many of physiognomy's scientific pretensions were frequently parodied by humorous and playful essays, but paradoxically these nevertheless helped to continue the discourse itself as a feature of public life and general conversation, particularly with respect to national differences. A prominent example in this period was George Jabet's *Nasology* (1848), republished from 1852 onwards as *Notes on Noses*. The book mocks physiognomy by declaring the establishment of a 'new science of nasology'. Arguing that mind determines the body ('We contend that the Mind forms the Nose, and not the Nose the Mind'), Jabet offers the reader the possibility of developing cognitive or other eminent forms of noses. Jabet concludes with a salient chapter 'Of National Noses', in which a range of differently shaped noses of different races or nations are illustrated and matched to national characteristics: 'Every nation', he avers, 'has a characteristic Nose.'[44] Here, as the Saxon confronts the Celtic nose, Jabet's humour moves into an angry discussion of the horrors of the conditions aboard the ships of emigrants trying to escape the Irish famine, which he argues was worse than that of the Middle Passage. This humorous invocation of racial science to make serious arguments for the Irish is not unique to Jabet, an ambivalent combination which may have contributed to Jabet's little volume receiving serious reviews alongside mainstream books on physiognomy.[45] Reading and defining the face remained a particularly important element for European racial theory. Eventually there really was a science of nasology, and books on physiognomy regularly included diagrams interpreting the different shapes of noses (one of Jabet's six classes of noses was 'the Jewish, or Hawk nose'). Jabet's burlesque becomes more sinister to later generations of readers as the jokey diagrams of different national noses foreshadow the noses subjected to Nazi anthropometrical instruments that were developed in exactly this mode of thinking.

Lavater's work was extended in the early nineteenth century by Franz Gall and Johann Spurzheim, who linked physiognomy, the art of reading the meanings of facial expression, to phrenology, also variously termed cranioscopy or craniology, the science of reading the shape of the skull. Phrenology, which 'by an external examination of the head, ascertains the particular talents, feelings and propensities of the individual examined', was first introduced to Britain, and denounced at the same time, by the *Edinburgh Review* in 1815, as a result of which Spurzheim himself went to Edinburgh and then stayed on to lecture there. Spurzheim won over his critics in Edinburgh in part because phrenology seemed to work within the norms of a medical community already focused on physiology and comparative anatomy, the science which Blumenbach himself had already oriented towards the study of racial difference. The classification of the varieties of humans was distinguished from other forms of scientific taxonomies in one particular aspect: unlike the difference between an oak and a beech, the distinction between different kinds of human being was made in part through value judgements. Natural differences were taken as signifiers of cultural differences, determined by differences between bodies. The study of physical differences in the human body, undertaken in natural philosophy, zoology and anatomy, was very rarely just that. Racial science always had a cultural, and therefore political, agenda. Its language, its thinking, its discourse, drew on a whole range of contemporary cultural assumptions evident in other practices from history to physiognomy. From Blumenbach onwards, it is rare to find any account of human physical difference without explicit value judgements attached to them. Only Prichard and his followers, dedicated to the unity of mankind in the context of the anti-slavery campaigns, could be said to have worked outside this paradigm.

Spurzheim's work was continued at Edinburgh by the Scotsman George Combe.[46] It was Combe who pioneered the linking of physical differences of the body with mental, moral and cultural differences, both between individuals and between nations. Physiognomy and phrenology provided the legitimating bridge between classifying the different ways people looked to attaching them to alleged differences between their minds and mental capacities, the immediately relevant question here being, however, as Charles Kingsley put it, whether 'the body is the expression of the soul, and is moulded by it' or 'as Combe would have it, the soul by the body'.[47] More generally, one of the reasons for the popularity of phrenology was that it questioned and diminished the role of environmental causes. As Roberto Romani observes in a discussion of Richard Cobden's enthusiasm for Combe, phrenology appealed to 'the urge in Britain, which went beyond phrenological circles, to belittle environmental causation in favour of the full independence and responsibility of individuals'.[48] Such virtues of individualism just happened to coincide with the precepts of Teutonism and Saxonism.

Combe, the pre-eminent authority on and exponent of the hugely popular science of phrenology, and founder of the Edinburgh Phrenology Society in 1820, had included short discussions of national characteristics in his *A System of Phrenology* (1819).[49] The *Phrenological Journal*, which began in 1823, recurred frequently to the topic. Combe soon found inspiration in the work of Joseph Vimont, above all in his magisterial and magnificent *Traité de phrénologie*.[50] Vimont was the first phrenologist to measure the crania of people of different ethnicities and to link skull shape and size to the study of racial difference. Phrenology was responsible for developing the techniques of measuring the skull with calipers that has now become indelibly identified with the sinister pretentions of scientific racism.

It was phrenology, too, with its affirmation that brain size corresponded to brain power ('that size in an organ . . . is a measure of power in its function; *i.e.* that small size indicates little power, and large size much power') that laid the foundations for the skull measurement system developed by the American anthropologist Samuel Morton to produce a hierarchy of different racial capacity based on brain sizes of skulls. Morton first broached his thesis that the difference of skull sizes between different races corresponded to a racial hierarchy in *Crania Americana* (1839).[51] Although he confined his own observations in this work to a footnote, Morton invited Combe to contribute an appendix on the differences of national character, entitled 'Phrenological Remarks on the Relation between the Natural Talents and Dispositions of Nations, and the Development of their Brains'. After a disquisition on the unchangeable differences between the races and the level of their civilizations,

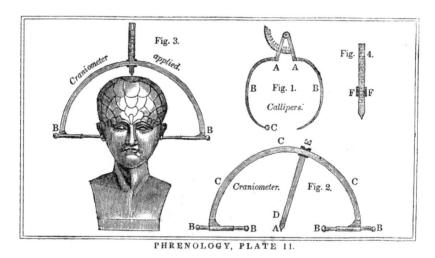

Figure 2.1
The Phrenologist's Own Book (Philadelphia, 1849), page 83.

starting with the Teutonic and Celtic races ('In France, Ireland and Scotland, the Celtic race remains far behind the Teutonic in the arts, sciences, philosophy and civilisation'), Combe spells out and endorses the implications of Morton's work:

> The phrenologist...has observed that a particular size and form of brain is the invariable concomitant of particular dispositions and talents, and this fact holds good in the case of nations as well as of individuals.
>
> If this view be correct, a knowledge of the size of the brain, and the proportions of its different parts, in the different varieties of the human race, will be the key to a correct appreciation of the differences in their natural mental endowments, on which external circumstances act only as modifying influences. Such, accordingly, is the light in which I regard this great subject.[52]

Crania Americana provides clear evidence of the direct link between the new discourse of race based on skull size and the established science of phrenology. The connection between them went further than skulls alone. In its accounts of the twenty-one organs of affective propensities and sentiments, and the fourteen intellectual perceptive and reflective organs, phrenology also developed much of the impressionistic, generalizing discourse of race that would continue for as long as racial theory was perpetuated. Consider Combe 'On the Cerebral Development of Nations':

> Dr Vimont, in his *Traité de Phrenologie*, has published a valuable chapter, in which he describes, among others, the characteristic features of the German, French, and English heads and nations with great accuracy.... We invite him to come to Scotland, and form his own judgement of our national heads. The SCOTCH lowland population, which has done everything by which Scotland is distinguished, excepting in the department of war, is a mixed race of Celts and Saxons. The long head of the Celts, is combined with the large reflecting and moral organs which characterise the Germans. The following is an average specimen of the Scotch lowland head:–

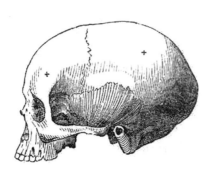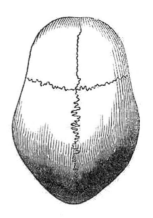

¹ Tome ii. p. 470.   ² *Lib. Cit.* vol. ii. p. 490.

The SCOTCH lowland head is rather large; and considerable variety of temperament exists among the people. In the labouring classes, the lymphatic and nervous, with an infusion of the bilious temperament, is very common; the hair is of a sandy colour; the skin pale, the figure heavy, but the eyes are blue and clear: The individuals are capable of long enduring efforts. The organs of Amativeness are considerable, and Philoprogenitiveness, and Adhesiveness, large: and domestic attachment is a striking characteristic of the race.... The organs of Acquisitiveness are generally large in the Scotch, and, taken in connection with large Self-Esteem, the result is a strong infusion of selfishness, or at least of attention to self-interest. Aided by Cautiousness, Secretiveness, Firmness, and the moral and intellectual organs, this combination renders them generally successful, when placed in competition with other nations, in the career of wealth; and it coincides also with the fact that the Scotch rapidly acquired capital when the markets of England and its colonies were opened to their industry.[53]

This shift between scientific discourse (the presentation of the images of the skulls) and an itemization of particular moral and intellectual qualities attributed to the race as a whole, with other casual observations added in, such as here the Scottish exploitation of the British Empire, would become entirely characteristic of the discourse of race. Though the scientific basis of phrenology was challenged from the 1840s onwards, it was still going strong in the 1870s, and its ideas survived in the culture at large as a form of popular science until the end of the century, indeed even into the twenty-first century in the use of terms such as 'high-brow' and 'low-brow', and in reference to people's 'direction bump' and the like.[54] As phrenology became discredited, the science of race switched its legitimating authority from phrenology to anatomy and zoology, but the discourse itself, and the style of observation, continued without interruption. So did much of the technology: the callipers and craniometer that had been the distinguishing instruments of phrenology were transferred to the realm of racial science. Although the analysis of bumps and depressions in the skull was discredited, questions of skull size and shape continued as central factors in racial analysis. The Englishman Marlow is still obliged to decline the doctor's request to measure his head as he sets off for the heart of darkness at the very end of the nineteenth century. In the same year, the American ethnologist William Ripley published a map of the cephalic index of the British cranial type. For the record, the indexes all lay between 77 and 79, 'with the possible exception of the middle and western parts of Scotland, where they fall to 76'.[55]

Many accounts of the history of 'race' point to the development of the science of race playing an important part in the increasing racialism of Victorian culture. Racialism, however, was a much broader phenomenon. The scientists provided a new ground and authority, and identified themselves with racialism just as the historical philologists had done, but they did not invent the sentiments. Racialized explanations developed in popular political discourse before the advent of scientific racialism as such. We have already seen examples of this in Thomas Arnold and Carlyle. So too, the popularization of ideas of race was the product of more accessible cultural forms than anatomy and ethnology on their own. They were often interlinked: in 1859, for example, an anonymous literary critic in Edinburgh published the first study of Shakespeare on the principle of race – with Iago as the Romano-Italic type, Hamlet as the Teuton, Macbeth as a Celt, Shylock as a Jew, and so on; in 1863, J. W. Jackson published a book on racial differences entitled *Ethnology and Phrenology as an Aid to the Historian*.[56] The discourses of physiognomy and phrenology and their definitions of racial characteristics also keyed into, and formed part of, the disquisitions on national character that followed Hume's essay 'Of National Characters' (1748) and which, as Roberto Romani and Peter Mandler have shown, could be said to constitute a minor genre of its own.[57] Hume, though perfectly capable of making remarkably racist statements when he felt like it, had emphasized the importance of 'moral causes' such as governments over 'physical causes' with respect to national character. Many writers though can be found alternating between the two. The passage of Carlyle discussed in the previous chapter shows the ways in which one could easily modulate into the other: in *Chartism*, a stinging critique of the English treatment of the Irish, who have been reduced to total poverty, is followed by an even more vitriolic attack on the Irish themselves for sinking so low.

Since 'nation' and 'race' were used interchangeably in this period, it is not surprising that writing on both race and national character shared an assumption that the two were closely allied: already in Kant's *Anthropology*, the discussion 'On the Character of Nations' is followed by a section 'On the Character of Races'.[58] National differences quickly moved into assertions of intrinsic racial differences between the people – who were then characterized with the qualities of the representative individual, or 'type'. Aside from being a popular topic for university prize essays, the subject of the English national character was generally more favoured by foreign Anglophiles or phobes such as Hyppolite Taine than the English themselves.[59] There was a series of publications in the 1830s: the opener, Irishman Richard Chenevix, a discredited chemist, was also an ardent advocate of phrenology, and the man who introduced Mesmerism into England.[60] His posthumous *An Essay Upon National Character* argued that all the elements that make up national character are as innate as they are in the individual, a fact which he considered phrenology put 'beyond a doubt'.[61] Bulwer Lytton's *England and the English* (1833), a book which J. S. Mill considered 'the truest ever written on the social condition of England', was largely concerned with that favourite theme of the Victorian intellectual, the intellectual's lament, lampooning English philistinism in favour of the more civilized culture of France.[62] Elsewhere Mill himself was fond of discussing national character, though always careful to downgrade the factor of race. In 1844, reviewing Michelet's *History of France*, founded on the clash of the Celtic and Germanic races, he argued that 'we think that M. Michelet has here carried the influence of Race too far, and that the difference is better explained by diversity of position, than by diversity of character in the Races'.[63] Mill preferred to emphasize social factors, rather than rejecting race outright and offering an alternative, such as climate, food and soil, in Henry Thomas Buckle, or language in Latham.[64] Despite arguing against the foregrounding of race, however, Mill himself was no less prone to use the racialized language of the stereotype, writing as if all the individuals of a nation are psychologically one and the same 'type', as in the following comments that he offered on the Irish character in 1846, observations which are hard to distinguish from the Tacitus-inspired sentiments of his racializing opponents:

> We have said it already, and we repeat it – the Celtic Irish are not the best material to colonize with. The English and Scotch are the proper stuff for the pioneers of the wilderness. The life of a backwoodsman does *not* require the social qualities which constitute the superiority of the Irish; it *does* require the individual hardihood, resource and self-reliance which are precisely what the Irish have not. . . . Instead of insisting, John-Bull-like, upon everything to himself, the demand of his [the Irishman's] nature is to be led and governed. He prefers to have some one to lean upon.[65]

Concluding that the Irishman should become more 'like his Celtic brother of France', Mill here shows himself apparently quite

69

comfortable working within the terms of a fixed Saxon–Celt dichotomy. The fact that the pre-eminent public figure of nineteenth-century Britain, who argued against an overemphasis on race, used language of this kind shows just how difficult it was to step outside its conceptual geography in this period.

No such considerations were to inhibit the nightwatchman for national character at the end of the century, the Australian politician Charles Henry Pearson. Recently returned to England, he made the widely publicized prediction in *National Life and Character: A Forecast* (1893) that 'the higher races of men' would shortly be thrust aside by the lower.[66] In the United States, Pearson's warning was taken to heart by the imperialist President Theodore Roosevelt. This *fin-de-siècle* paranoia showed that some things, at least, had changed over the course of the century. In 1838, a writer on colonization in the *Phrenological Journal* had remarked: 'It may be deemed a cold and mercenary calculation; but we must say, that instead of attempting an amalgamation of the two races, – Europeans and Zealanders, – as is recommended by some persons, the wiser course would be, to let the native race gradually retire before the settlers, and ultimately become extinct. This is the natural course of events when a superior race establishes itself in a country peopled by an inferior one.'[67]

Chapter 3
Moral and Philosophical Anatomy

Race 5: The Transcendental Anatomy
of Robert Knox

When the linguist and historian J. M. Kemble appealed in *The Saxons in England* to 'the personal appearance of the peasantry in many parts of England' as proof for his historical argument about the Saxons, it marked the emergence of a new factor in academic discourse. Arnold had appealed to race, but he never suggested that his students should go outside into the street and test his remarks by checking out how Teutonic the faces of the people of Oxford looked. Race had now become embodied. It had also become permanent. The English weren't just historically descended from Saxons and Celts: Saxons and Celts could still be found milling together on the streets.

In Kemble, this comes as a minor observation, almost unnoticed among the painstakingly accumulated details of his historical evidence. The following year, however, saw the publication of a work that for the first time substantially connected ideas about the Saxon to the new racial science that had been developing since the latter part of the eighteenth century: Robert Knox's *The Races of Men* (1850).[1] Making this link gave the Saxonist account of England a whole new disciplinary dimension. For Knox was both an advocate of the new anatomically based racial science that was emanating from Paris and

Edinburgh, and a Saxonist of what appeared to be an extreme persuasion.

Knox used to be remembered less for his book on the races of men than for his role as a receiver of corpses in the Burke and Hare scandal, the result of the incompatibility between the demands of the Royal College of Surgeons of Edinburgh (of which Knox was a fellow) for anatomical training for medical students and the legal difficulty of obtaining corpses for dissection. A military surgeon on the field at the Battle of Waterloo, who later studied in Paris with Cuvier and Geoffroy Saint-Hilaire, he returned to Edinburgh in 1822 to become the assistant of Dr John Barclay in his well-known extramural anatomy school in Surgeon's Square. Among those who enrolled at that time was the comparative anatomist and palaeontologist Sir Richard Owen, who developed similar interests to those of Knox. In 1826 Knox took over the school, assisted by William Fergusson, who was later to become President of the Royal College of Surgeons of England, John Reid, and subsequently by his brother Frederick, also a surgeon, and rapidly became the most popular teacher of anatomy in Edinburgh, an achievement which did not endear him to his colleagues.[2] He was widely acknowledged as one of the best anatomists of his time: G.T. Bettany, in the first 1892 *Dictionary of National Biography*, described him as 'among the greatest anatomical teachers'. At Edinburgh, his regular lectures were given to classes of up to five hundred. With as much as two-thirds of the whole Edinburgh medical school in his class, Knox reckoned to have taught between five and six thousand students, many of whom went on to become eminent surgeons and anatomists themselves, in both Britain and the United States.[3] On Saturday mornings Knox also gave popular public lectures on 'Comparative and General Anatomy, and Ethnology', in which he broached his more comprehensive philosophical views, particularly those relating to race.[4] Knox was also the founder and first curator of the Edinburgh Museum for Comparative Anatomy.[5] Although a commission of enquiry, which he himself initiated, cleared Knox of wrongdoing in the Burke and Hare 'resurrectionists' case (one of many which led to the passing of the Anatomy Act in 1832), his professional career suffered thereafter in Edinburgh's milieu of professional rivalry that had forced even Charles Bell to seek work in London. Knox continued to lecture on anatomy, but with epidemics in Edinburgh, the retirement of Professor Alexander Monro Tertius from the Edinburgh Chair of Anatomy in 1846 (last of a line whose family had held the chair continuously for 126 years – Monro, Darwin remarked, 'made his lectures on human anatomy as dull as he was himself'), and the decline of the Edinburgh Medical School itself, the numbers attending Knox's school dwindled.[6] He turned more and more to writing.

Knox, whose interests involved not just anatomy, zoology, ethnology, geography, meteorology and natural history, but also the philosophical 'transcendental anatomy' that he had learned in Paris from Etienne Geoffroy Saint-Hilaire, had hitherto published scientific articles in journals such as the *Lancet*, the *Edinburgh Philosophical Journal*, and the *Edinburgh Medical Journal*, some of which were collected in his *Memoirs: Chiefly Anatomical and Physical* of 1837.[7] Another of Knox's early interests was in accurate representations of human anatomy; from the 1820s onwards, he edited or annotated several collections of plates or engravings. In the 1840s and 1850s he published books in the area of anatomy and aesthetics, translations of French anatomical and zoological works, and anatomy textbooks which were regarded as the best in the field.[8] In 1842 Knox started to travel away from Edinburgh, to London and Paris. In 1846 he began to give series of lectures on 'The Races of Men' to various philosophical and literary societies and institutions in Newcastle, Manchester (where they were reported in the politically radical *Manchester Examiner*), Liverpool, Birmingham and London.[9] From June 1848 to February 1849 these lectures were published in twenty-four weekly parts in a general practitioner's journal, the *Medical Times*, reaching a broad readership of contemporary physicians.[10] In 1850, Knox's revised version of the lectures, *The Races of Men: A Fragment*, illustrated with wood engravings by the sculptor Richard Westmacott, RA, was published in London and in Philadelphia, then the centre of medicine and racial science in the US.[11] Though frequently criticized for his forthright and sometimes vituperative rhetoric, which with its rhetorical emphasis on the 'facts' of the unerring laws of nature in many ways resembled Carlyle's, Knox was soon being routinely cited in the subsequent international literature on race in the nineteenth century. The paradoxical reception of the book was pinpointed by the writer of Knox's obituary in the *Lancet*: 'Dr Knox will be best remembered by his work on the "Races of Men", which has been largely read, freely found fault with, and yet highly praised.'[12]

Whether it is true or not that Knox 'revolutionised altogether our study of the races of man', as was claimed after his death, he gave an upfront version of the new thinking which produced a transformation of the prevailing basis of ethnography, the science of races, into an anthropology based on anatomical and 'moral' differences.[13] An illustrative moment in this respect comes with the report that Lord Lyndhurst, author of the notorious 'aliens in blood, in language, and religion' speech on the Irish in the House of Lords in 1836, was comforted when Dr Robert Druitt, editor of the *Medical Times*, read passages to him from *The Races of Men*. Lyndhurst subsequently sent a message to Knox expressing his delight in the book, and expressing his wish 'to see the work circulated in the best English society'.[14] Though Lyndhurst was a close friend of Disraeli, whose early views on race are often cited together with Knox's, it is unlikely that Knox's work ever achieved that kind of genteel dissemination, apart perhaps from his book *Fish and Fishing in the Lone Glens of Scotland* (1854). It did circulate, however, in the scientific world of anthropology, medicine and the natural sciences. In other works, such as *A Manual of Artistic Anatomy* (1852), *Great Artists and Great Anatomists* (1852), *A Manual on Human Anatomy* (1853) and in his translations and editions, Knox missed no chance to emphasize the relations of the body to race; paradoxically, however, for one who invoked Saxon supremacy, in these works he clearly identified his own aesthetic interests as Celtic rather than Saxon. Through all these books, his many contributions to medical and scientific journals (including twenty-eight in the *Lancet* alone), his articles in popular weeklies such as the *Illustrated London News*, and his public lectures which he continued till his death, Knox's ideas infiltrated the medical, scientific and aesthetic spheres, and, as will be shown, coincided with a new element discernible in public discourse, particularly in relation to Ireland.

In 1858 Knox was made an honorary fellow of the Ethnological Society of London; in 1861 he was elected foreign member of the Anthropological Society of Paris, an indication of his international esteem, and the following year, the year of his death, a new, extended edition of his *The Races of Men* was published.[15] From the late 1850s, Knox's career had revived in a dramatic way when he and his work were taken up by the anthropologist James Hunt. Knox was credited by its members with playing a central influential role in planning the formation of the Anthropological Society of London.[16] Hunt was his most enthusiastic disciple, and it was he who initiated the break away from the allegedly moribund Ethnological Society to found the Anthropological Society of London (now the Royal Anthropological Society) in 1863, in order to shift the methodological basis of anthropology from what was regarded as the discredited language paradigm to the contemporary focus on anatomy. Although Knox died before its meetings began, Hunt subsequently took every chance to promote Knox's work in the society and its journals. Characterizing Knox as 'the great modern British anthropologist', Hunt included essays by Knox in the first volume of the *Anthropological Review*, the journal of the Anthropological Society, and habitually invoked his work thereafter. In 1868, declaring 'Let Dr Knox instruct us from his grave', the Society published an edited compilation of Knox on the Celt in order to offer an anthropological view of the current Fenian disturbances, declaring: 'Fenianism startled John Bull, and taught him that there may after all be something in Comparative Anthropology'.[17]

'The number of great English minds that owe their first scientific *impetus* to Knox's teaching and personal influence are enormous' wrote his disciple C. Carter Blake in 1871, reviewing Lonsdale's *The Life of Robert Knox*.[18] Knox was always a controversial figure, and few of his readers accepted his more speculative observations. They pointed out at the time that his arguments were often paradoxical, though a love of paradox was a characteristic in fact of many racial theorists, for example de Gobineau. But they all read him. As Evelleen Richards has argued in a detailed study of the institutional afterlife of Knox's influence, while his adoption by the Anthropological Society had the effect of perpetuating his views into the mainstream of Victorian anthropology, the international institutionalization of his work came at a cost.[19] For Hunt and his colleagues dropped the political radicalism so evident in his work and used Knox to justify very different views, such as the Anthropological Society's support of Governor Eyre and the South during the American Civil War. The paradoxes of Knox's radicalism and his racialism were resolved for the causes of British imperialism and American slavery, both of which he abhorred.

Knox's *The Races of Men* appeared at the time of a sudden explosion of books on race which, taken together, show the striking shift that was taking place towards a zoological emphasis in the study of human beings.[20] Prichard's death in 1848 marked the beginning of the end of the dominance of the earlier generation of liberal-minded ethnologists who had championed monogenesis, anti-slavery, environmental explanation and a linguistic taxonomy for human difference. The decline of R. G. Latham, Prichard's disciple, is indicative of this transformation. After a decade of writing successful books on grammar and the English language, in the 1850s Latham turned to publishing a series of ethnological surveys in which the peoples of Britain, the colonies and Europe were classified according to linguistic rather than racial categories. In 1862 he argued, against the powerful Max Müller, that India was not the Aryan motherland, 'an eccentricity' which, as the DNB puts it, 'destroyed his reputation' (the idea of the Scandinavian origin of the 'primitive Aryans' was later revived by Isaac Taylor and Thomas Huxley and was subsequently taken up with enthusiasm by Nazi ideologues).[21] Though Latham was laudably reluctant even to employ the term 'race', A. H. Sayce argued that his Aryan thesis was itself the result of a confusion between language and race.[22] If the issue with Knox's writing was its over-vehement rhetoric, the real problem with Latham's 'glossological ethnography' (as D. W. Mackintosh described it) was, more prosaically, its sheer unreadability.[23] As Huxley lamented in 1890, Latham's 'attacks upon the Hindoo-Kooshite doctrine could scarcely have failed as completely as they did, if his great powers had been bestowed upon making his books not only worthy of being read, but readable'.[24] Faced with general neglect by his peers, Latham descended into an impoverished alcoholism.[25]

Latham lost his institutional support almost at the moment when Knox found it, for after the publication of *The Origin of Species* in 1859, the Ethnological Society was taken over by Huxley and the Darwinists, who despite their rivalry with the Anthropological Society were much closer to Knox in their views than to Prichard or his disciple Latham.[26] Knox's relation to the evolutionary theories of Chambers and Darwin was complex. Darwin, who studied medicine in Edinburgh in 1826–7 at the time when Knox had just taken over from John Barclay in the Anatomy School and was giving his Saturday morning lectures on Ethnology, was familiar with Knox's views on 'transmutation' or evolution on a basis of immanence, which he cites in *The Descent of Man* (1871).[27] While he considered races unalterable, Knox's evolutionary theory also allowed for 'transitions of organic beings from one form to another' by saltatory descent.[28]

Though Knox was an anatomist, there is in fact almost nothing about anatomy as such in *The Races of Men*. In Knox's day, anatomy was not just a pedagogical science teaching the layout of the body's organs to medical students. It involved philosophical questions about form and function, as well as the origin and necessity of each organ's development. Like his pupil Owen, Knox was inspired by Geoffroy Saint-Hilaire's 'transcendental anatomy' which was founded on the idea of 'homology', that is that different parts in different animals would nevertheless perform the same functions. As Darwin put it in *The Origin of Species*:

What can be more curious than that the hand of a man, formed for grasping, that of a mole for digging, the leg of the horse, the paddle of

77

the porpoise, and the wing of the bat, should all be constructed on the same pattern, and should include the same bones, in the same relative positions? Geoffroy St. Hilaire has insisted strongly on the high importance of relative connexion in homologous organs: the parts may change to almost any extent in form and size, and yet they always remain connected together in the same order.[29]

Knox followed Geoffroy in looking for universal laws of form in the anatomical structure of all living beings.[30] For the latter, these were shared 'transcendental' forms, not necessarily linked by an evolutionary process, which demonstrated, as Knox put it, the great law of 'the unity of the organization in all living beings throughout all time'.[31] Knox's interest as a scientist was less in tracing the general laws of this universal homology of form than in investigating its other side, namely variety (or diversity), its origins, the laws that had produced it, and how they continued to operate as a factor in society and history. This was the basis of his 'moral' or 'philosophical' anatomy: through the category of race, and the effects of racial variety, Knox sought to show the operation of natural law on human history and society. In that respect, though differing with respect to evolution, he anticipated the arguments of Herbert Spencer.

The Races of Men, therefore, is not about biological race in the sense of providing anatomical accounts of racial difference: in the exposition of the book, the emphasis on race largely falls on enduring cultural characteristics. Knox in fact is contemptuous of what he calls 'those miserable, trashy, popular physiologists' such as Combe (p. 32). In this way he anticipates the contemporary move away from physical anthropology, which began with Blumenbach, towards an investigation of 'the mental and moral characteristics of mankind' which would culminate with the founding of the Anthropological Society in 1863.[32] What he offers, following L. A. J. Quetelet, whose *Treatise on Man and the Development of His Faculties* he translated in 1842, is a book of 'moral anatomy', that is, an analysis of the rule of natural law on social and political life.[33] Quetelet developed the use of statistics to discover laws within the apparently random activities of human behaviour, the technique that would turn into the discipline of sociology. Quetelet had demonstrated the statistical regularity of marriage, birth, suicide, murder, crime and so on, arguing that though each one might be the action of an individual agent, taken together such human activity was predictable. Knox interpreted him to mean that human behaviour and morality, the disposition and characteristics of individuals and of nations, were also governed by natural law, just as for animals; he was sympathetic to reformers such as Quetelet who foregrounded this view. For Knox, natural law formed the basis of his two fundamental theses: that the specific characteristics of the different human races were unalterable, and that the races themselves were adapted to survive only in the places on earth where they had originated. In an appendix to his Quetelet translation, in the first treatise on what his follower James Hunt would call 'ethnoclimatology', Knox presented statistical evidence as the basis of his claim that Celt and Saxon could not survive outside their own climates, an argument that would be a major thesis of *The Races of Men*.[34]

If not Carlyle, then it was the influence of Quetelet's statistical method that led Knox to insist always, like Gradgrind, on 'the facts'. In Knox's moral anatomy, the facts always reduced to race, and race in his account always linked the physical type to its social and mental characteristics. This tendency can be demonstrated most simply from Westmacott's illustrations of the Saxon and Celt, the implications of which go back to Tacitus' account of the solitariness of the German as opposed to the gregariousness of the Celt.

In figure 3.1 the five Celts are portrayed as 'a group', impoverished and overfertile, crowded together and profligate, spilling out of the edges of the picture. The mention of Marylebone, the Kilburn of its day, identifies them as Irish immigrants. The Africanoid nose of the man on the right, a standard characterization of the Irish for much of the nineteenth century, particularly in the cartoons in *Punch*, suggests their racial identity as non-European others.[35] The Saxon on the other hand is not represented directly at all, but rather through his

Figure 3.1
Richard Westmacott, 'A Celtic Group: such as may be seen at any time in
Marylebone, London', from Robert Knox, *The Races of Men* (1850), page 52.

comfortable mansion, which Knox describes as 'Standing always
apart, if possible, from all others' (figure 3.2). What's remarkable
about this image – repeated three times in the book – is that there
is no representation of any Saxon physiognomy at all – no biological
racialism evident here. The bourgeois Saxon embodies his instinctive
racial purity, freedom and love of liberty in his property, home and
solitariness, just as in Tacitus. It's only when the image is enlarged

80

Figure 3.2
Richard Westmacott, 'A Saxon House: standing always apart, if possible, from all others', from Robert Knox, *The Races of Men* (1850), page 40.

that you see two tiny genteel female figures sitting on a bench in the garden on the right. As with Thierry, Knox thus also suggests that the racial difference between Saxon and Celt corresponds to class differ-ence – and nothing suggests class differences in Britain more quickly than the three forms of British homes, detached, semi-detached and terrace, the respective dwellings of the upper, middle and lower classes.

For his 'moral' anatomy, Knox also drew on an older tradition of Scottish cultural and ethnic historiography, some of which was distinguished by its strongly negative attitude towards the Celts. In that sense, his interests come closer to the tradition of Scottish historians such as MacCulloch, to whose work he refers, than to that of many contemporary anthropologists.[36] Another influential figure in this tradition was the Scottish historian John Pinkerton, who, in his *Dissertation on the Origin and Progress of the Scythians or Goths* (1787), eulogized the Goths at every opportunity while declaring the Celts

> to be mere radical savages, not yet advanced even to a state of barbarism; and if any foreigner doubts this, he has only to step into the Celtic parts of Wales, Ireland, or Scotland, and look at them, for they are just as they were, incapable of industry or civilization, even after half their blood is Gothic, and remain, as marked by the ancients, fond of lyes, and enemies of truth. . . . to say that a writer is a Celt, is to say, that he is a stranger to truth, modesty, and morality. . . . characters of nations change; characters of savage RACES never.[37]

Compared to Pinkerton, Knox's attitude towards the Celts was almost enthusiastic. He wrote that 'Ireland contains in her Celtic population the elements of a great race, were she not politically enslaved'.[38] Yet, exactly like Carlyle, he then blames the victims themselves.

Merging Pinkerton's diatribes against the Celts with Thierry's view of history as the product of racial antagonism, and drawing on the discourses of physiognomy, phrenology and physiology, Knox argued that it was the animosity between races – an idea derived from natural history of an instinctive repugnance between different species – that determined the course of history. All racial differences, according to Knox, produce antagonisms. Interpreting nationalism as merely a form of race consciousness, he claimed that the outbreak of nationalist revolutions based on ethnic identities in 1848, which contemporary newspapers and journals described as the year of 'the war of the races', proved the historical thesis about race and nationality that he had been advancing in his lectures.[39] By combining history with racial theory, Knox turned the dominant view of English history as a triumph of the Saxons over the Celt into a foundational principle of racial struggle; he used the thesis of racial antagonism to turn the historical conflict between Celt and Saxon into a story of a 'natural' racial war between them. As a result, he portrayed the Celt not just as an illegitimate pretender to the superior Saxon's rightful territory, but as a group whose presence threatened the racial homogeneity of England as a nation, 'England' being identified with the whole of the British Isles:

> The really momentous question for England, as a *nation*, is the presence of three sections of the Celtic race still on her soil . . . and how to dispose of them. The Caledonian Celt touches the end of his career; they are reduced to about one hundred and fifty thousand; the Welsh Celts are not troublesome, but might easily become so; the Irish Celt is the most to be dreaded. . . .
>
> The Norman government of England has, it is true, done its best and its worst in Ireland. If you wish to see what such a dynasty can do, go to Ireland; still, the source of all evil lies in *the race*, the Celtic race of Ireland. There is no getting over *historical facts*. Look at Wales, look at Caledonia; it is ever the same. The race must be forced from the soil; by fair means if possible; still they must leave. England's safety requires it. I speak not of the justice of the cause; nations must ever act as Machiavelli advised: look to yourself. (pp. 378–9, emphasis in original)

Even his most enthusiastic supporter, James Hunt, was moved to remark at this point that 'Knox appeared to let his pen run away with him here'.[40] As Knox knew very well, the Celts were already being forced to leave: his comments were written in the context of the time of the Irish famine. He had himself offered a scientific explanation of the cause of the potato blight, blaming a parasitic fungus. The real cause, he added, however, was feudalism, and the immediate solution to the famine would be to open the ports.[41]

Aside from the starkness of his views, and the power of his vigorous upfront manner of expression, Knox's work was unusual to the degree that he focused his distinctions predominantly between the different European races. Unusually, therefore, for a book on 'the races of men', Knox spends only one chapter on what he calls 'The Dark Races of Men': for the most part, he is interested only in distinguishing between white peoples. Attacking Blumenbach and Prichard for misleading the public with the label 'Caucasian', because it implied a vast harmonious racial category for all Europeans, Knox announces that

> the object of this work is to show that the European races, so called, differ from each other as widely as the Negro does from the Bushman; the Caffre from the Hottentot; the Red Indian of America from the Esquimaux; the Esquimaux from the Basque. (pp. 44–5)

The opening chapter indicates his priorities by being devoted to the 'Saxon or Scandinavian Race': 'No race interests us so much as the Saxon' writes Knox (p. 9). The supreme qualities of the Saxon are then progressively differentiated from gypsies, Copts, Jews, Celts, Germans, Slavs and Sarmatians. Since Knox considers the true Saxon to be Scandinavian, he argues that there are in fact three races in Britain – Celts in the Scottish Highlands, Wales and Ireland, Scandinavian Saxons on the eastern coasts of Scotland and England, and Flemish Belgians in the South – the invading Angles and Danes, he claims, never really established themselves outside London.

While he envisages a Britain from which the Celts have been expelled, Knox is not, however, an orthodox Saxonist. He reinterprets the historians' traditional Saxon supremacist argument about the Saxons being the true English. Though aligning himself politically with the historians, he disputes their arguments from the point of view of ethnography. Putting Saxonism on a new racial foundation means that he corrects its earlier unscientific formulations, taking issue with Arnold in particular by contesting the expression 'Teuton'. 'Teuton', he contends, is meaningless in ethnographical terms, for the Germans are not simply Teutons – they are rather made up of at least two races, Saxon and Slavonian, corresponding to their two religions, Protestant and Catholic (p. 341). Knox therefore avoids the terms 'German' or 'Teuton', preferring 'Saxon' or 'Scandinavian' (not to be confused with Latham's idea that the Scandinavian was in turn the origin of the Aryan). He describes the Saxons as 'a race of men, differing from all others physically and mentally' who originally dwelt in Scandinavia, around the various shores of the Baltic, from Norway

84

to the north and east of the Rhine in Northern Germany. Asking what restless qualities led this race to spread itself northwards and southwards in Caesar's time, and subsequently migrate to South Africa, North America and Australia, he answers:

> To me it seems referrible [*sic*] simply to the qualities of the race; to their inordinate self-esteem; to their love of independence, which makes them dislike the proximity of a neighbour; to their hatred for dynasties and governments; democrats by their nature, the only democrats on the earth, the only race which truly comprehends the meaning of the word liberty. (p. 46)

Like Kemble before him, Kingsley and even Henry James afterwards, Knox portrays the Saxon as inherently migratory. While proclaiming the Saxon's instinctive racial superiority, Knox, with his strong 'Celtic' aesthetic interests, is nevertheless quite upfront about the Saxon's qualities of boorishness, anti-intellectualism, lack of aesthetic sense ('In the fine arts, and in music, tastes cannot go lower'), and his 'inordinate self-esteem'. His portrait of the Saxon is brutally unflattering and often sarcastic – 'a profitable war is a pleasant thing for a Saxon nation'. He even criticizes the Saxon for being racist. All the same, he announces that the Saxon is about to be 'the dominant race on the earth', its 'republican empire' in America, 'destined some future day to rule the world'[42] Knox's ambivalence towards the Saxon can be linked to the apparent paradox of his work first emphasized by Michael Biddiss, namely that though his racialism today appears very much on the right, politically, in the terms of his day, Knox was a radical materialist, a republican who wished to extend the rights of man to include women and non-Europeans. He was highly critical of slavery, colonialism and 'Sanitary' laws directed against prostitutes, whose rights as women he thought should be acknowledged.[43] This republican materialism in itself gave further grounds for his unpopularity with the still Calvinistic establishment in Edinburgh.

Racial supremacist as he was, and not fearful to apply to European races ideas of extermination that were being freely used in the context of non-European races, Knox was nevertheless no devotee of Arnold's fantasies of Teutonic imperial racial expansion. His republicanism means that though he agrees with Arnold that the Saxon is a naturally colonizing race (colonizing in the sense of settler colonies), he has no sympathy with British colonialism in terms of its political administration – even in Ireland. For Knox, the Saxon's colonizing impulse produces what might be termed colonial anti-colonialism, or diasporic anti-imperialism, that is, the effect that free-born colonizing Saxons will always resist any forms of metropolitan imperial control.[44] Characterizing Saxons as essentially Protestant, democratic, independent and self-reliant, and more attached to the soil than to any nation, Knox invokes the American War of Independence to prove his claim that Saxons will colonize, but never remain long as colonists subject to the Crown. His belief in the independent spirit of Saxons is such that he suggests that if Ireland were to be repopulated with Saxons, as he himself had suggested, it would inevitably become independent and even republican, in due course. This kind of consequence is typical of Knox's paradoxical logic:

> Then will come, a hundred years hence, a more momentous question for England: a *Saxon population* in Ireland will assuredly forget that they ever came from England. . . . Then will come the struggle of self; the Saxon against Saxon. A Saxon colony in Ireland! But long before that, the tri-colour flag may wave over the United States of Great Britain and Ireland. This is the march of the Saxon onwards to democracy; self-government, self-rule; with him, self is everything. (p. 379, emphasis in original)

The same qualities lead Knox, like Jefferson before him, to regard the present government and aristocracy in Britain as a Norman legacy that restricts Saxon freedom: 'its views and policy are antagonistic to the Saxon race it governs' (p. 5), he claims, looking forward to the more 'natural' Anglo-Saxon republic in England. Knox's combination of strong republicanism with racialism helped to make his work popular in the United States. Alongside the Americans, he

86

is sympathetic to the Boers of South Africa and their resistance to British colonial policy, as also, characteristically, to the South African 'Kaffirs' who are resisting invasion. He is completely upfront about the motives and unscrupulous and unseemly practices of settler colonialism, of which he had direct experience in South Africa. For Knox, however, this is the product of an unstoppable racial drive entirely immune to the moral issues at stake, of which he was more aware than most. As a racialist, he is nevertheless quick to praise Africans for their military prowess ('the correctness of Knox's views as to indigenous races holding their own against their conquerors is well instanced in Algeria', commented his biographer Lonsdale in 1870, following a lead from Knox himself), and also shows sympathetic interest in the case of minorities such as Jews and gypsies.[45] The paradox of Knox's racialism was that he was, you might say, a Scottish self-hating Saxon.

In that context, it is noticeable that one of Knox's closest friends was an Englishman from Jamaica who became naturalized in France, William F. Edwards. Edwards provides the link that was the most original aspect of Knox's book in the English-speaking world, namely his use of the findings of contemporary racial science to provide an analysis of contemporary history. For Knox, it was not just that British history was the determined product of racial conflict, but that the natural law of racial characteristics could be used to explain historical events, such as the American Revolution, and thus to provide the basis for decisions on future policy and action, for example in British policy in Ireland.

Race 6: Hybridity: W. F. Edwards

Knox's radical extension of Thierry's argument into the realm of natural science was, as he himself points out, in fact not his own: he relied on a connection between the disciplines of history and race that had already been developed by his friend Edwards, who had been the first to link the principles of comparative anatomy to

Thierry's history. The Thierry brothers had argued that English and French history was the product of the conflict of different races, an idea that as we have seen had already been taken up by historians in Britain. With a common sentiment that, as Knox put it, 'race is everything in human history',[46] the originality of Edward's book lay in the fact that he strengthened Thierry's argument of the racial determination of history by invoking the authority of the new racialism of comparative anatomy. Thierry's racialist historiography implied the permanence of races, enduring through time. It was enough for him, as it was for Thomas Arnold, to assert their continuing presence. In his *Des caractères physiologiques des races humaines, considérés dans leur rapports avec l'histoire, lettre à M. Amédée Thierry, auteur de l'histoire des Gaulois* (1829) Edwards gave an anthropological basis to Thierry's arguments and suggested the mechanisms by which, in countries like France, or England, the latter's arguments about the persistence of races through history could be substantiated through racial analyses of their living populations.[47] Here Knox and Edwards connect with Kemble.

Edwards' book, *Des caractères physiologiques des races humaines*, was widely credited by French anthropologists and raciologists in the nineteenth century as being the founding text of French ethnology. The distinguished anthropologist Paul Broca called Edwards 'the first author who clearly conceived and formulated the complete idea of race'.[48] Edwards' importance was the result of the fact that he succeeded in combining the purely physiological analysis of human difference (which had been well established in France since Cuvier) with the contemporary historical accounts of the moral, intellectual capacities of different nations evident in their histories and cultures. If race became the general explanatory category of nineteenth-century analysis in the humanities and social sciences, it was the result of this particular combination of physical and cultural difference. Edwards' contribution was to combine these new features in a decisive way by allying physiology and anatomy to history; to do this he produced an apparent solution to the problem of how racial difference could be combined with a history of racial fusion. Edwards' interest in the role of race in national history meant that, like Knox, his own sphere of interest was focused on Europe. This was particularly problematic for tracing a racial genealogy. It was all very well to claim permanent difference between Europeans and Africans. Europe, by contrast, was historically documented as made up of a composite of races that had successively invaded and colonized the European landmass, and was frequently used by the monogenists as a refutation of the idea of permanent racial differences. How, therefore, if countries like Britain and France were made up of successive different races, could Thierry claim that their histories were the product of inter-racial antagonisms? If it was admitted that the English or the French were made up of more than one race, would not the populace have long since become mixed, in the manner which Walter Scott suggests gave rise to the mixed language of English? And if races had become biologically mixed, how could they be characterized in the manner of the historians as belonging to particular races, such as Celts or Saxons?

The particular contribution of Edwards was to provide an answer to this question through a new theory of racial mixture, or hybridity. The increasing emphasis, from 1848 onwards, on the permanence of racial types, and their inalienable difference from each other, had led to an ever-greater preoccupation with the implications of racial mixture. Edwards' thesis provided the answer to an argument about racial mixing that went to the heart of contemporary debates about race, namely, were all humans one species, or should the different races of men be considered to be distinct and different species? In the context of arguments about slavery, this was a highly charged question. Polygenesis, or the belief that the different races should be described as different species, was first widely considered in the eighteenth century. But not only did this contradict the biblical account of all men and women being descended from Adam and Eve ('And hath made of one blood all nations of men': Acts 17.26), there was also an apparently insuperable scientific barrier to its general acceptance, in as much as the generally accepted definition of species was that the product of any sexual union between different species was infertile. The mule, the product of a horse and a donkey, was the central example of this principle. The widespread appearance in the colonies of mulattoes, the product of unions between white and black, apparently refuted the argument that human beings were made up of different species. Monogenists such as Prichard argued for the correctness of the biblical account in which all humans are portrayed as descended from a single source; they claimed that the variety of features of the different races were the product not just of climatic difference but also of racial intermixture which could produce new races with new physical and mental characteristics.

The prolificness of inter-racial unions did not, however, stop many writers from claiming that mulattoes were indeed mules, if not in the first generation, then definitely by the second or third.[49] This anecdotal argument was put on a more scientific footing in 1829 by Edwards, who proposed a more sophisticated version which came to be called the law of decomposition.[50] His interest in the racial composition of whole nations enabled him to side-step the more or less impossible question of whether individual unions over several generations had produced fertile offspring or not. Looking at populations as a whole allowed Edwards to formulate the question in a different way. He pointed out that at a national level it was rarely the case that two populations of exactly the same numbers came to mix; historical and geographical factors meant that in general intermixture took place only between a large population and a small alien group (for example, the Norman conquerors in Britain), in which case the smaller would be absorbed by the larger, unless it remained isolated for political or religious reasons, as in the case of the Jews. For Edwards, as for Knox, the Jews were a decisive example of the permanence of racial types. Not only, he argued, were portraits of Jews in Egyptian wall illustrations or in Renaissance paintings still recognizable as Jews, but the Jewish diaspora provided definitive evidence that climate did not change human physical features, as Prichard and the monogenists had claimed. In the same vein, Edwards pointed to other examples of the fixity of morphological types, such as the case of domestic animals taken from the Old World to the New. Ideas of the unalterability of race and the refusal of races to mix were allied by others to the Indian caste system, in so far as it was understood. As De Quincey put it in 1822: 'Even Englishmen...cannot but shudder at the mystic sublimity of castes that have flowed apart, and refused to mix, through such immemorial tracts of time.'[51] Even Englishmen.

What, though, if the mixtures were more equal? Would they not mix and fuse? In the *Histoire des Gaulois* (1828), Thierry had argued that the ancient conflict of the Celts (or Gauls) and Belgae was still being played out in French history. Edwards was clearly attracted to the assumption in this argument that the two races, far from merging one into another, had continued in their separate ways, with the tension between them accounting for the dynamics of French history. Edwards' contribution was to suggest to Thierry that this racial difference was still discernible at a physical level in the population of France. In order to make this argument, Edwards differentiated between different kinds of racial intermixture: he distinguished between what he considered absolutely different races and what he called closely allied races ('distant' and 'proximate'). Unions between radically different races, he argued, produced hybrid 'half-breeds' whose progeny would degenerate and eventually die out.[52] But with similar races, the case was very different. Here Edwards cited the experiments of a Swiss scientist named Jean-Antoine Colladon (1755–1830) who had researched into the laws of hybridization.[53] Colladon had crossed white and grey mice, and reported that the product of these unions was not an indistinct mousey colour but mice which were definitively either grey or white. This led Edwards to claim by analogy that when European races were crossed with each other, the children similarly preserved intact the exact characteristics of just one of the parental races. Although he allowed the possibility of the production of intermediate types, Edwards suggested that these would in time revert to one or other of the original types. In what was to become the dominant anthropological theory of hybridity in the nineteenth century, racial fusion was thus impossible: it was a theory of permanent separation, of a natural apartheid between the races. This theory was already being voiced with the authority of law by Chambers in 1844 ('It is also ascertained that the external peculiarities of particular nations do not rapidly change. There is rather a tendency to a persistency of type in all lines of descent, insomuch that a subordinate admixture of various type is usually obliterated in a few generations'). By the 1860s it was widely accepted throughout Europe and America as received scientific knowledge.[54]

Edwards used his science in order to substantiate a ready-made thesis about race that had been developed by contemporary historians. Science came to the aid of history, which meant that science itself was already ideologically determined. Edwards' theory became the standard reference point for the new American Anthropological School developed by S. G. Morton and Josiah Nott.[55] The attraction of the thesis in the United States was that it allowed apologists for slavery to claim that blacks and whites were entirely distinct races that would never succeed in intermixing, and that the white race would remain predominantly Anglo-Saxon despite the arrival of other European immigrants. In Britain, rather unexpectedly, Edwards' best-known and most influential admirer was Matthew Arnold.

The tendentiousness of Edwards' evidence from Colladon for the origin of this thesis is striking. The widespread acceptance of the idea throughout the nineteenth century leads one to ask how it could have been taken as fact by even the most reputable scientists such as Darwin or Taylor, and how it was still being cited by writers in the twentieth century.[56] Edwards' work was substantiated and somewhat revised in 1860 by Broca's full study of hybridization among animals (including humans), a work which became the standard reference for the subject.[57] The phenomena with which this science was trying to deal were in fact outside the scope of its technical capacity, and were only understood with the gradual and belated acceptance of Mendel's theory of genetics in the early twentieth century.[58] Edwards' law of human hybridity, namely that mixed races will always die out or revert to their original type, according to whether they were proximate or distant, was modified but not seriously attacked until the 1930s. Although Edwards' law seems so counter-intuitive, one reason why it survived in anthropological circles must have been because without it, the whole 'scientific' analysis of discrete races would have fallen apart.

So Edwards' law enabled the 'mingled' population of Europe to be viewed as a living history of its still distinct different races, allowing a nuanced theory of the hybridity of the English population, whereby it could be admitted that they were racially mixed, but without losing their fundamental separate ethnic identities. For this reason, statements about the 'mongrel' or mixed identity of the English cannot in themselves necessarily be interpreted as refusing the idea of race – as, for example, in Sir Arthur Keith's 'it is often said, that we British are a mixed and mongrel collection of types and breeds' of 1919.[59] As late as 1956 the celebrated art historian Nicholas Pevsner could still claim in his classic *The Englishness of English Art*: 'To this day there are two distinct racial types recognizable in England, one tall with long head and long features, little facial display and little gesticulation, the other round-faced, more agile and more active.'[60] Pevsner's source for 'the racial components of the English and their influence on art' was what he calls a 'very remarkable' book published in 1942 by the Nazi collaborator art historian Dagobert Frey, *Englisches Wesen in der bildenden Kunst* (*The English Character as Reflected in English Art*), whose opening chapter 'Angelsächsisches und keltisches Volkstum' sets up the ethnological basis for presenting English art as a dynamic product of the racial tension between Saxon and Celt.[61] Just as for Knox, it is the Celt's 'fast-moving intensity and aesthetic desire for form' that Frey argues has always provided the fundamental stimulation for the development of English art.[62]

In the 1860s, meanwhile, inspired by Edwards' thesis, practically minded anthropologists began to look for the English in the surviving descendants of the successions of invaders of the lands. The crucial question was: were they going to turn out to be Saxons or Celts?

Chapter 4

The Times *and Its Celtic Challengers*

In *The Races of Men* Knox claimed that *The Times* had stolen his ideas about race and history from his earlier lectures:

> The views which I had so long adapted of human nature, human history, and the future, had led me long ago to foresee the approaching struggle of race against race. The evidence appeared to me so clear that I felt greatly disappointed on finding so few disposed to acquiesce in the views I had adopted. But now that the question can no longer be concealed, the London press has honoured me with a notice which I did not, I confess, aspire to. One leading journal, at least, has fairly reprinted nearly all my view in the form of leaders, to which, of course, no name was attached.[1]

There is no direct evidence for this claim, though the similarity of views on occasion remains striking. Knox's intervention was certainly remarkably timely, and had the effect of substantiating the particular political racialism that *The Times* had been developing since the early 1840s, whereby the paper characterized the English as Saxon and the Irish as inferior Celts, with the Welsh and the Scots Highlanders generally thrown into the Celtic pale as well. *The Times'* racism towards the Irish was on many occasions just as extreme as that of Knox.

Punch, whose negative attitude to the Irish has been well documented, was merely, as Emerson observed, a comic version of *The Times*. But it was *The Times* that had the real power, prestige and circulation at the highest levels, and it was *The Times* that dominated English reactions to Ireland in the 1840s. Emerson remarked:

> No power in England is more felt, more feared, or more obeyed. What you read in the morning in that journal, you shall hear in the evening in all society. It has ears every where, and its information is earliest, completest, and surest. It has risen, year by year, and victory by victory, to its present authority.... It has its own history and famous trophies. In 1820, it adopted the cause of Queen Caroline, and carried it against the king. It adopted a poor-law system, and almost alone lifted it through. When Lord Brougham was in power, it decided against him, and pulled him down. It declared war against Ireland, and conquered it.[2]

The development of *The Times'* campaign against the Irish leaders, and the Irish people, as Celts to English Saxons, began very soon after the appointment in 1842 of a new editor, John Thadeus Delane, who was just 23 years of age. Like the owners of *The Times*, John Walter II and III, Delane was hostile to Irish Catholics and, particularly, to Daniel O'Connell.[3] Delane himself had a Protestant Irish background: he was a descendant of the Delanys of Mountreth, Queen's County (now Mountrath, County Laois) in Ireland, a town notorious for its Orangeism and violent Protestant hostility towards Catholics. When his branch of the family emigrated to England in the eighteenth century they strategically changed the 'y' at the end of their name to an 'e' to mask their Irishness.[4] Before joining *The Times*, according to Henry Wace, Dean of Canterbury and principle leader writer for the paper from the 1860s, Delane 'had attended the hospitals for some terms. He was always fond of medical and surgical knowledge.'[5] He had studied in Paris under François Magendie, regarded as one of the greatest physiologists of his time, known for his pioneering research into the central nervous system. Magendie is, however, more generally remembered for his controversy with Scottish anatomist Sir Charles Bell over his emphasis on the need for vivisection (which Bell deplored on humanitarian and religious grounds), and his refusal to use ether to diminish the pain of his subjects in his experimental surgery on humans or animals. Delane's studies under Magendie begin to account for the similarities that Knox noted between his own views and those of *The Times*: both men had studied physiology in Paris, the centre of contemporary medicine committed to racialized perspectives.[6] Delane's background in the physiology of race was augmented by his assistant, George Dasent, who came from a prominent West Indian colonial family. Dasent was a Scandinavian and Icelandic scholar, who, after studying with Jacob Grimm in Germany, spent four years in Stockholm, studying the Sagas. His first book, *The Prose or [sic] Younger Edda, commonly ascribed to Snorri Sturluson* (1842), was dedicated to Thomas Carlyle, whose views on slavery in the West Indies he shared.[7] All the contemporary currents of 1840s racialism – French physiology, German historical philology, Carlyle's robust anti-Irish Saxonism – came together in the two editors of *The Times*.

Neither Delane nor Dasent wrote the leaders of *The Times* in this period, and the variety of opinions expressed in them reflects the range of their different authors. But Delane was responsible for the overall political line that the paper took: 'He controlled with the utmost thoroughness every branch of it. . . . he kept strictly in his own hands the initiative of all that was to appear in the paper, and especially of the leading articles.'[8] It was he who would appoint '*The Times* Commissioner to Ireland'.

The Times and the Politics of the 1840s

In the 1840s, while some of the quarterlies, particularly the *Edinburgh Review*, and among the newspapers, the *Morning Chronicle*, were sympathetic to Irish Catholics, offering economic analyses for Irish ills, most newspapers, including the *Standard* (its editor, Stanley Lees

Giffard, was Anglo-Irish), *Punch* and the *Scotsman*, were generally hostile. A paradigm of Saxon Britain versus Celtic Ireland, of industrious Protestants versus impoverished Catholics, was articulated particularly in the columns of *The Times*, which, selling 40,000 copies a day, was the country's predominant newspaper, and, as Mill put it, a power in the state. Although *The Times* had supported Catholic emancipation in the 1820s, under Delane's editorship it fixed upon Daniel O'Connell, who was both Catholic and a supporter of the Whigs, as its particular enemy.[9]

In 1840, O'Connell (known as 'The Liberator' for his success in achieving Catholic emancipation in 1829) had set up the Repeal Association in Ireland and in 1843 initiated what *The Times* famously characterized as 'monster meetings' in his drive against the Union. The combination of O'Connell's campaign, which was not violent but raised the spectre of violence (he was jailed, in 1844, for 'intimidation'), his activism in parliament against the Union, and subsequently against the Irish Poor Law in the context of the ever increasing intensity of the Irish famine after 1845, and Peel's Irish Coercion Bill passed in 1846 to put down Irish unrest, together with the Young Ireland rising of 1848, meant that from 1843 onwards the Irish question was ever at the forefront of British politics – it never really left it until the 1920s. While recent commentators have argued for the importance of Empire in the formation of English identity in the nineteenth century, there was really only one part of the Empire that was fundamental to it, part of it and yet not part of it, and that was Ireland. In fact, the English would never have become English if it hadn't been for Ireland. And Ireland would probably never have quite become 'Ireland' if it hadn't been for the Irish emigrants in America.

During this time, Irish politicians and writers created a new nationalist rhetoric, most notably articulated by O'Connell, William Smith O'Brien, leader of Young Ireland, the *Freeman's Journal* and the new weekly, *The Nation*, edited by Thomas Davis. Davis, an admirer of Augustin Thierry, developed a nationalist identification of Ireland with Irish language, culture and history, as part of a long struggle against English rule. *The Times* did not directly respond to O'Connell's or *The Nation's* arguments which were articulated in terms of specific issues and grievances about Ireland's anomalous relation to England, but rather characterized the new nationalism of the repealers in terms of a division of Celt against Saxon, deliberately assimilating nation to race. Nationalism was presented as a form of racial or 'caste' identification, and *The Times'* first response was to challenge it in those terms. In 1843, a leader writer asked: 'Who in the world, we should like to know, is trying to raise a dissension between Saxon and Celt . . . who in the three kingdoms would think of raising *this* dissension, excepting only Mr Daniel O'Connell?'[10] Nationalism was assumed to involve nothing but race. A leader written the following year shows *The Times* following the strategy of opposing Irish nationalism by providing an account of the racial heterogeneity of the whole British nation:

> The present key to the favour of Mr O'Connell is "nationality." . . .
> But Providence, which placed Ireland alongside and within sight of
> the noblest island in the world . . . most clearly had another, and far
> better intention, tha[n] that we too [*sic*] should ever be divided realms.
> It is the very strength of this nation that it has triumphed over so many
> petty nationalities. These, broken and digested, have become the
> manifold and various elements of her power, her wondrous versatility,
> her fitness for all climates, for all occupations, for all enterprizes.
> Whatever is noble and energetic in this quarter of the world, has
> contributed to its formation: our race is not one, but many. We are
> British, Celt, Gaelic, Phoenician, Roman, Saxon, Dane, Norman; and
> there is scarce a family of any but the lowest and most predial class
> which carries not in its blood the traces of lesser and more recent
> introductions, the welcome refugees from foreign tyranny to this
> hospitable soil.[11]

This rather liberal, cosmopolitan tone, to modern ears, masks the degree to which by representing Irish demands solely as a matter of perverse racial identification, they could be disregarded. From the columns of *The Times*, a reader would assume that the categories of

Celt and Saxon were the dominant form in which Irish demands were being made. Aside from Thomas Davis' poems signed 'A True Celt', however, there is little sign of this.[12] Neither O'Connell's speeches, nor the editorials of *The Nation*, voice a rhetoric of the kind used by *The Times*:

> There seems to brood over Ireland a heavy curse, which can neither be expiated by calamities nor mitigated by time. . . . we are told . . . of the mixture of hostile races as a mischief not less fatal than the confusion of repulsive creeds. The Saxon and the Celt, – this is the cause of Irish tumult, or Irish bloodshed, and Irish misery. 'The Saxon lord, the Celtic serf'. . . .
>
> We are not now reasoning on the absurdity of such a belief. We are stating it as an ominous fact in the history of Ireland, that a prejudice, which elsewhere has been dissipated by circumstances or modified by time, is there more potent than ever. In other lands time has blended the conquered and the conquerors into one common family. Alliances have fused the most hostile, interest has reconciled the most repugnant races. . . . Who in England now thinks of Saxon or Norman? What rational man in Scotland cares for Gaelic or Saxon descent? . . . how nobly and how gainfully have national antipathies and particular jealousies been sacrificed at the shrine of that comprehensive patriotism which has inspired the descendants of the Normans, the Saxon, and the Highlander to forget all but their common faith and fealty to Great Britain?
>
> And yet in Ireland this unhallowed potency of traditionary hate still prevails – more dangerous because concentrated within narrower limits. . . .
>
> The Celtic peasant fires at his half-Saxon landlord, the half-Saxon landlord avenges himself by debarring his half-Celtic neighbour from the rights granted to him by a Saxon parliament![13]

While initially using the mixture of races in Britain as a way of attempting to refute Irish nationalism, it was not long before *The Times* itself began to utilize the opposition of Celt and Saxon as a way of blaming the Irish for their plight during the famine ('we do not doubt that, by the inscrutable but invariable laws of nature, the Celt is less energetic, less independent, less industrious than the Saxon. This is the archaic condition of his race').[14] These sentiments were largely initiated by the reports of Thomas Campbell Foster, whom Delane had sent as '*The Times* Commissioner' to Ireland, a title designed to make Foster sound less like a reporter than an impartial state official compiling a government Blue Book – though to judge by the unreflecting prejudice displayed against the Welsh by the three authors of the notorious 1847 *Report of the Commission of Inquiry into the State of Education in Wales*, Government Commissioners were in practice very similar.[15] From August 1845 to January 1846, Foster, who himself cheerfully admitted he had no previous knowledge of Ireland, sent in some thirty-six reports to the paper 'On the Condition of Ireland'.[16] Primed with *The Times*' views on the Irish Poor Law debate, these articles portrayed an Ireland divided between indolent Catholic peasants, who made little attempt to utilize the natural resources at their disposal, and self-reliant, energetic Protestants of the northern counties. This division, hitherto conceived in terms of the Catholic–Protestant antimony, was reconceived so that it was portrayed in terms of a fundamental racial difference between Celt and Saxon:

> It is because the poor Celt is prepared to put up with bad fare, and worse clothing and shelter, that he is *made* to put up with them. It is because the man of Saxon descent *will* live comfortably and well, or, if his exertions cannot accomplish this, make his grumblings heard and *felt*, that he *does* live comfortably and well. Let any man of observation travel through the Celtic population of the county of Leitrim into the adjoining mixed population of the county of Fermagh, and I think he must be convinced that *race* has more to do with the distinguishing characteristics of Ulster than either politics or religion.[17]

Foster, though largely ignoring the famine, was by the same token opposed to the sending of any famine relief, even in the face of an appeal from Queen Victoria. The final insult, he argued, was when the Irish 'call upon the Government to do something for the benefit of Ireland, with English money, the produce of English enterprise and English industry!' *The Times* itself would subsequently also voice its disapproval about charity relief being sent to Ireland from England during the famine ('So there is to be another collection for Ireland' opined a leader in *The Times*) and published many complaints from clergymen correspondents about 'an attempt so ill-advised as again to fatten the lazy Celt on the daily bread of the industrious Saxon'.[18] Sending the Irish charity became particularly resented in the context of increased Irish militancy in 1848 accompanied by 'one incessant whine for English money'.[19]

Foster's 'crochets about the inferiority of the Celtic race', as Mill described them, and his representation of the fundamentally racial causes of the famine, were adopted as the view of *The Times* itself.[20] From 1846 onwards, *The Times* began to profile the reasons for the failures of the famine in terms of racial difference, with the Saxon praised for those qualities of honest hard work and self-reliance so promoted by Carlyle, while the Celt was characterized as irredeemably idle, the Irish a 'wretched, squalid, destitute people'.[21] In December 1848, for example, a leader repeated Foster's comments about the incongruity between the richness of the soil and fisheries of the west of Ireland and the abject state of the people, adding:

> If we ask the cause of this distressing anomaly, the answer is, that the people are Celts. An unmixed, aboriginal race, swarms on those shores, and multiplies not indeed beyond the resources of the country, for they have not been tried, but beyond the resources of idleness and the spontaneous produce of the soil. For three hundred years there has been a continuous succession of attempts to infuse the Anglo-Saxon spirit into these miserable imbeciles, and make them feel the dominion of man over nature.... So far it is all in vain.[22]

At the same time, as the epithet 'aboriginal' suggests, the paper increasingly compared the difference between the Irish and the English to that between European and non-Europeans races.

> ...our plantations are not fringed with Caffres or Red Indians; our downs are not scoured by Bedouins or Calmucks; our conquerors and our conquered are not wholly unmixed. So far there seems no discrepancy which a few generations might not be thought enough

to overcome. Yet, within 24 hours of this great metropolis there are differences which...may well compare with the more picturesque diversities to which we have alluded. England and Ireland, each as a whole, are strange opposites.[23]

> To say that Irishmen, speaking the English tongue, and living under an English Government, cannot be taught English habits, practise an English economy, and flourish under English institutions, is to brand them with a stigma which no man has as yet ventured to affix to the 'barbarians' of New Zealand. An intercourse of 20, and a dominion of less than 10 years, sufficed to make the tribes of New Zealand adepts in the English language, and imitators of English customs, and suitors in the English law courts. Is there any Irishman who will insult his countrymen by a defence which assumes their inferiority to the 'savages' of the Pacific?[24]

The comparison of the Irish to the Maoris would be repeated in a different context by Darwin in *The Descent of Man*.[25] The issue for the leader writers of *The Times* was whether it would ever be possible to 'Saxonize the Celtic mind', or whether the devastating phenomena of death and emigration of evicted peasants during the time of the famine would provide a golden opportunity for repopulating the country with Saxons, as Knox was already suggesting in his lectures.[26] In 1848, an editorial commented:

> In a few months we might imagine half of Tipperary and the whole of Mayo would be completely divested of that encumbrance, a pauper peasantry; and the place of the ejected tenants supplied by a new race with new habits from the farmyards of Norfolk or the wealds of Yorkshire. According to some, and these are not the most highly coloured accounts, there are tracts of land from which the emigrant has swept the last remnant of his last crop, lying in gloomy waste for the bold occupation of some Saxon adventurer.[27]

Most of the extravagant sentiments in relation to the Irish, therefore, that can be found in Arnold, Carlyle or Knox, can also be found in the columns of *The Times* during this period. While books by particular authors cannot in themselves individually be held responsible for the development of a general discourse of race, if, as many commentators have noted, a change of thinking and expression with respect to race is discernible in Britain in this period, an influential source for this shift can be found in the daily columns of *The Times*, a paper which prided itself on forming political opinion. At the end of the decade, a more permanent institutionalization of *The Times'* racialized perspective came from another source, from a book whose sales figures reached comparable numbers to those of the circulation of *The Times* itself: Macaulay's *History of England*. As Romani argues, whereas many earlier historians of the nineteenth century, from J. Millar to H. Hallam to Samuel Smiles, had concurred in portraying the state of Ireland as a testimony to the injustice of English misrule, Macaulay reoriented the story into one more like that of Thierry: of a colonized country inalienably divided by race, religion and class:[28]

In his [the Irish Roman Catholics'] country the same line of demarcation which separated religions separated races; and he was of the conquered, the subjugated, the degraded race. On the same soil dwelt two populations, locally intermixed, morally and politically sundered. The difference of religion was by no means the only difference, and was perhaps not even the chief difference, which existed between them. They sprang from different stocks. They spoke different languages. They had different national characters as strongly opposed as any two national characters in Europe. They were in widely different stages of civilisation. Between two such populations there could be little sympathy; and centuries of calamities and wrongs had generated a strong antipathy. The relation in which the minority stood to the majority resembled the relation in which the followers of William the Conqueror stood to the Saxon churls, or the relation in which the followers of Cortes stood to the Indians of Mexico.

The appellation of Irish was then given exclusively to the Celts and to those families which, though not of Celtic origin, had in the course of ages degenerated into Celtic manners. These people, probably somewhat under a million in number, had, with few exceptions, adhered to the Church of Rome. Among them resided about two hundred thousand colonists, proud of their Saxon blood and of their Protestant faith.[29]

For as long as Macaulay's *History* remained the most popular history of England, so long were generations of British brought up on his analysis of Irish history in which the fundamental political difficulty was presented as that of the incompatibility of race.

Celtic Challenges

While in earlier decades the Saxon myth had served attempts, in Linda Colley's phrase, to forge the nation, by the 1840s, as the language of *The Times*, Knox and others suggests, its self-defining relation to Celtism had become bound up with an anti-Irish racism.[30] The more English industrialization increased English prosperity, the more English success was identified with intrinsic Saxon racial characteristics, and contrasted to Celtic lethargy and poverty in Ireland. Anti-Irish racism in the nineteenth century has been charted in L. P. Curtis' well-known studies, and though it is customary to suggest that the picture has now become more nuanced, the critique of Curtis that is most often cited by the revisionists makes some startling arguments that are hardly persuasive.[31]

As with language and race, so too with the Celts the philologists propagated a myth which they subsequently came to deny. In the nineteenth century some people argued that racially Celts were not even Europeans, that they were racially affiliated to Africans, and therefore were illegitimate inhabitants even of Ireland. Thanks to Curtis' studies, it is well known that the Irish were often represented as having what were called Africanoid features, as in Knox's illustration of 'The Celtic Group'. Technically, this characterization of the 'Black Irish' rested on the claim that the Celtic languages were not Indo-Germanic, a suggestion mooted by writers as various as Pinkerton and Friedrich Schlegel, but which had been challenged by Prichard in *The Eastern Origins of the Celtic Nations* as early as 1831, where he demonstrated the relation of Celtic languages to Slavonian, German and Pelasgian. Once in circulation, however, popular myths take a long time to die. Prichard's linguistic argument about the

104

'origin and mutual affinity of the European nations' did not really have sufficient impact to change widespread popular assumptions about the Celts. In 1857, therefore, nine years after Prichard's death, R. G. Latham published a second edition, in which he expanded Prichard's original 194 pages to 387.[32] A long opening 'supplementary chapter' allowed Latham to research and to spell out Prichard's arguments much more clearly, showing in particular just how widely the Celts had been dispersed throughout Europe. Together with Adolphe Pictet's *De l'affinité des langues celtiques avec le sanscrit* (1837) and Johann Kaspar Zeuss's *Grammatica Celtica* (1853), these works changed the academic consensus, at a time when the European public was far more receptive to assimilating the Celts within the European language and racial family. Given that few would claim the Celts to be Teutonic, the term 'Indo-Germanic' was eventually modified to 'Indo-European' to accommodate this change.[33] However, while the philologists changed their mind, in England the idea remained abroad that the Irish Celts were, as Macaulay casually implies, a degenerate race. Every time there was a new campaign for Irish independence, with the Fenians, with Gladstone's Home Rule Bills, Unionists would revive the racial stereotype. As the sociologist and politician John Mackinnon Robertson observed in 1897: 'there is a certain psychological compulsion, so to speak, on nearly all opponents of Irish nationalist claims, to revert in some way to the attitude of race prejudice'.[34]

The Times' rhetoric of Saxon versus Celt had formed a response to the emergence of a new form of Irish nationalism in the 1840s, articulated not only by O'Connell, but by the Young Ireland movement in their paper *The Nation*. For the most part, it is salutary to compare their clearly reasoned arguments, and lists of Irish grievances, with the bombastic rhetoric of *The Times*. The English paper interpreted nationalism as Celtism, but while the contributors to *The Nation* may have perceived England as Ireland's natural enemy (they were, paradoxically, admirers of Carlyle on the basis of his excoriating critiques of the English government), they generally used the term 'Irish' rather than Celt. By 1848, however, the Irish nationalists of *The Nation* themselves began to invoke the Celt as part of their rhetoric as they moved into the advocacy of armed revolution with Gavin Duffy's arrest and the brief editorship of Jane Elgee (known as Speranza, in 1851 she married Sir William Wilde, the Surgeon Oculist to the Queen who was also a pioneer of Irish ethnology and the Celtic Revival; in 1854 she would give birth to Oscar Wilde). *The Nation* could be said to have pioneered the 'Celtic Revival', but for the most part its actual language remained more directly political (and was always English).

While the Teutonic identity for the English was being still advocated so forcibly in the 1840s, it was also being subverted at that very time by the agitation in Ireland. This left three possible positions with regard to Irish politics on both sides of the water:

1 Extirpation: at its most extreme, for English Saxonist hardliners and some absentee Irish landlords, an ethnic cleansing of the Catholic Irish, by emigration or extermination, and repopulation by Protestant English Saxons.
2 Independence: the nationalist advocacy of Ireland for the Irish, with a Celtic revival at a cultural level (after the fall of Parnell this would also be identified with Catholicism) and the expulsion of the English (Saxons).
3 Ethnic and cultural assimilation: the alternative English response to demonizing the Irish as degenerate and unassimilable was to argue against an untrammelled Saxonism in favour of the virtues of the Celts, suggesting that the English themselves were a mixture of Celt and Saxon. Among the Irish ascendancy, English liberals and moderate conservatives, most were generally prepared to concede a broader national identity that would include Ireland, involving a dialectic of some sort between Celt and Saxon, occasionally mediated by other minor ethnicities, such as the Jews. The implication was that the Irish could be integrated culturally and politically with the English. This was not to Saxonize the Irish, in the manner of *The Times*, but to undo the opposition itself. In order to solve the problem of Ireland, in other words, English and even some Irish

106

writers began to try to change the ethnic and cultural identity of 'England' to one which would accommodate the Irish. This mixed identity, it was thought, would also resolve ethnic and religious difficulties within Ireland itself.

This third option would steadily gain ground, gradually producing a reformulation of English identity from the 1840s onwards, in part as a response to Irish agitation. The English began to remake themselves to include the Irish. This political argument was facilitated by the fact that at the same time, a host of ethnologists and anthropologists, themselves often from the peripheries of the UK, particularly Wales and the West Country, began to challenge the idea that the English were exclusively Saxon. Claims might be made on the basis of history and the English language, but in terms of the new racial science, even Knox admitted at times that the English, as they were, were a 'mongrel crew'.[35]

Knox may have been the first of the new racialists, but in a sense he was the last of the Saxon supremacists, particularly given his under-belly of Celtic sympathies. The racial discourse that he helped to unleash, and which he used to challenge the Teutonism of Dr Arnold, turned out to be the very discourse that would be used against Saxon supremacism, specifically with respect to the claim that the English were exclusively Saxon. The paradox here is that in this context racial theorists, for the most part blamed by history, in this case turned out to be the good guys.

Celtic Challenge 1: Thomas Price

The discourse of Saxonism was soon opposed through the promulgation of a counter-discourse of Celtism. A constant stream of writing on the history and literature of Celts had been developing since the eighteenth century in English, French (particularly) and German. In Britain, since the publication of Macpherson's *Ossian* (1761), the literary and aesthetic enthusiasm for Celtism formed a romantic counter-discourse, or counter-spirit, to mainstream whig-gish Saxonism.[36] Indeed, extraordinary to relate in the context of all the statements about them that we have encountered so far, it should now be confessed that the Celts themselves were really an eighteenth-century invention, created once again by philologists, and then deployed in order alternately to contest and to counter the power of the ideology of Saxonism. Saxon supremacy had in some sense been possible precisely because the Celts did not exist. The Oxford English Dictionary confirms this – it can muster only two entries for the term 'Celtic' before 1700. The few uses of the word 'Celt' before 1700 invoked the term according to the original Roman use of 'Celtae' to describe the peoples of Western Europe generally, including those living in Northern Italy and Spain. The Romans actually never used the word to describe the inhabitants of so-called Celtic Britain. Like 'Latin America', it was an ethnic invention of the French – the first use of the term 'Celt' in the modern sense occurred in English in 1706 in a translation of Paul Yves Pezron's *Antiquité de la nation et de la langue des Celtes, autrement appellez Gaulois* of 1703. Originally used to describe the speakers of Breton and the inhabitants of Brittany, regarded as descendants of the ancient Gauls, with the gradual recognition of the Breton language's links to Cornish, Welsh and Irish and Scottish Gaelic, the term 'Celtic' was extended to other languages in the same family. With the inexorable identification between race and language of the time, the term 'Celt' then came to be used for the inhabitants of Cornwall, Wales, Ireland and Scotland, who were given a common ethnological identity on the basis of their linguistic affinity – because their lan-guages were all interrelated they must have been, so the argument went, a single racial group. By contrast, ethnographers today argue that the idea that the Celts were a single people with a common culture is a modern invention – there were only individual tribes with their own particular cultural identities.[37] The category of the Celts came to describe all those who were not Saxon, and all those who were in some sense marginalized by dominant British society. Once united as Celts, they could be demonized as the largely

Catholic 'other' of the successful Protestant Saxon, or celebrated as the marginalized cultural alternative to boorish John Bull.

By the nineteenth century, thanks to the timely invention of tradition, the Celts were well established as an authentic ethnic group identified in Britain with the nations of France, Ireland, Wales and with the Scottish Highlanders.[38] Eighteenth-century Romantic literary Celtism was soon extended into the more contestatory regions of history and ethnography. Just as common elements of the variants of the language had been identified, so too, as we have seen, stereotypical characteristics of the people were produced, largely from Scotland. Like the Irish, the Welsh, however, were not content to acquiesce in their own denigration. In 1829, the same year Edwards published his letter to Amédée Thierry, the scholar the Rev. Thomas Price, already known as a talented speaker at the Welsh Eisteddfods (he would later write the first history of Wales in Welsh), published an *Essay on the Physiognomy and Physiology of the Present Inhabitants of Britain, with Reference to their Origin, as Goths and Celts*, in which he contested the racial differentiations between the Celt and the Goth by the Scottish historians Pinkerton and MacCulloch:

> The system, which PINKERTON and his disciples have adopted, is the following:
> *That the Gothic and Celtic races were originally and generically different: that this difference has ever been clear and distinct, in their physiognomical, physiological, and moral character;* neither time nor accident having had power to change it, so that the Gothic breed or race is as *distinct*, and as *distinguishable* from the Celtic, at this day, as it was two thousand years ago.
> The respective characteristics of the two races they assert to be as follows.
> The Gothic tribes, it is said, were and still are red, or yellow-haired, blue-eyed, fair complexioned, large of limb, and tall of stature. The Celtic, on the other hand, dark-haired, dark-eyed, of swarthy complexion, and small in stature.[39]

Arguing that physical differences were not the result of race but of accidental causes, the purpose of Price's book was to deny these absolute racial differences altogether, and to contest the prejudices which followed from them:

> But it is not only in this instance, that the love of system carries its supporters into the extreme of prejudice: for this Gothic blood is made to engross all the virtues of the kingdom. For example, it is usual, when discussing the merits and origin of our admirable constitution and national liberty, to attribute all these advantages to the German origin of the Saxons. The representation of the people in parliament, trial by jury, rights of free citizens, all originated, it is alleged, in the German woods!!! (p. 87)

To deny such generic distinctions, Price argues from history and against race. Citing the historical accounts of the different invasions of the country, he suggests that 'many parts of England contain a greater portion of Celtic blood than is generally supposed'. From this, he even goes on to make the claim that the specific qualities of the English are indebted to racial mixture:

> if mixture of blood has any influence upon the moral character, it is well for Britain that such streams of Celtic or other blood have flown into the veins of the English, from Wales, from Scotland, and from Ireland, &c, for the last few centuries. Doubtless the energy of Britain is more indebted to this than to any predominance of Saxon blood. (pp. 90–1)

These arguments would be repeated again and again for the rest of the century. Price attempts to prove his observations by taking the reader on a brief ethnological tour of local physiognomies in different areas of the country, showing the absurdity of the fact that 'the physiognomical distinctions between Goths and Celts have been as strenuously insisted upon, as if the present English exhibited their *universal character of red hair, blue eyes, and gigantic stature*' (p. 87).

The denial of inherent racial difference nevertheless gets Price into a new problem, for he must account for the physical differences of the people he sees in other terms. Committed to Prichard's

110

Enlightenment ideas of racial difference being explained by climate and habit, Price finds his solution in the environment:

> in Britain the dark-coloured eye [black or grey] is always found to prevail in the neighbourhood of COAL MINES; and where COAL is used as the general fuel; while, on the other hand, the light or blue eye belongs to those districts, in which that mineral is not used. (p. 36)

Price's explanation, accounting for the relative darkness or fairness of the population by their proximity to coal mines, however implausible, would be once again seriously proposed by R. G. Latham in the 1860s.[40] It offered a solution to the difficulty of on the one hand denying race, and yet at the same time explaining physical differences within limits of relatively small localities. Although Price denies the influence of race, he nevertheless continues to use the category, as for example in the quotation emphasizing the mixture of blood between Goth and Celt. This also points to the problem of how he can then sustain, as he wished to do, a specific interest in Celtic culture. While Price comments that 'it would be difficult, from mere external aspect, to distinguish . . . between a Scotchman and an Englishman', and suggests that instead of being distinguished by race, the Irish 'may be divided into two great classes, − *the well fed* and *the ill fed*', he also argues that uniquely 'in the Principality of Wales, the Celtic race and language have always predominated' (pp. 97, 103). The physical isolation of the Welsh has allowed them an ethnic and linguistic purity unavailable in the rest of the kingdom, and it seems impossible for him here to avoid the term 'race.' Price's text shows the conceptual and rhetorical difficulties of simultaneously denying the racialization of the category of Celt and Saxon, and attempting to redress the power balance between them in order to argue for the value and worth of Celtic culture. By denying race he makes his Celtophilia illogical. It was for this reason that Irish nationalists and their sympathizers would take a different tack − accepting the racial categories, they would make a counter-argument for the value of the Celts as a race. In a comparable way to the proponents of *négritude* in the twentieth century, rather than denying race, they would challenge and reinscribe the values attached to the different racial characterizations.

Celtic Challenge 2: George Ellis, John M'Elheran

The publication of Knox's book stimulated not so much ripostes, quarrelling with his remarks on the importance of race as such, as contributions from ethnologists concerned to redeem and redefine the Celt from his unflattering account. In November 1848, Knox himself reported that in response to his article in *The Medical Times* on 'The Celt in Ireland', he had received 'a very valuable communication on the ancient races of Ireland, from W. R. Wilde, Esq. of Dublin'.[41] Four years later, in 1852, George Ellis, an Irish doctor, published *Irish Ethnology Socially and Politically Considered: Embracing a General Outline of the Celtic and Saxon Races: with Practical Inferences*. Ellis accepted Knox's argument for a fundamental distinction between Celt and Saxon, but resisted the claim of hierarchy, suggesting rather that greater and more accurate knowledge about both Celt and Saxon 'would be found the most efficacious means of terminating mutual animosities, and insuring the mutual advantages of a close and lasting union'.[42] Ellis's book is unusual in that its further aim is to inquire into areas of political economy – he examines issues of education, land, capital and alternative power sources to coal – that would enable the Irish to transform themselves out of the destitution for which they were typically blamed on racial grounds. Unexpectedly, however, his criticism of the English turns out to be that they have not paid enough heed to the question of race, and that as imperialists they have been too egalitarian in their attitude towards other races in their empire:

> This light estimation of the subject of race is carried further still. The conduct of England towards her various dependencies, however generous and noble in intention, (occasionally it is the reverse) is marked,

especially of late years, by a similar infatuation – acted on in principle, though not perhaps expressed in language, viz. that although nature may have endued the different races of the world with characteristic differences in feature, colour, and bodily configuration, yet that in all she has constituted the mind alone essentially alike, requiring only time and circumstances to alter and assimilate it to that standard with which an Englishman is best acquainted – his own; – that therefore all men, however incapable of being converted into Englishmen in bodily appearance, may yet be easily adapted by proper education and training, carried on through a few generations, to receive the same moral and intellectual bias, the same ideas of liberty, the same prepossessions in favour of order and submission to the law, in a word, to become thoroughly English in mind while thoroughly foreign in blood; – and further, as a legitimate practical corollary from such views, that the same laws, restrictions, and privileges which are found suitable to the full development of the energies of the people of England, must of necessity be equally suited to the corresponding improvement of all other races under the English government.[43]

Here, in his critique of the utilitarian mode of management of the Empire, Ellis implicitly brings out the liberal aspect of Macaulay's oft-criticized *Minute on Indian Education* – that is, that he at least allows for some kind of equality between the Indians and the English through education.[44] The problem with the English is thus that they have assumed that all men are capable of 'being converted into Englishmen'. In his opposition to this universal idea of Englishness as a convertible ethnic currency, Ellis, for all his defence of the Celt and desire for union between Celt and Saxon, is closer to Knox: though resisting the latter's thesis of racial antagonism, he thinks that an equitable treatment for Ireland can only be effected through the employment of a local knowledge modulated to their particular racial differences and idiosyncrasies.

Though Ellis's politics are unusual, his emphasis on the qualities of the Celt is typical of the responses prompted by the anti-Celtism of Knox and *The Times*. The earliest challenges, in the 1850s, came not from professional ethnographers or anthropologists, but as an

editorial in the *Medical Times* proudly remarked, from those with
a similar medical background to Knox – anatomists, doctors,
surgeons.[45] In 1852, the same year as Ellis's book, by which time it
had been developing its racialist discourse for the best part of a decade,
The Times published a remarkable letter from John M'Elheran, an Irish
doctor and ethnologist (and one of the many who had studied under
Knox in Edinburgh), to which it gave the heading:

Irish IMPUDENCE

Sir, – Until I found you wilfully shutting your eyes, I was bound to
assume that your contempt of the Celtic race arose from ignorance, and
in my former letters, which you have smothered, I treated you with as
much courtesy as if you were a great advocate of truth. But now I see
you have a persistent prejudice. What is he, 'this godlike Anglo-Saxon'
whom you insultingly hawk about the world as an object of worship?
From a long and careful examination of the race I can tell you what the
Saxon is: – A flaxen-haired, bullet-headed, pig-eyed, huge-faced, long-
backed, pot-bellied, bad-legged, stupid, slavish, lumbering, sulky boor,
whose moral state is a disgrace and regret to England. This is the
prevailing character of your Saxon population, who form a wretched
and decreasing minority, and who are physically and morally the same
as when first they came prowling from the forests of the north. . . .

. . . your Saxons hold a very inferior position in number and importance. There are some fine men amongst them, and they are
capable of improvement; but they have not the cranial capacity nor
the physical energy of a dominant race. Their inferiority of complexion and figure, their obesity, their weak legs and scanty beard, their
small brain in proportion to their long spine and large flat faces are
marks of inferiority. The best of your people are Britons and Gauls,
and Highland Scots, who as masters or foremen invariably walk over
the heads of your Saxons; the hard-working Irish who push your
clodhoppers out of the labour market in docks, railways, and factories,
and will ferret your Saxons out of the coal mines, as they are doing in
the south of Scotland, or whenever they are placed on an equal
footing with regard to education &c. The intelligent and progressive
English are Celts of 'various hues,' as ancient historians and bards
described them.

114

In this letter, M'Elheran offered what was probably the least flattering account of the Saxon since Hazlitt's portrait of John Bull (notice how he used 'Briton' in its original meaning here). Having praised the Celt, M'Elheran, never one for half-measures, gives equal space to attacking *The Times*' anti-Irish racism:

> Sir, your Saxon tradition is false, and you are heaping dung on the graves of your forefathers; you are ballooning with a hoax, and I cannot expect that you will at once let the foul wind out of your vanity, and tumble down to the level of Celts whom you regard as inherently unprogressive, wretched, dirty, lazy, superstitious, murdering ruffians, a contrast to the 'go-ahead Saxon', the noblest and best of created beings, 'the foremost race on earth'. Your blinded, almost blood-thirsty, hatred of the Irish, your 'No Irish need apply', your gloating over the exterminations, and famine, and death in Ireland and the Highlands, your heartless, selfish speculations on the Celtic exodus from your rod of iron . . . prove that your prejudice is not the result of mere ignorance but of wickedness. Your infidel, material theory of race, created and justifies oppression and assassination in Ireland. It makes landlord and tenant look upon each other as aliens. It excites persecution against the poor Irish in England and Scotland. It adds gall to sectarianism. It fulfills your heart's desire of preserving castes – the policy of barbarian conquerors in all ages. You do well, sir, to fasten the Saxon lie.[46]

Taken overall, the lively invective of M'Elheran's style somewhat undermines the effective basis of his argument. It helped to get it known, however. In 1857, Knox heard that his former pupil had read a memoir to the New York Academy of Medicine, in which accusing him of promoting 'Anglomania' in the US, M'Elheran had dismissed the 'carnivorous Saxon' as the 'outer rind of humanity', and claimed that the Celts had become predominant in America.[47] Knox quickly responded, in characteristic robust style, with an article in *The Lancet*, 'New Theory of Race: Celt *v.* Saxon' in which he defended his position, pointing out his extensive praise of the Celt, but questioning the thesis of Celtic predominance in the US.[48] In fact Knox had been misinformed – the New York Academy of Medicine article consists of a rather sober scientific review of the different races of man.[49] The text to which Knox is referring may have been M'Elheran's 'Celt and Saxon: Address to the British Association on the Ethnology of England' of 1852.[50] Or he may have got wind of M'Elheran's forthcoming full-scale vitriolic attack on Saxon arrogance and oppression in *The Condition of Women and Children Among the Celtic, Gothic, and Other Nations*, published the following year in 1858, shortly before M'Elheran's death. 'The virtues of the English, and the dirt and debasement of the Irish, are well known wherever 'The Times' and 'Punch' and all that tribe circulate' he wrote.[51] In riposte, he offered a powerful critique of Saxon attitudes, practices and injustices, showing the civility of the English by focusing on their treatment of women and children (the book includes a chapter entitled 'English Niggers', an exposé of the treatment of boy chimney sweeps); its publication solely in Boston, however, meant that it remained little known in England. As in the letter to *The Times*, M'Elheran's anti-Saxonism ('the very dregs and offal of the white population in America') extends to the counter-claim that the English and Americans who matter are predominantly Celtic ('the divine spark of genius radiates from the Celtic centre of the world. The talent and energy of Great Britain and America belong to the Celt, not to the flaxen-haired, small-brained, and grossly-organized Saxon').[52] M'Elheran ends, nevertheless, with the positive comment that 'Revelation and science teach me that Saxon and Celt are brothers'. As in the case of Price, a contestation of Saxon supremacism cannot in the end make a counter-claim of an equally sweeping Celtic supremacism. Saxon England had to be accepted to some degree, so the effective way to argue against it was to claim an ethnic mixture.

Knox responding to his former pupil was one thing. More surprising was that M'Elheran's challenge to the racism of *The Times* was also powerful enough not only for Delane to publish it in the first place but also to feel compelled to make a response. While *The Times'* leader writers varied in tone from week to week in their attitude towards the Irish – sometimes more vituperative, sometimes more conciliatory – in this instance, the writer was inclined to be defensive, claiming innocence, becoming conciliatory and offensive all at once to the correspondent it described as 'an enraged ethnical philosopher with a Mac to his name':

> In those remarks which our position impels us to make on Irish shortcomings and Irish excesses a spirit of challenge often induces us to refer to the race of the people who thus painfully obtrude themselves on our attention. We picture a man lounging before his cabin, in a constant dishabille, scheming how much he may overreach his landlord and the law, and we call him a Celt. We describe a coast population that will neither catch fish themselves, when they come to be caught, nor allow others to catch them, and we observe by the way that they are Celts, and that none but Celts could act so ridiculous a part. We speak of the constant use to which roadside hedges, stone walls, bludgeons, and bog-holes are applied in certain parts of Ireland, and remark that no race, of at least the British Isles, make a principle and practice of assassination, the Celtic only excepted. Indeed, there really is no denying that the persons and peoples who distinguish themselves in this unhappy way are very pure Celts. There are different families of Celts in Ireland, and there are mixed Celts, but the less mixed the Celt, the more tenacious he is of his birthplace and soil, the more inhospitable to strangers and averse to changes, the more degraded he is sure to be found.

At this point, however, the writer becomes noticeably more conciliatory:

> Of course, we don't deny, we never have denied, the inheritance of some peculiar powers and virtues in the Celtic race. We have not denied that the Irish Celt is a much nearer cousin than the ordinary Englishman to the brilliant Parisian, to the Italian, even to the Greek. For anything we have said, it may simply be the accident of position that prevents the Tipperary man from governing the world at this moment. And we must add, that it has never been our custom to set up the 'Saxon' or the 'Anglo-Saxon' as the rival and contrast of the

Celt. The word 'Saxon' may have dropped occasionally from our pen when it was not easy to find a better substitute. . . . It is not our boast, because we know it is not the fact, that the English people at large are 'Saxon', or 'Anglo-Saxon'. We have repeatedly pointed out . . . that the English owe their great versatility and other practical powers, as well as the mixed elements of their social and political fabrics, to the very heterogeneous composition of their race. It has been observed in this place that almost any man that you meet in the Strand, unless he be actually and entirely a foreigner, has Saxon, Celtic, Gaelic, French, Flemish, Dutch and German blood in his veins. The average English-man is a born cosmopolite, and to that mixed composition he owes the universality of his moral affinities and mental powers. No country in Europe has harboured so many migrations, whether as conquerors, as allies, as refugees, or simply as guests, and no people are so free from the follies of nationality.[53]

Admitting to its typical anti-Irish characterization of Celts, *The Times* thus disengenuously (and given the historical record, untruthfully) nevertheless tries to disengage itself from the charge of enforcing racial antagonism through its championing of English Saxonism. The writer here returns to the position, voiced at the beginning of the previous decade, that the English are in fact ethnically mixed, and makes the bolder claim that the Englishman is a 'born cosmopolite', free from the 'follies of nationality'. This astonishing retreat is, of course, marked most of all by the fact that Delane decided to publish M'Elheran's letter at all. What it most likely signals is an awareness that after 1848, promulgating 'a conflict of races', and hence nation-alities, was a dangerous tactic politically for the English establishment, whether with respect to the United Kingdom or the Empire. The writer continues:

That word ['Englishman'] has long ceased to be the denomination of a race, for there is no race of 'Englishmen'. In its most restricted sense it means that heterogeneous multitude residing in what is called England; and in that larger sense, which public spirit, loyalty, common sense, and convenience all conspire to recommend, it means the whole population of the British Isles. As it happens, we are very ill off for a denomination, the legal title of this realm being one of the most unwieldy dimensions. We are forced to personify the whole empire in the title of England, and we have really no alternative but to call the average gentleman of these isles an Englishman.[54]

There are three instructive and significant statements here: that there is no 'race' of Englishmen, who are heterogeneous in racial terms; that 'Englishmen' includes the whole population of the British Isles; and that the whole Empire is personified 'in the title of England'. Here, in response to the prospect of a separate Celtic nationality on its doorstep, the leader writer expands the semantic reference and range of the word 'Englishman'. The Englishman is no longer the man from England. The word becomes a more general, delocalized term that denotes the whole population of the British Isles, thus including the Irish, the Scots and the Welsh. In the same way, the term 'England' comes to personify the whole of the British Empire around the world. Here, for the first time, we find a statement of a new larger identity for England and Englishness. From this time onwards, Englishness would never again, as it were, be entirely about itself.

At this point, as if having glimpsed something more than he saw, the leader writer abandons his conciliatory tone, returns to the attack, with much talk of indolence, murder and pig-sties, and challenges M'Elheran to prove that the Irish are not Celts. Nevertheless, the publication of his letter signals a new moment in the thinking of *The Times* with respect to Ireland and race. M'Elheran, as *The Times* must have sensed, was not speaking alone.

Celtic Challenge 3: Richard Tuthill Massy

The offensiveness of *The Times*' statements about the Irish was soon criticized again by another Irishman, Richard Tuthill Massy, in his *Analytical Ethnology: The Mixed Tribes in Great Britain and Ireland, and the Political, Physical and Metaphysical Blunderings on the Celt and Saxon Exposed* (1855).[55] Tuthill Massy, who reprints the whole of M'Elheran's letter at the back of his book, remarks:

> It is sad to mark the blunderings made upon this great question of race by the *Times*, potent now for good and now for evil. Many of its articles, written as though the liquid flowing from the editorial quill was wholly gall, are a disgrace to the nation, and stand out all the more marked by injustice and cruelty, when the dispatches of every mail from the Crimea, where the real Celts and the real Saxons are contending with the Russian tribes, tell of Celtic order and Saxon confusion. But, as regards race, or the science of races, and their varieties, the invectives of the *Times* against the Irish are wholly destitute of truth. (pp. 157–8)

In the context of these comments on *The Times*, it is noticeable that Tuthill Massy's book originated as a direct response to the equally virulent prose of Knox's *Races of Men*. Tuthill Massy's initial reaction to reading Knox was to write to the *Medical Times*, the periodical which had been printing Knox's lectures. In two articles, published simultaneously with Knox's lectures, Massy had added his views on the physical bodily differences between Celt and Saxon.[56] These are further elaborated in *Analytical Ethnology*, where the reader is offered contrasting descriptions not just between Saxon and Celtic heads, as one might expect, but a whole range of bodily differences, including, for example, a bizarre illustration comparing the Celtic with the Saxon hand (figure 4.1). After the hand, Tuthill Massy then proceeds to compare the Celtic against the Saxon foot – both of which he claims predicate intelligence and the passions far more accurately than anything to be found in phrenology (figure 4.2). Tuthill Massy's enthusiasm for female Celtic feet in particular knows no bounds. As with Thomas Price, while at one level Massy contests racialism, at a physiological level in his account of ethnic difference he in fact emphasizes – far more than Knox – various anatomical differences of the body. As a doctor, his observations are made up of specific

120

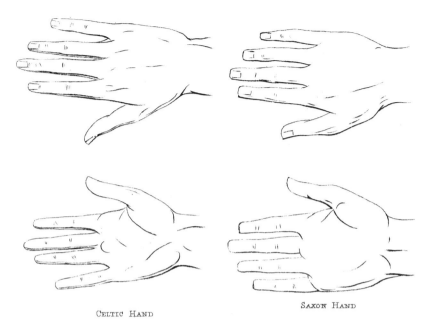

CELTIC HAND

SAXON HAND

Figure 4.1
Richard Tuthill Massy, *Analytical Ethnology* (1855), facing pages 16 and 19.

comments on the varying shapes of different body organs, accompanied by general cultural and anecdotal observations devoted to proving 'the blunderings of the men who would have us think of England as wholly and exclusively Saxon'.[57]

In this way, Tuthill Massy contests aspects of Knox's book, while criticizing others, such as the writers of *The Times*, who engage in racialized discourse. Above all he is concerned to argue against the idea of the Celt and Saxon as antagonistic races, suggesting instead that the British are essentially a 'mixed race': 'From the analysis which I have already made', he declares, 'it must have been manifest even to the most superficial reader, that no pure race exists in the British Isles' (p. 109). Mixed or not, Tuthill Massy also counters Knox with a vigorous defence of the Celts, criticizing English policy

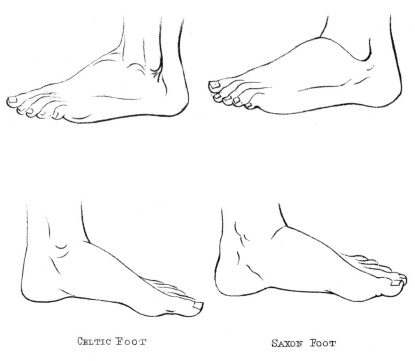

CELTIC FOOT   SAXON FOOT

Figure 4.2
Richard Tuthill Massy, *Analytical Ethnology* (1855), facing pages 24 and 26.

in Ireland and praising the Irish particularly for their poetic imaginative spirit, as Matthew Arnold would a decade later. As with M'Elheran, a defence of the Celts necessarily involves a critique of the Saxons. Here, at the opening of his chapter on 'The Celt in England', he humorously interrogates John Bull, his reader, by mocking the talk of the portly Saxonist:

'What is it, sir? Why, who ever heard of the Celt in England? Celtic England! It's all nonsense! We are Saxon, sir – downright Saxon! Saxon to the back-bone! Why, sir, isn't it a fact that two of our kings – I think George the First and George the Second – could hardly ever speak English? I know they could not speak it correctly;

and there were several others of the same power and eminence, who were our rulers, from Saxony – from Saxony, sir!

And so John walks off, with his portly air and his comfortable digestive organs. You will find him ere long taking his nap quietly over 'Celtic England'. To-morrow he will be talking about Anglo-Saxon rule, Anglo-Saxon power, Anglo-Saxon everything. The evening, perhaps, will find him, forgetful and dreamy, listening to the oratory which comes forth, as a gushing stream, from the eloquent lips of his Celtic brothers. But the House of Lords and the House of Commons may be flooded with their eloquence . . . yet John will still talk of the 'Anglo-Saxon', 'our institutions', 'our language', 'our Shakespeare', 'our Milton', 'our Byron', 'our Saxon poets'.

'Can you write poetry, John?'

'No! nor do I wish. I can find something better to do than to write nonsense!'

And this is the true feeling of the real Saxon mind; at least, of what men now call Saxon – that word which has been spoken and sung, echoed and re-echoed, placed in all conceivable positions, until one has been sickened with the very absurdity of its use.

While contesting Saxon supremacism, Tuthill Massy does not deny ethnic distinctions between Saxon and Celt, but rather, as Arnold would, characterizes the differences as ones of mental and cultural polarities, contrasting the utilitarian plain sense of the Saxon with the poetic, imaginative mind of the Celt. England and English culture, he argues, is the product of both racial and cultural intermixture between the two:

> To speak, indeed, of English poets, is to speak of men whose claims none will dispute. The wide wide world is filled with the fame of the Bard of Avon – England's Muse. Men would give all they have to be English, for Shakespeare's sake alone. But if the greatest writers and the profoundest thinkers are correct in their views of the Mental History of Race, we must rank the great and immortal man, who has thus thrown a glory around the English name, with the now fallen and degraded Celt. All poets, ethnologically speaking, must be Celtic. (pp. 36–8)

Like Price, while 'casting shame upon the reckless abuse of race' (p. 162), Tuthill Massy's objection to race is not to the concept as such, but to Knox's dialectical view of it, in which different races are equated with antagonistic species fighting for the same territory. Races, Tuthill Massy suggests in the manner of Prichard, are not fixed biologically but can be changed by climate, diet or history. This allows him to then argue for the integration of the British people on non-racial grounds: 'Sprung originally from one stock, men may yet be led onwards and upwards towards one standard of perfection. But ere this can be done that jealousy of race, which had made one man an oppressor and another a slave, must be destroyed' (p. 198). Tuthill Massy's ethnology, like Prichard's, remains firmly grounded in the Christian egalitarian discourse of the anti-slavery movement. At another level, however, he repeats and extends the discourse of race.

Celtic Challenge 4: The Comparative Anthropology of England and Wales

The ethnologists who defended the Celts thus became by contrast if anything more 'scientifically' racialist than their Saxonist antagonists. As we have seen, Knox's intervention, though written from a know-ledge of contemporary anthropology, in fact draws as much on the discourse of phrenology and of 'moral and philosophical' anatomy as that of ethnology. The defence of Celtism, on the other hand, emanated from the new scientific racialists themselves, many of whom were Welsh or Irish, who wanted to define the racial and cultural identities of the population of the British Isles (including the Irish) with much greater specificity. Saxon supremacism was therefore finally success-fully challenged through invoking contemporary racial science. The result was not a denial of English ethnicity, but a redefinition of it in new, scientific terms. As racial science became more sophisticated, and as ethnologists began to test out the thesis that the English were racially Saxons, the more it became apparent that not just historically,

culturally and linguistically, but also racially, the English were irretrievably mixed. In terms of modern preconceptions, therefore, the
paradox was that in the case of English ethnicity, far from proposing
a new racialized identity for the English as constituting a pure race, it
was racial science that was used to disprove the racial exclusivism of
Saxonism.

From the 1860s onwards, the claims of the Saxon supremacists
were increasingly put to empiricist tests that sought to determine ever
more accurately the exact details of the origin of the English. It
was the development of scientific racial theory that enabled this
project. One major work corroborated the Saxonist thesis. Inspired
by Samuel George Morton's *Crania Americana* (1839), the eminent
craniologists J. B. Davis and J. Thurnam published *Crania Britannica.
Delineations and Descriptions of the Skulls of the Aboriginal and Early
Inhabitants of the British Isles* (1856–65, dedicated, like Kemble's
Saxons in England, to Queen Victoria), and argued that the Anglo-
Saxon skulls that they had disinterred greatly resembled those of
modern Englishmen, providing a vindication of 'the true derivation
of the essential characteristics of our race from a Teutonic origin'.[58]
Like Knox, Davis and Thurnam argued against Prichard that races
were effectively unalterable, and relied on the Edwardsian model of
racial mixture to deny the possibility of racial fusion. However,
though surviving skulls could be claimed to be Anglo-Saxon, their
repeated assertion that what they call 'our race' was essentially Teutonic and utterly incompatible with the Celt was already being challenged through an ethnography of the present. As ethnography and
the scientific techniques of classification of racial difference developed, the possibility became apparent that the population of Britain
could be scientifically analysed to discover the actual racial composition of the British, as Edwards had argued. The historical claims of
the British stock were subjected to modern, scientific ethnographic
analysis. Although those who challenged the Saxon supremacists
tended inevitably to espouse the Celtic alternative, they made their
arguments by charting in some historical detail the successive waves
of invasions of the British Isles by different European peoples, which

they then proved by analysis of contemporary racial types. Ethno-graphic surveys enabled them to argue that the English were, after all, in fact basically Celtic, with some later racial admixture by Saxons and others. This counter ethno-history was so successful that by 1885 the eminent ethnographer John Beddoe was to write:

> It is not very long since educated opinion considered the English and lowland Scots an almost purely Teutonic people. Now the current runs so much the other way that I have had to take up the attitude of an apologist of the 'Saxon' view.[59]

In Britain this was the result of the fact that from the 1860s attempts had been made, particularly by Beddoe himself, to test or prove history by ethnic monitoring of the living population of Britain. An early example of such contemporary ethnography can be found in Daniel Mackintosh's 'Comparative Anthropology of England and Wales', first given as a paper to the Ethnological Society in 1861 and then published, in an extended version, in the *Anthropological Review* in 1866. Arguing 'that distinct, hereditary, and long-persistent races or types can be traced in different districts of England', Mackintosh produced a geographical map of the highly diverse different racial types.[60] For the first time, what was presented was not a map showing the various historical invasions by different peoples, but a contempor-ary map of the different ethnic 'types' (figure 4.3).

Mackintosh argues that the living population literally embody the signs of their hereditary descent and thus manifest signs of their 'typical distinctions'. In a long discussion designed to justify his ability to identify ancient racial types in the present, he rehearses Edwards' theory of hybridity and the permanence of type in order to arrive at his conclusion that he feels justified in 'classifying the types which come under our notice as if they were unalterably fixed', after which he proceeds to spell out the different 'types' to be found around the country (figure 4.4).[61]

Though ethnological in its presentation, Mackintosh's analysis shows that the discourse of race, now presented as a form of

126

MAP TO ILLUSTRATE
THE
COMPARATIVE ANTHROPOLOGY
OF
ENGLAND AND WALES.
BY
D. MACKINTOSH, F.G.S.

The areas are not coloured, because the boundary lines cannot be precisely defined.

Figure 4.3
Daniel Mackintosh, 'Comparative Anthropology of England and Wales', *Anthropological Review* 4:12 (1866), facing page 16.

Figure 4.4
Daniel Mackintosh, 'Comparative Anthropology of England and Wales',
Anthropological Review 4:12 (1866), facing page 1.

anthropological science, still drew heavily on the impressionistic and personalized style of the earlier sciences of physiognomy and phrenology. He begins by classifying four separate Welsh or Cymrian types (his figures 1–4), giving their individual 'mental characteristics' – one of which, suitably enough, is 'extreme tendency to trace back ancestry' (p. 9). He then follows this with their 'moral condition', which he announces for the working class at least is higher than the English working class – 'at book and music shops of a rank where in England negro melodies would form the staple compositions, Handel is the great favourite; and such tunes as *Pop goes the Weasel* would not be tolerated' (p. 12). The first of these Welsh types is described, in notably ambiguous language, as

> stature various, but often tall – neck more or less long – loose gait – dark brown (often very dark) and coarse hair – eyes sunken and ill-defined, with a peculiarly close expression – dark eye-lashes and eyebrows, eye-basins more or less wrinkled. The face was long, or rather long, narrow or rather narrow, and broadest under the eyes. There was a *sudden sinking in under the cheek-bones*, with denuded cheeks. The chin was rather narrow and generally retreating, though sometimes prominent. The nose was narrow, long or rather long, much raised either in the middle or at the point, and occasionally approaching the Jewish form (see fig. 5).[62]

Having elaborated the four types of North Wales, Mackintosh moves on to South Wales, where the Cymrian type gives way to what he calls the British and Gaelic types (types 12 to 14). The Gaelic physiognomy is described as characterized by a bulging prognathous upper jaw with receding chin, and a turned up Africanoid nose with 'yawning nostrils' (p. 15). Gaelic mental characteristics are characterized in terms which anticipate Arnold's, but which also conform to the general stereotype of any characterization of the Celts as a race:

> *quick in perception*, but deficient in depth of reasoning power; headstrong and excitable; tendency to oppose; *strong in love and hate*; at one time lively, soon after sad; vivid in imagination; extremely social, with a *propensity for crowding together*; forward and self-confident; deficient in application to deep study, but possessed of *great concentration*

in monotonous or purely mechanical operations . . . want of prudence and foresight. (p. 16)

In the South of England, by contrast, lives the Saxon type, illustrated by types 19 to 21. One fatherly 'Anglo-Saxon' male is significantly represented both as larger in size and at the centre. At this point, it is noticeable that Mackintosh, despite his name, becomes much more sure of himself in his description. The Saxon has regular features and familiar characteristics:

> mouth well formed . . . chin neither prominent nor retreating; nose straight, and neither long nor short . . . general smoothness and roundness. . . . *Saxon Mental Characteristics.*– Extreme moderation; absence of extraordinary talents, and equal absence of extraordinary defects, mind equally balanced; character consistent, simple, truthful, straightforward and honest . . . not brilliant in imagination, but sound in judgement . . . tendency . . . to have limited intercourse with neighbours. (p. 17)

Though his face features so largely, the Anglo-Saxon male (type 20) does not represent the Anglo-Saxon in the modern sense, says Mackintosh. In anthropology, the word can only mean a combination of the Saxon and Anglian types, the key mental characteristic of which is summed up in the word 'indomitable'. Nevertheless, as we shall see, it is significant that he conflates the two at this point. Finally, completing the ethnological picture, on the Eastern side, are to be found Anglian (types 17, 18, 22), Jute (types 24, 25) and Danish (types 26, 27, 28). The living population of England and Wales, as the map indicates, can be shown to be made up of a composite of descendants of the country's ancient invaders, still individually visible and classifiable. The 'British', we might note, are largely confined to the West. Just as M'Elheran used 'Briton' to denote the peoples in England at the time of the Roman invasion, so here Mackintosh uses the term 'British' not for the people of Great Britain in general, but rather to describe those who survived in the West after the Saxon invasion.

John Beddoe's *The Races of Britain*

Despite its relative particularity in terms of regional mapping, Mackintosh's study shows that the more difficult problem for a proper scientific analysis was how to survey people with anything like an impartial scientific accuracy rather than the impressionistic and stereotyped observations characteristic of the older disciplines of race such as phrenology and physiognomy, whose discourse still lingered on. By the 1860s some ethnographers were beginning to take a more impersonal scientific approach. John Beddoe spent a lifetime going round the cities of Britain and Europe classifying the people in them by means of their eye and hair colour, attempting to chart the exact ethnicity of the population of the British Isles. He took almost two decades to collect the data for his *The Races of Britain*, which was published in 1885.

After beginning with a detailed historical account of the different racial invasions, the evidence for which had been sifted fairly comprehensively by 1885, Beddoe reveals his detailed findings of the racial composition of Britain.[63] His scientific method was not to measure skulls, in the manner of Davis and Thurnam, but to register racial signifiers that could be observed without the subjects being aware of it. Clearly the skin colour used to determine the differences between European and non-European races was of little use here. At the same time, the science of modern physiognomy required complex anthropometric measurements and appropriate machines which in turn required the consent of their subjects – something not easy to obtain if you were trying to survey the whole population. So Beddoe turned instead to the earlier physiognomical categories of the specific signifiers of hair and eye colour which he considered 'so nearly permanent in races of men as to be fairly trustworthy evidence in the matter of ethnical descent' (p. 297). These, he argued, allowed him to determine the exact racial characteristics of the inhabitants of the British Isles. To conduct his investigations, he went round the country concealing small cards in the palm of his hand, on which he marked down the characteristics of those walking in the streets about him. His *Races of Britain* contains endless pages of his results, of which figure 4.5 is but one. While he argued that the mix of people was changing, Beddoe too continued to believe in the fixity of individual 'type' enduring as distinct physical forms. In the manner of Mackintosh, he produced his own representations of the characteristic 'types' from the different regions (figure 4.6). Though of higher quality than Mackintosh's sketches, Beddoe's illustrations come across as somewhat stereotypical portraits. The drawings, however, were based on his own photographs of real people, now housed in the Royal Anthropological Institute. Ripley's *The Races of Europe*, published fifteen years later in 1900, uses many of Beddoe's photographs of these 'types'(figure 4.7), and they were used once again as late as 1923 by H. J. Fleure (figure 4.8) in his *The Races of England and Wales*.[64]

Beddoe's work was designed to produce an exact scientific analysis of the racial composition of the British Isles. However, as Mackintosh's map already suggests, it was difficult to demarcate the different areas with any exactitude. Beddoe's solution was to produce a composite portrait of the racial composition of the area. Using his data of hair and eye colour, he expressed this according to an abstruse mathematical formula, which he called the 'Index of Nigrescence':

> A ready means of comparing the colours of two peoples or localities is found in the Index of Nigresence. The gross index is gotten by subtracting the number of red and fair-haired persons from that of the dark-haired, together with twice the black-haired. I double the black, in order to give its proper value to the greater tendency to melanosity shown thereby; while brown (chestnut) hair is regarded as neutral . . .
>
> $D + 2N-R-F =$ Index.
>
> From the gross index, the net, or percentage index, is of course readily obtained.[65]

Colour of Hair and Eyes in several Districts of the United Kingdom, from Personal Observation.—ENGLAND, continued.

Colour of Hair	Number	Sex	EYES LIGHT					Eyes Light	EYES INTERMEDIATE OR NEUTER					Eyes Neuter	EYES DARK					Eyes Dark	Indices	
			Red	Fair	Brown	Dark	Nig.		Red	Fair	Brown	Dark	Nig.		Red	Fair	Brown	Dark	Nig.		Gross	Per Cent
208. Bewdley	500	both	17·5	38·5	171·5	62	2·5	292	1	2	20	25	2	50	2	4·5	33	102·5	16	158	165	...
Per cent.	...	...	3·5	7·7	34·3	12·4	·5	58·4	·2	·4	4	5	·4	10	·4	·9	6·6	20·5	3·2	31·6	...	33
209. Worcestershire, central, rural	700	both	19	92	213·5	133	1·5	489	2	2	23	31	2	60	4	5	27·5	100·5	14	151	175·5	...
Per cent.	...	...	2·7	13·1	34·8	19	·2	69·8	·3	·3	3·3	4·4	·3	8·5	·6	·7	3·9	14·3	2	21·5	...	25·1
210. Worcestershire, N.W. forest and rural district	500	both	11·5	42·5	164	82·5	5·5	306	3	1	29	24	4	61	1	4	33·5	82·5	12	153	..	..
Per cent.	...	...	2·3	8·5	32·8	16·5	1·1	61·1	·6	·2	5·8	4·8	·8	12·2	2	·8	6·7	16·5	2·4	...		33·7
WARWICKSHIRE.																						
211. Birmingham...	310	m	7·5	42·5	76	42·5	2·5	171	2·5	6·5	18·5	18	1·5	47	...	4·5	21·5	57	9	...	..	..
	357	fem	19·5	55	94·5	40·5	·5	...	...	6	16	17	...	...	2·5	5	26	65	9·5	...	..	..
Total...	667	both	27	97·5	170·5	83	3	...	2·5	12·5	34·5	·5	1·5	...	2·5	9·5	47·5	122	18·5	...	134·5	...
Per cent.	...	...	4	14·6	25·6	12·4	·4	57	·4	1·8	5·2	5·2	·2	12·8	·4	1·4	7·1	18·3	2·8	30	...	20·1
212. Stratford-on-Avon fair, mostly country folk ...	125	m	4·5	17	32	17·5	1	72	...	2	5	7	...	14	...	...	6	26·5	6·5	39	41·5	...
	175	fem	3	26	41	24	...	94	1	1	10	9	...	21	2	2·5	15·5	35	5	60	42·5	...
Total...	300	both	7·5	43	73	41·5	1	166	1	3	15	16	...	35	2	2·5	21·5	61·5	11·5	99	84	...
Per cent.	...	...	2·5	14·3	24·3	13·8	·3	55·3	·3	1	5	5·3	...	15	·7	·8	7·2	20·5	3·8	29·3	...	28·2
213. Rugby	53	♂♀	2	4	12·5	7	1·5	27	...	3	7·5	1·5	...	12	·5	·5	2	9	2	14	...	...
Per cent.	...	...	3·8	7·5	23·6	13·2	2·8	51	...	5·6	14·1	2·8	22·6	·9	·9	3·8	17	3·8	26·4	...	50	
	1	2	3	4	5	6	7	8	9	10	11	12	13	14	15	16	17	18	19	20	21	22

Colour of Hair	Number	Sex	EYES LIGHT					Eyes Light	EYES INTERMEDIATE OR NEUTER					Eyes Neuter	EYES DARK					Eyes Dark	Indices	
	1	2	3	4	5	6	7	8	9	10	11	12	13	14	15	16	17	18	19	20	21	22
NORTHAMPTONSHIRE.																						
214. Heyford, Flure, Stowe, Bugbrook, Weedon (Sth. West Northamptonshire)	119	m	3·5	16	38·5	16	...	74	...	1	4	4·5	·5	10	1·5	·5	6·5	23	3·5	35	29	...
	61	fem	2	4·5	18	6·5	...	31	...	...	2	4	...	6	1	...	4	18	1	24	24	...
Total...	180	...	5·5	20·5	56·5	22·5	...	105	1	6	8·5	·5	16	2·5	·5	10·5	41	4·5	59	...	...	
Per cent.	...	...	3	11·4	31·4	12·5	...	58·3	...	·5	3·3	4·7	·3	8·8	1·4	·3	5·8	22·8	3	32·8	...	30
215. Northampton	155	m	4	13·5	59·5	22·5	·5	100	1	1	1·5	8·5	...	12	...	5	5·5	29	9	44	...	...
	145	fem	5	16	47·5	17·5	2	88	...	1	9	5	...	15	1	1	10·5	27	2·5	42	...	...
Total...	300	...	9	29·5	107	40	2·5	188	1	2	10·5	13·5	...	27	1	1·5	16	56	11·5	86	...	...
Per cent.	...	...	3	9·8	35·6	13·3	·8	62·6	·3	·7	3·5	4·5	...	9	·3	·5	5·3	18·7	3·8	28·6	...	31·1
216. Peterborough	113	♂♀	...	18·5	34·5	12·5	·5	66	1·5	·5	6	4	1	13	...	...	10·5	21·5	2	34	...	...
Per cent.	...	...	...	16·4	30·5	11·1	·4	58·4	1·3	·4	5·3	3·5	·9	11·5	...	...	9·3	19	1·8	30	...	21·7
OXFORDSHIRE.																						
217. Oxford, city	720	both	31	85	246	80	3·5	446	4·5	9	37	35·5	...	86	5	6	51·5	111	14·5	188	...	...
Per cent.	...	...	4·3	11·8	34·2	11·1	·5	62	·6	1·2	5·1	4·9	...	11·9	·7	·8	7·1	15·4	2	26·1	...	17
218. Oxfordshire, militia	66	m	2	9	24	4	...	39	...	6	1	...	7	...	2	8	10	...	20	2	3	
219. Do., peasants	30	most m	·5	5·5	11	4	...	21	...	...	2	...	2	...	...	4	3	...	7	3	10	
BUCKS.																						
220. Aylesbury	100	♂♀	4·5	20	25·5	9	...	59	3	2	4·5	7·5	1	18	...	1	4	15	3	23	...	9
BEDFORDSHIRE.																						
221. Dunstable	112	m	2·5	16	32	14·5	1	66	...	1	4	5·5	·5	11	1	...	4	26·5	3·5	35	...	...
	128	fem	5·5	17	32·5	20	...	75	...	1	6	6	...	13	...	1	6·5	30	2·5	40	...	...
Total...	240	both	8	33	64·5	34·5	1	141	...	2	10	11·5	·5	24	1	1	10·5	56·5	6	75	73	...
Per cent.	...	...	3·3	13·7	26·9	14·4	·4	58·7	...	·8	4·2	4·8	·2	10	·4	·4	4·4	23·5	2·5	31·2	...	30·4

Figure 4.5
John Beddoe, *The Races of Britain* (1885), pages 182–3.

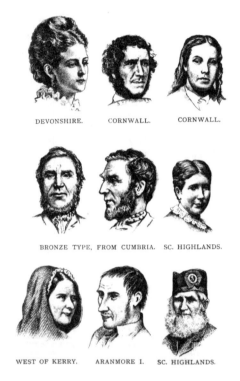

DEVONSHIRE.   CORNWALL.   CORNWALL.

BRONZE TYPE, FROM CUMBRIA.   SC. HIGHLANDS.

WEST OF KERRY.   ARANMORE I.   SC. HIGHLANDS.

Figure 4.6
John Beddoe, *The Races of Britain* (1885), page 287.

Beddoe reckoned that this abstruse formula was 'more apt to represent ethnological truth' than the rival German method of 'separating
and estimating the pure blond and pure brunet types' (p. 86). It
allowed him to construct maps of Britain and Europe that showed
the relative comparative 'nigrescence' of each district. Figure 4.9 is
a visual representation of Beddoe's 'Index of Nigrescence' in its
German version from Dagobert Frey's *Englisches Wesen in der bildenden Kunst* of 1942.

As a result of his research, Beddoe came to the conclusion that the
people of the country were getting darker. As well as simply tracking

Figure 4.7
William Z. Ripley, *The Races of Europe* (1900), between pages 308–9.

the alleged ethnic origins and proportions of the various parts of the British Isles, Beddoe's research also suggested the increasing melanosity of the population as a whole, though he was reticent in his conclusions about why this literal 'denigration' was happening. As a man of modern science, Beddoe was less speculative than Price or Latham with their coal mines. However, a single paragraph is revealing:

in the absence of trustworthy evidence as to a change of colour-type in Britain, in the direction of light to dark, it is best to rest upon the undoubted fact that the Gaelic and Iberian races of the west, mostly

Figure 4.8
H. J. Fleure, *The Races of England and Wales* (1923), between pages 102–3, 104–5.

Figure 4.9

'Haarfarbenverbreitung in Großbritannien und Irland, Dunkelhaarigkeit in den mediterran-keltischen westlichen Rückzugsgebieten', Dagobert Frey, *Englisches Wesen in der bildenden Kunst* (1942), reproducing a version of the 'Index of Nigrescence' from J. Beddoe, *The Races of Britain* (1885), as reinterpreted in W. Z. Ripley, *The Races of Europe* (1900), page 318.

dark-haired, are tending to swamp the blond Teutons of England by a reflux migration. At the same time, the possible effects of conjugal selection, of selection through disease, and the relative increase of the darker types through the more rapid multiplication of the artizan class who are in England generally darker than the upper classes, should be kept in view. (p. 298)

Here Beddoe summarizes his overall thesis of the increasing 'nigrescence' of the English, covertly implying their degeneration. His description of a 'reflux migration' suggests that the Celts have returned from their fringes to 'swamp the blond Teutons of England'. In other words, people from the so-called Celtic peripheries have been pouring into the expanding industrial towns of England. As Grant Allen put it rather differently from Beddoe five years before in his essay 'Are We Englishmen?', 'since the rise of the industrial system the Kelts have peacefully recovered their numerical superiority. They have crowded into the towns and seaports, so that at the present day only the rural districts of Eastern England can claim to be thoroughly Teutonic.'[66] The relaxed language used to describe Irish immigration has changed very significantly from the paranoia of Carlyle. By this stage, the focus of immigration paranoia had shifted to the East End of London.

In Beddoe the phenomenon of Irish immigration is extended to the observation that the spawning working class in general tends to be darker than the upper classes. The exact extent of this discrepancy would, however, never be known. Beddoe was involved in a later attempt of the Anthropometric Committee of the British Association for the Advancement of Science to carry out a systematic survey of the British Isles, comparable to Risley's Census of India.[67] But it collapsed from lack of funds and from the impossible complexity of the precise anthropometric scientific data demanded. Many people, apparently, also objected to having their heads measured. Despite energetic efforts by the Anthropometric Committee of the British Association for the Advancement of Science, a proposed Imperial Bureau of Ethnology for Greater Britain was never established.[68] Though local surveys were carried out, including one in Ireland by Dr William Wilde, and though commentators such as T. Rice Holmes were still arguing as late as 1936 that 'statistics of nigrescence and of cranial measurements retain their value', the exact racial composition of the British population as a whole was never determined through contemporary scientific analysis.[69] In the terms of the day, it was a hopeless task: the population was not only the product of successive migration movements of the past, but during the course of the century it had drained out of the countryside into the city, producing an irreducible mixture. By 1885, internal migration within Britain had been enormous. With or without this mixture, however, Beddoe's work was taken thereafter as evidence that the English were irretrievably heterogeneous as a race.

Racial mixture, however, could be projected in a variety of different ways.

Chapter 5

Matthew Arnold's Critique of 'Englishism'

'What is England?' Arnold and Celtic Literature

Far away from the erudite anthropological analyses of eye and hair colour on the streets of English towns, it was Matthew Arnold, more than anyone else, who was responsible for transforming the ideology of the English as Teutons back into a more inclusive account of ethnic mixture. Though his arguments were made about literature and culture, they were nevertheless underpinned by reference to the researches of contemporary historical philology and ethnology. Arnold first challenged Saxon supremacism in his *On the Study of Celtic Literature* (1867), followed two years later by the best-known and most influential attack on the English-as-Saxons in *Culture and Anarchy*.[1] The subtext in these writings was that Arnold himself was engaged in an oedipal struggle, challenging the Teutonism of his father, Thomas Arnold, as he himself makes clear:

> I remember, when I was young, I was taught to think of Celt as separated by an impassable gulf from Teuton; my father, in particular, was never weary of contrasting them; he insisted much oftener on the separation between us and them than on the separation between us

and any other race in the world; in the same way, Lord Lyndhurst, in words long famous, called the Irish, 'aliens in speech, in religion, in blood'. (pp. 299–300)

It was above all by contrasting them to the Celt, for which in his case read the Irish, rather than any other race, that Dr Arnold had created the identity of the English. Now, however, his son announces that philological science has shown that the Irish are part of the Indo-European family, and this new knowledge has a direct political effect:

> In the sphere of politics, too, there has, in the same way, appeared an indirect practical result from this science; the sense of antipathy to the Irish people, of radical estrangement from them, has visibly abated amongst all the better part of us; the remorse for past ill-treatment of them, the wish to make amends, to do them justice, *to fairly unite, if possible, in one people with them*, has visibly increased. (p. 302, my emphasis)

Science now insisting, Arnold notes, that 'there is no such original chasm between the Celt and the Saxon as we once popularly im-agined', the English are no longer English by virtue of not being Irish. On the question of the racial identity of the English, the son triumphed over the father, substituting what might be termed a progressive, inclusive cultural conservatism for the paternal exclusive arch-toryism. Arnold's essay on Celtic literature constituted a major challenge to the ideology of a Saxon supremacism which had in-creasingly adopted an anti-Irish and anti-Welsh Celtism as part of its rhetoric. Influential as it was, as we have seen, Arnold's essay represented only one of a range of different responses that had emerged since the 1840s from critics, anatomists, ethnologists and physiognomists. Arnold was, however, by far the best known of them, and what was distinctive about his essay was that he brought to bear on the issue the whole range of different disciplinary knowledges – literary, historical, philo-logical, ethnological and physiognomical – all assembled together for the first time.

Against his father's Teutonism, Arnold argued that English culture was as mixed as its people (including himself: his mother was Cornish). Unexpectedly, he discovered a way of putting the two together in Emerson. In *English Traits* (1856), Emerson had argued that English culture was a product of a racial dialectic. At the beginning of the chapter on 'Race' in that book, he cites Knox approvingly in terms of the primacy he places on race. Trying to put his finger on what makes the English so powerful and inventive, Emerson, like Knox, finds only one answer:

> It is race, is it not? that puts the hundred millions of India under the dominion of a remote island in the north of Europe? Race avails much, if that be true, which is alleged, that all Celts are Catholics, and all Saxons are Protestants; that Celts love unity of power, and Saxons the representative principle. Race is a controlling influence in the Jew, who, for two millenniums, under every climate, has preserved the same character and employments. Race in the negro is of appalling importance. The French in Canada, cut off from all intercourse with the parent people, have held their national traits. I chanced to read Tacitus 'On the Manners of the Germans,' not long since, in Missouri, and the heart of Illinois, and I found abundant points of resemblance between the Germans of the Hercynian forest, and our *Hoosiers*, *Suckers*, and *Badgers* of the American woods.[2]

Though Emerson finds 'pungent and unforgettable truths' in Knox's writings on race, fully accepting his thesis of race as a determining factor in human society and culture, and comparing his discovery of this natural law to those of Dalton and Newton, he quarrels with the claim of the 'ingenious anatomist' that racial difference inevitably produces the antagonism of a war between the races in every case.[3] Against Knox's doctrine of the unalterability of race, Emerson draws on Robert Chambers' *Vestiges of the Natural History of Creation* (1844) in order to allow some mediating influences of environment and evolution.[4] The result, he suggests, is that 'the English character' is constructed according to a dynamic interaction of a racial dialectic which has been subsumed into the higher form of the genius of the nation:

The English composite character betrays a mixed origin. Everything English is a fusion of distant and antagonistic elements. The language is mixed; the names of men are of different nations – three languages, three or four nations; – the currents of thought are counter: contemplation and practical skill; active intellect and dead conservatism; world-wide enterprise, and devoted use and wont; aggressive freedom and hospitable law, with bitter class-legislation; a people scattered by their wars and affairs over the face of the whole earth, and homesick to a man; a country of extremes. (p. 29)

'A true-born Englishman's a contradiction', as Defoe had put it: Emerson, no less than Knox, sees this as the product of natural law. He modelled this dialectic of antitheses on Samuel Taylor Coleridge's 'law of polarities', which he had encountered in the latter's *On the Constitution of Church and State*. According to Coleridge's *Naturphilosophie*, all powers in nature evolve an opposite as their condition of emergence, towards which they tend to unite.[5] Emerson transforms Coleridge's abstractions via Knox's racial determinism into the genius of England itself:

I can well believe what I have often heard, that there are two nations in England; but it is not the Poor and the Rich; nor is it the Normans and Saxons; nor the Celt and the Goth. These are each always becoming the other.... But the two complexions, or two styles of mind – the perceptive class, and the practical finality class – are ever in counterpoise, interacting mutually; one, in hopeless minorities; the other, in huge masses; one studious, contemplative, experimenting; the other, the ungrateful pupil, scornful of the source, whilst availing itself of the knowledge for gain; these two nations, of genius and of animal force, though the first consist of only a dozen souls, and the second of twenty millions, for ever by their discord and their accord yield the power of the English State. (pp. 153–4)

Emerson's account of 'the English duality' (p. 141), a cultural and racial dialectic in which English culture is made up of an interaction – not just a general mixture – between two peoples of different casts of mind, one intellectual, one practical, was to form the basis of Arnold's better-known characterization of English culture as a dialectic between Saxon and Celt in *On the Study of Celtic Literature* (1867) and between Hellene and Hebrew in *Culture and Anarchy* (1869). In both instances, Arnold too represents the one as mediating the other, disturbing it and supplementing it. It was entirely symptomatic that what would become the dominant account of English culture – still prevalent in many ways today – should have been invented by an American.

A different America, however, to that of Emerson's Anglophile New England was soon to play its part in the creation of new ideas of English ethnicity. Emerson, the friend of Carlyle and his circle, spoke a little too soon in *English Traits* in 1856 when he announced that *The Times* had vanquished Ireland.[6] Two years later, James Stephens was to form the Irish Republican Brotherhood in Dublin, committed to win Irish independence through violent insurrection; the following year John Mahoney founded a branch of the Fenians in New York. During the American Civil War (1861–5), sympathetic British treatment of the Confederates meant that American politicians in the North made regular threats to invade Canada either in retribution or, should the South succeed in secession, in compensation. By the end of the Civil War, the Fenians in turn had gained military experience, were rumoured to have an army of half a million men, and to have collected a million dollars in funds. They then threatened to invade Canada in their own right – no longer with respect to issues relating to the Civil War, but as a means of demanding Irish independence.[7] In 1866 the raids began, and though unsuccessful, they continued through to 1871. Arnold's essay was published in 1867, the year of an attempted Fenian uprising in Ireland, an abortive Fenian raid on Chester Castle, the rescue of the Irish-American Fenian leader James Kelly from a prison van in Manchester, and the first Fenian terrorist bombings of London.[8] In 1867 the ship carrying the last group of convicts to be sent to Western Australia included 62 Fenians: rumours spread that a Fenian vessel had embarked in pursuit in order to liberate its prisoner passengers, and a British navy

144

vessel immediately set sail for Perth.[9] In April 1868 in Sydney, a Fenian tried to assassinate the Duke of Edinburgh, the son of Queen Victoria, who was making a tour of Australia and New Zealand; after hearing of Fenian demonstrations in New Zealand, the Duke quickly cancelled the rest of his trip and returned home. The development of a new form of terrorism in England, aided by the new compact explosive weapon of dynamite which was almost impossible to detect (Alfred Nobel had begun manufacturing it in 1866), and the internationalization of the Irish struggle across Australia, New Zealand, Canada and the United States – with the *de facto* support of an American government more or less hostile to British interests – meant that Irish discontent came once again to the foreground of British politics. Though the country was not seriously threatened, it produced a sense of insecurity whose effects would continue to be felt for decades to come. It was no longer possible complacently to blame the Irish as victims lacking in energy and resourcefulness. The Irish had asserted themselves internationally, with a powerful ally in the United States, and had to be accommodated. And this is what Arnold tried to do.

Though addressed in the first instance to the 'good' Celts (the Welsh), rather than the bad ones (the Irish), Arnold's *On the Study of Celtic Literature*, written at this time of these renewed anxieties about Ireland and the Irish, was, as he states explicitly, meant as a political, conciliatory essay. Its final aim, to send 'a message of peace to Ireland' (p. 386), in certain respects anticipated Gladstone's mission, when elected the following year, 'to pacify Ireland'. Whereas the liberal Gladstone controversially pursued the disestablishment of the Protestant Church of Ireland and subsequently Home Rule, Arnold's more conservative object was to offer conciliation through the project of English assimilation of the Celt. Instead of Saxonizing Ireland, Arnold suggested that if Celtic Ireland would come to England, by abandoning its Irish language and the worst of its Irish ways, he would offer compensation by showing how England was already part Celtic, and therefore in a sense already part Irish. The living Celtic languages, Arnold, like the leader writers of *The Times*, fervently believed, must die out in favour of English, but in recompense he offered a Celticized English culture in which the Celts would have their place, which he called for to be embodied institutionally in a Chair of Celtic at Oxford University. Though the offer of an Oxford professorship (which it was not in Arnold's power to give anyway) seems in retrospect rather minimal in comparison to Home Rule or independence, a minor cultural rather than a political concession, Arnold's essay did have two significant effects: it promoted a new mediated identity for the English and was influential in Ireland in supporting the movement later known as the Celtic Revival (the beginnings of which can be dated back to the 1840s). Arnold uses science, linguistic and racial, to make his argument. It is science, he suggests, which offers a reconciling power, to which he adds the contribution of his own domain, literature, science that can undo Teutonic racism and change English attitudes towards Ireland.

Arnold's essay, divided into six sections, falls into three main strands of elaboration about the Celts: linguistic (historical philology), ethnological (including ideas of 'national genius'), and aesthetic (oratory, plastic arts, religion and the Celtic literary style, melancholy, natural magic). Despite this attention, it becomes clear that Arnold is interested in isolating the Celtic element not so much to discover the identities in their own right of the Irish or the Welsh, as to allow him to identify the Celtic element in the English. The country, he argues, must be made one through a common language, English. Not for him, Gladstone's liberal encouragement of Welsh that would make such an impression on Gandhi (who would thereafter write only in Gujarati):

> The fusion of all the inhabitants of these islands into one homogeneous, English-speaking whole, the breaking down of barriers between us, the swallowing up of separate provincial nationalities, is a consummation to which the natural course of things irresistibly tends; it is a necessity of what is called modern civilisation, and modern civilisation is a real, legitimate force; the change must come, and its accomplishment is a mere affair of time. (pp. 296–7)

146

As for *The Times* on occasion, Englishness here becomes the category that transcends nationality and provinciality. However, at this point of arguing for the 'legitimate force' of modern civilization that breaks down minorities and swallows them into 'one, homogeneous, English-speaking whole', Arnold parts company with his 'brother Saxons'. For he finds Welsh and Irish literature, or Celtic literature more generally, of great interest, an embodiment of the 'Celtic genius' which he does not wish to get lost in the milieu of the militant Saxon desire to 'improve everything but themselves off the face of the earth':

> We may threaten them with extinction if we will. . . . It is not in the outward and visible world of material life that the Celtic genius of Wales or Ireland can at this day hope to count for much; it is in the inward world of thought and science. What it *has* been, what it *has* done, let us ask to attend to that, as a matter of science and history; not to what it will be or will do, as a matter of modern politics. It cannot count appreciably now as a material power; but, perhaps, if it can get itself thoroughly known as an object of science, it may count for a good deal, – far more than we Saxons, most of us, imagine, – as a spiritual power. (pp. 297–8)

Arnold, here speaking as a Saxon, makes it clear that he has absolutely no sympathy with the politics of Irish or Welsh nationalism, with what he calls 'political and social Celtism'; rather, he wishes to break down all forms of estrangement and 'radical antagonism' (p. 300), generating a new sense of 'kinship and kindliness' that will help to work against the threat of what he memorably characterizes as a Celtic 'malignant revolution'. Just as it was erroneous science that helped to create the gulf that resulted from his father's unalloyed Teutonism, so modern science now offers the means through which reconciliation can be made possible. As Arnold puts it: 'Science's reconciling power . . . on which I have already touched, philology, in her Celtic researches, again and again illustrates' (p. 330). Philology has shown 'a law of ultimate fusion, of conciliation', as it illustrates the deep affinities of words across different languages. Philology, as

147

Jones and Prichard had believed, provided a basis for bringing unlike peoples into one, making the invisible visible. Arnold's demonstration of the philological relation of Celtic to English allows him to argue that English, far from being an alien language to Welsh or Gaelic, is already a synthesis of them:

> By the forms of its language a nation expresses its very self. Our language is the loosest, the most analytic, of all European languages. Are we, then, what are we? what is England? I will not answer, A vast obscure Cymric basis with a vast visible Teutonic superstructure; but I will say that that answer sometimes suggests itself, at any rate, – sometimes knocks at our mind's door for admission; and we begin to cast about and see whether it is to be let in. (pp. 334–5)

So the relation of Celtic to Teutonic is *not* an inverted linguistic equivalent to Marx's base–superstructure model, with an invisible Celtic culture the base to the visible superstructure of English economics. Except that in fact it is so like it, that Arnold leaves it at the door, knocking to be let in – which allows him to suggest that it may well be.

While Arnold leaves philology knocking at the door asking for reconciliation and union, he appeals to another science, which brings a similar message of conciliation, that of ethnology. Like philology, ethnology reconciles Celt with Saxon by setting them within a larger division:

> ...meanwhile, the pregnant and striking ideas of the ethnologists about the true natural grouping of the human race, the doctrine of a great Indo-European unity, comprising Hindoos, Persians, Greeks, Latins, Celts, Teutons, Slavonians, on the one hand, and, on the other hand, of a Semitic unity and of a Mongolian unity, separated by profound distinguishing marks from the Indo-European unity and from one another, was slowly acquiring consistency and popularising itself. (pp. 300–1)

Here, remarks Arnold, 'sympathy or antipathy, grounded upon real identity or diversity in race', grew in men of culture, so that their

148

intellectual affiliation with Hebrew culture through their religion was replaced by that of 'the Teuton's born kinsfolk' of Greece or India. The science of ethnology, he suggests in an echo of Knox's argument, teaches us 'which way our natural affinities and repulsions lie'. Arnold means to use this to imply a Saxon affinity for the Celt: what he suggests in this passage is that in England in the nineteenth century, English antipathy to the Celt was being neatly replaced by that to the Semitic, even to the extent, as in Emile Burnouf, of purging the Christian religion of its Semitic elements.[10] Yet Hebraism, Arnold would argue in *Culture and Anarchy*, remains a central part of the 'English genius'.

'We have seen how philology carries us towards ideas of race which are new to us' (p. 335), announces Arnold. How far can this new science take us? Affinity alone, linked to the ancient past, is not 'potent' enough. The empiricist English prefer documented historical fact, as painstakingly elaborated by Thomas Wright in his oft-reprinted history, *The Celt, the Roman, and the Saxon* of 1852, to transcendental meta-categories such as Aryan.[11] Contact and mixture between peoples who had by then formed their own national characteristics, on the other hand, is an altogether very different matter:

> ... here in our country, in historic times, long after the Celtic embryo had crystallised into the Celt proper, long after the Germanic embryo had crystallised into the German proper, there was an important contact between the two peoples; the Saxons invaded the Britons and settled themselves in the Britons' country. Well, then, here was a contact which one might expect would leave its traces; if the Saxons got the upper hand, as we all know they did, and made our country be England and us be English, there must yet, one would think, be some trace of the Saxon having met the Briton; there must be some Celtic vein or other running through us. ... even as a matter of science the Celt has a claim to be known, and we have an interest in knowing him, yet this interest is wonderfully enhanced if we find him to have actually a part in us. The question is to be tried by external and by internal evidence; the language and the physical type of our race afford certain data for trying it, and other data are afforded by our literature,

genius, and spiritual production generally. Data of this second kind belong to the province of the literary critic; data of the first kind to the province of the philologist and of the physiologist. (pp. 336–7)

Here Arnold begins to bring the different discourses together. Though some continue to deny it, the Celt, according to Arnold, has 'a part in us': the geological metaphor manages also to suggest Celtic blood running through our veins. This Celtic element in the English can be proved by both 'external and by internal evidence'. The philologist and physiologist can locate the former, while the skill of the literary critic can discover the latter.

> The province of the philologist and of the physiologist is not mine; but this whole question as to the mixture of Celt with Saxon in us has been so little explored, people have been so prone to settle it off-hand according to their prepossessions, that even on the philological and physiological side of it I must say a few words in passing. (p. 337)

He must do this before he can make his literary argument for isolating the Celtic element in the English, because he has first to contend with the still common Saxonist view that all the Celts had been exterminated on English soil. It is in order to claim that the English population is preserved as a mixture of Celt and Saxon, that Arnold invokes the work of the first person to link history with ethnography: W. F. Edwards. Arnold remarks accurately that Edwards' book 'attracted great attention on the Continent', adding that 'it fills not much more than a hundred pages, and they are a hundred pages which well deserve reading and re-reading' (p. 339). His interest in Edwards' work results from his central thesis that Europeans, though physically mixed, continue to bear the physical, psychological and moral characteristics of their particular racial forbears.

In his essay, therefore, Arnold develops a new formulation of the older historical myth that the English were made up of a composite of Celtic and Saxon races. He does this by giving an Emersonian twist to the standard Arthurian account: instead of an integrated fusion of the

Celts, Saxons and Normans, Edwards allowed him to argue that the English were made up of a dialectic of still distinct Celts and Saxons. In Edwards' theory, it will be recalled, between allied races the progeny would revert to type. If you crossed a Celt with a Saxon, you didn't get a mixed race child, for the child would turn out to be either a Celt or a Saxon (if not in the first, then in the second or third generation), rather in the same way as it would either be a girl or a boy. This meant that the English could happily think of themselves as a 'mongrel' nation of mixed racial descent, without being threatened with the degeneracy that was supposed to follow on from the mixture of like and unlike races. They were mixed, but not hybrid. Unlike the Arthurian myth which represented the English as a composite people, an unspecified amalgamation of Celt, Saxon and various others, Arnold's version of British history argues for a dialectical continuity between the races. Edwards' thesis allows him to suggest that there has been no racial fusion, only mingling and 'admixture'. For Arnold, it was only in the realms of English literature that a cultural fusion took place between the Celt and Saxon; the task of the literary critic was to detect and chart the harmonious literary, strictly textual resolution of this racial dialectic.

While invoking the work of contemporary philologists and physiologists to prove the existence of 'Celtic elements in any modern Englishman', Arnold himself offers two additional tests for which he volunteers himself as his own expert:

> As there are for physiology physical marks, such as the square heads of the German, the round head of the Gael, the oval head of the Cymri, which determine the type of a people, so for criticism there are spiritual marks which determine the type, and make us speak of the Greek genius, the Teutonic genius, the Celtic genius, and so on. Here is another test at our service; and this test, too, has never yet been thoroughly employed. (p. 340)

European and some English critics, he notes, have argued that without a certain Celtic element, 'England would not have produced a

Shakespeare'. But no one, he comments, has actually shown specifically how this Celtic element has influenced English literature. This, then, can be his particular contribution:

> Unlike the physiological test, or the linguistic test, this literary, spiritual test is one which I may perhaps be allowed to try my hand at applying. I say that there is a Celtic element in the English nature, as well as a Germanic element, and that this element manifests itself in our spirit and literature. (p. 341)

In seeking to isolate the qualities in English culture and literature that Arnold characterizes as Celtic, Arnold begins by defining the nature of the 'English genius'. Here he essentially follows the earlier discourse of race, which pre-dated that of racial science, namely that of history and national characteristics. This brings Arnold closer to earlier writers whose observations did not claim the status of science, and who advanced a discourse of national stereotypes. Arnold duly describes the Celt in clichéd terms as 'sentimental', 'impressionable', 'sociable', 'hospitable'. His test of national genius is hardly an original one: what is individual is the way in which he brings all the different discourses of race together in a single synthesis. Cumulatively, they ground his desire to integrate the Celtic with the Saxon. In order to accommodate the Irish, Arnold changes the ethnicity of the English so that instead of being not Irish the English become partly Irish. Whether in or out, the Irish were always part of what it meant to be English.

Hybridity and Anarchy

In so far as literature resolves the antagonistic alternation between Celt and Saxon, Arnold's dialectical model could be seen to have expanded Emerson's by effectively incorporating and subsuming the two incompatible historical myths of origin of British history. Even in *Culture and Anarchy* (1869), where Celt and Saxon give way to the

Hellene and Hebrew (to which they are already linked in passing in *Celtic Literature*), and where the function of reconciliation is assigned to culture more generally, Arnold has simply extended the gendered race-character associations of Celt and Saxon into the cultural origins of the English – now classical civilization and the Bible. Only culture offers a harmonious and aesthetic resolution to the fractured historical ethnographic genealogy of the English nation.

In suggesting this synthesis that occurs specifically at the level of culture, Arnold seems to have accepted the arguments of Knox, Emerson and his own major source for information on the Celts, Ernest Renan, that the races themselves were antagonistic.[12] For the question inevitably arises of why, instead of invoking Edwards, did he not more simply suggest a racial as well as a cultural amalgamation? Why did he go out of his way so carefully to preserve the distinction? Apart from his awareness of the received scientific view, another reason why he would have been attracted to the thesis of a continuing racial separation was that at this time mixed, hybrid races had a common political connotation with things that were not dear to Arnold's heart: liberalism and anarchy.

While it may have been politically convenient to argue that a fusion between the different races of Britain towards a common cultural and political identity was desirable, Arnold's terms, such as mingling or admixture, allowed him to imply a physical mingling without a physical blending. His attraction to the idea that the different races could maintain their distinct racial characteristics can be allied to the fact that contemporary commentators not only argued that racial hybrids were intrinsically degenerative, but if a majority of the population then they developed into a chaotic form of 'ethnic commotion' that produced political anarchy.[13] By the 1850s it was a commonplace to point to the alleged racial anarchy (that is, racial intermixture) of South America and identify the political instability of its states with what was considered the 'raceless chaos' of its population, to cite Houston Stewart Chamberlain's later description of the degenerate Roman Empire before it was redeemed by the Teutons.[14] Correspondingly, as we have seen, the political stability of Britain was associated with the constancy of its racial type, and the pure pedigree of the English breed. The argument was made in a very forthright fashion in 1867, the year Arnold not only published *On Celtic Literature* but also delivered his lectures on 'Culture and Anarchy', in an article by the novelist, philologist and popular theologian Frederic Farrar, author of the popular *Eric, or Little by Little* (1858). Farrar, who was eventually to become Dean of Canterbury Cathedral, was a noted philologist and, like Arnold, an admirer of Renan. The same year, 1867, he was elected a fellow of the Royal Society on Darwin's nomination. In a review of J. S. Mill's *Principles of Political Economy, On Liberty* and *On Representative Government*, Farrar associates the 'anarchy' of racial mixing with the 'doing as one likes' philosophy of liberalism – the very object of Arnold's attack in *Culture and Anarchy.* Mill's error is specified as his 'unwise rejection of the racial element' in his political philosophy, and his lack of consideration of the differing aptitude of 'the various races for political liberty'. These 'deficiencies and misconceptions', in Farrar's eyes, are augmented by his lack of reference to

> hybridism, as an obstruction to the formation and maintenance of a stable government. It is, of course, quite legitimate in logic, for the man who does not believe in race, to deny or ignore the existence of half-castes. But, unfortunately nature will not so ignore them, as Mexico and the South American republics have found to their cost. Where the parental elements are very diverse, the hybrid is himself a fermenting monstrosity. He is ever a more or less chaotic compound. He is in conflict with himself, and but too often exhibits the vices of both parents without the virtues of either. He is a blot on creation, the product of a sin against nature, whom she hastens with all possible expedition to reduce to annihilation. He is not in healthful equilibrium, whether mental or physical, and consequently cannot conduce to the stability of anything else. He is ever oscillating between his paternal and maternal proclivities. His very instincts are perverted. He unites the baseness of the negro with the aspirations of the European; and while the creature of ungovernable appetite, longs for that liberty which is only compatible with self-command. Such are the

many-coloured many-featured 'curs' that abound in most of the colonial populations of modern times, produced...by our having overstepped the boundaries of nature in the mixture of races.[15]

This from the man who, as the *Dictionary of National Biography* puts it, 'exerted a vast popular influence upon the religious feeling and culture of the middle classes for fully forty years'. As in the United States during the Civil War, where the idea of racial mixing was always associated with the political amalgamationism of the Union-ists, liberal attitudes towards race – or even the rare instance of the denial of race, as was almost the case in Mill – were associated by those on the right with racial and political anarchy. Arnold's pointed self-affiliation to the work of Edwards shows that he shared with both Edwards and Knox the same basic presuppositions about the per-manence of racial types, a natural mechanism preventing racial mix-ing, as a guarantor of political stability and counter to contemporary working-class and Irish disorder. Even as Celts, the Irish were tur-bulent enough – if the Celts and the Saxons had been able to hybridize, then things could have got far worse. For Arnold, Edwards' theory of a biological process of natural racial separation avoided the political problems associated with hybridity, while at the same time allowing him to challenge his father's Teutonism and offer a typically English compromise to the racial identity of the English.

The Eisteddfod

Arnold provided the most important, and the most comprehensive, of a series of intellectual challenges to Saxon supremacism in the 1850s and 1860s. The majority of those invoking ethnological sci-ence shared with him the racialist assumption that the physical survival of the Celt could be based on some version of Edwards' theory of the workings of hybridity. Critics have suggested that Arnold himself was unaware of the contemporary ethnographic context of Celtic challenges.[16] This is unlikely, not only because the question of race was so well developed in *The Times* and the quarterlies after 1848 ('Race is the order of the day' announced a *Times* leader in 1866), not only because Arnold's own major source for his ideas on the Celts, Ernest Renan, was profoundly racialist in his thinking, but also because Arnold himself begins his essay by telling us of how he went to the Eisteddfod at Llandudno and heard the recitation of the prize compositions there.[17]

These compositions were written in answer to the offer in 1864 of a prize of 100 guineas (the money was contributed by a Welsh judge, A. Johnes), for the best essay on 'The Origin of the English Nation' – in English, Welsh, French or German. It is characteristic that in this period even an event designed to promote Welsh cultural revival should focus its attention on the origin of 'the English nation'. A correspondence in *The Times* that followed the Eisteddfod that year focused on the other paradox, that much of the gathering was conducted in English, not Welsh. One of the unsuccessful essays written for this competition was by the Welsh ethnologist Luke Owen Pike, and became the basis of his book, *The English and Their Origin: A Prologue to Authentic English History* (1866), in which he advanced the thesis that analysis of the historical, philological, physical and psychical characteristics of the English shows them to be predominantly Celt.[18] To guard himself against any charges of 'unconscious plagiarism' Pike provided a list of works consulted. Two years later the Welsh educationist Thomas Nicholas published another of the unsuccessful prize essays as *The Pedigree of the English People* (1868) and unwisely omitted Pike from his list of works consulted – unwise given that Pike worked for his day job as a barrister. Nicholas' argument about the mostly Celtic character of the English was so close to Pike's that the latter successfully took him to court for plagiarism (the case, however, was dismissed on appeal). This did not stop Nicholas' more comprehensive work going into five editions between 1868 and 1878, to Pike's one.[19]

Pike begins by asking whether any laws have been established in ethnology, the first of which is the role of race. Here he cites Knox, for whom 'race is everything, and the surrounding circumstances ... nothing', against Buckle, for whom race is nothing and for whom 'man owes his disposition and character solely to ... climate, food, and soil'.[20] Pike finds Buckle's determinism, which denies any connection between ancestor and descendant apart from a common environment, as extreme in its own way as Knox's, and argues that Darwin offers a better explanation of the mechanisms of hereditary transmission. However, according to Pike, this still leaves open the question of what happens when races mix. Having broached the question of hybridity, he notes that on this issue the authorities, Knox, Paul Broca and Georges Pouchet, are all in agreement: 'these three writers deny that all the races of mankind are, for any length of time, prolific one with another'. Pouchet's position was similar to Knox's, if closer to the simplicity of Thierry: 'two distinct races divide Great Britain between them'.[21] Pike notes, however, that Broca, who wrote what became the standard textbook on human hybridity, allows that some closely related groups, such as the Cymry and Celt, may be prolific: this he calls 'hybridité eugéné-sique'.[22] Broca in fact developed four different degrees of hybridity, from complete infertility (agenesic) to full fertility (eugenesic). For the latter category, Prichard and Latham's examples of hybrid races having been refuted, Broca established his own, through an inspired counter-reading of Knox – the French: 'Dr Knox, in praising in his own manner the Celtic race, has not perceived that unconsciously and contrary to his own system, he wrote the apology of a strongly mixed race.'[23]

On the basis of Broca's argument, together with a demonstration of some inconsistencies in Pouchet, Pike concludes that the laws of human hybridity have yet to be established. Despite the general consistency of anthropologists on this question throughout the nineteenth century, Broca opened the door to the possibility of mixture for closely 'proximate' races. This would become central to the racial ideas of Herbert Spencer (for whom proximate races could procreate with positive evolutionary results producing heterogeneity, while the 'incongruity' of distant races would lead to infertility), and allow the possibility of positive results for the mixture of allied races ('the Englishman is like a built-up gun barrel, all one temper though welded of many different materials', Rudyard Kipling would later claim).[24] The problem for the Celtophiles, however, remained that they were in a sense forced to be scarcely less determinate than the Saxonists – for if the history of the nation was one of racial fusion, how could you plausibly argue for the continuing influence of the Celts, as Celts? Only by bracketing off the law of hybridity as not yet established can Pike make his general argument for Celtic predominance in Britain.[25]

Although Pike was certainly correct that his rival, Nicholas, follows a comparable format to his own book, and ultimately makes the same argument for Celtic predominance, there is a fundamental difference in Nicholas' approach, which is that he inclines towards Latham's language-based model, which allows him to avoid the question of hybridity altogether. Nevertheless, starting from his analysis of the 'pedigree' of the English people, he still uses the language of race, commenting how 'the Race relations of the English people are in our day gaining increased attention' and announcing that the object of his work is 'to trace, step by step, that process of race-amalgamation which has issued in the compound people called English'.[26] The secret of the English race, he announces, is 'the complexity of its origin'. Unmixed races have been far less successful. Offering the reader elaborate comparative tables of the discernible distinctly different qualities of Celt and Saxon, he claims that the English are a compound of the best of both. Does that mean that Celts and Saxons have therefore now altogether disappeared? Not quite. Nicholas subtitled his book *An argument, historical and scientific, on English ethnology, showing the progress of race-amalgamation in Britain from the earliest times, with especial reference to the incorporation of the Celtic aborigines.* If the races have been amalgamating from the earliest times, then the question that follows is how they have also maintained their separate identities. This contradiction was doubtless why later editions bore a revised subtitle, *An argument, historical and scientific, on the formation and growth of the nation: tracing race-admixture in Britain from the earliest times, with especial reference to the incorporation of the Celtic aborigines*. As in the case of Matthew Arnold, the use of the term race 'admixture' as opposed to 'amalgamation' preserves a nice ambiguity, semantically allowing both fusion or a more ambiguous mingling of the different races where each is preserved as an alien element, according to the preference of the reader. As late as 1934, the historian G. M. Trevelyan would still be adhering to the same paradigm, calling the first book of his *History of England*, 'The Mingling of the Races'.[27]

In one unusual way, Arnold himself came close to Pike. Expanding on Latham's arguments, Pike claimed that the Celts were actually physically descended from the ancient Greeks. When in *Celtic Literature* Arnold sets up his argument for English literature as a dialectic of the Celt and the Saxon, he himself also alludes to the similarities between the Celts and the Greeks – a connection that would be developed fully in *Culture and Anarchy*.[28] In that book the Saxons are also supplanted, in this case not by the Jews as such, but by Protestant Hebraism. Arnold, it seems, transformed the literal discussion of the origin to the English via the Aryan and Semitic categories of historical philology which he cites in *Celtic Literature*, to metaphors of English cultural filiations. When we consider that at this time Pike was arguing that the Celts were really descended from the Greeks, it may have been that Arnold was also thinking of it being a real possibility. Even with respect to Hebraism, it will be recalled that the Anglo-Israelite movement in this period was also claiming that the Anglo-Saxons were really the true descendants of the Jews.[29] Where race is concerned, at times it seems as if anything is possible.

The eventual winner of the Eisteddfod prize was none other than John Beddoe. He spent almost twenty years developing his Eisteddfod prize essay of 1868 into *The Races of Britain*, published in 1885, a work which, as we have seen, gave definitive corroboration to Arnold's thesis. From the moment Arnold arrived in Llandudno, therefore, far from having a tangential relation to such discussions, he became a central part of them. His *On Celtic Literature* was itself quickly picked up by contemporary ethnologists, such as Nicholas, whose work in its way also comprises an elaborately worked ethnological version of Arnold's argument.[30] The years of the Fenian 'outrages' in the 1860s were thus marked by a simultaneous explosion of Celtic challenges to the Saxon thesis.

The Times and 'A New Sort of Englishman'

Arnold first announced the thesis of *Celtic Literature* in a letter to Hugh Owen, the Chairman of the 1866 Eisteddfod. Published in the *Pall-Mall Gazette,* it was duly reported, and ridiculed in *The Times.* Arnold's letter is actually couched closer to the terms of *Culture and Anarchy,* focusing on the abjection of the English aristocracy and philistine middle class, but instead of offering 'culture' as a palliative it ends with a direct statement of how only the Celt can renew them:

> Now, then, is the moment for the greater delicacy and spirituality of the Celtic peoples who are blended with us, if it be but wisely directed, to make itself felt, prized, and honoured. In a certain measure the children of Taliesin and Ossian have now an opportunity for renewing the famous feat of the Greeks, and conquering their conquerors. No service England can render the Celts by giving you a share in her many good qualities can surpass what the Celts can at this moment do for England by communicating to us some of theirs.[31]

The Times responded robustly to this impertinent prospect of England being conquered by the Celts, and duly denounced Arnold's remarks as 'arrant nonsense':

> We are to be invaded by the Welsh language and literature, by Welsh harps and bards.... we must protest against such proceedings [the Eisteddfod] as one of the most mischievous and selfish pieces of sentimentalism which could possibly be perpetrated. The Welsh language is the curse of Wales.... Their antiquated and semibarbarous language...shrouds them in darkness.... For all practical purposes Welsh is a dead language.[32]

160

Arnold in turn replied to this ridicule by explicitly setting his argument in *Celtic Literature* in opposition to *The Times*. In a remarkably upfront political statement, he squarely laid the blame for the disastrous English rule of Ireland at its door:

> The *Times*, however, prefers a shorter and a sharper method of dealing with the Celts. . . . *Cease to do evil, learn to do good*, was the upshot of its exhortations to the Welsh; by *evil*, the *Times* understanding all things Celtic, and by *good*, all things English . . . when I read these asperities of the *Times* . . . I said to myself, as I put the newspaper down . . . '*Behold England's difficulties in governing Ireland*'. (p. 391)

While not repeating his startling claim that the Celts will reconquer their conquerors, the essay repeats the reconciling message of showing the role of Celtic within English, the benefit of knowing about the Celt and things Celtic, and the value of Celtic culture. What Arnold drew from the Eisteddfod was the perception that the Welsh had produced a cultural solution to a political problem. In the book version he added an Introduction in which, again explicitly set in opposition to the arguments of *The Times*, he offered an additional elaboration of the implications of the essay for English identity. The publication of his articles on Celtic literature, he relates, brought a large response from Welshmen and Irishmen, and what Arnold noticed was how hostile to the English they all were. 'Who', he asks, 'can be surprised at it, when he observes the strain of the *Times* in the articles just quoted, and remembers that this is the characteristic strain of the Englishman in commenting on whatsoever is not himself?' Attitudes like those of *The Times*, Arnold argues, are what produce the sense of 'estrangement and dislike':

> . . . the Welsh and Irish obstinately refuse to amalgamate with us, and will not admire the Englishman as he admires himself, however much the *Times* may scold them and rate them, and assure them there is nobody on earth so admirable. (p. 394)

What is required, Arnold announces provocatively, is nothing less than a new sort of Englishman. Unexpectedly, it seems, Arnold was an early proponent of the 'new man'. At this time when the bull-like Englishman needs to transform himself, however, *The Times* only criticizes the Celts:

> And this is the moment, when Englishism pure and simple, which with all its fine qualities managed always to make itself singularly unattractive, is losing that imperturbable faith in its untransformed self which at any rate made it imposing, – this is the moment when our great organ [*The Times*] tells the Celts that everything of theirs not English is 'simply a foolish interference with the natural progress of civilisation and prosperity'; and poor Talhaiarn, venturing to remonstrate, is commanded 'to drop his outlandish title, and to refuse even to talk Welsh in Wales!' (p. 395)

'Englishism', Arnold argues, invoking a term first used in Kaye's *History of the Sepoy War* a couple of years earlier, is losing its faith in itself. 'New ideas and forces' are stirring in England, almost all of which are, by contrast, 'the friend of the Celt'. Ministers of these new ideas, such as Arnold, will work towards perfection by promoting them, and in doing so remove the grounds of the 'Celt's alienation from the Englishman'. Arnold ends by calling for the substitution of the old kind of Englishman, the Saxon Englishman of *The Times*, with 'a new type, more intelligent, more gracious, and more humane' – in other words, more Celtic.[33] The aim of Arnold's essay was nothing less than to change the ethnicity of Englishness itself.

The Slow Demise of Teutonism

Despite all the Celtophile work charted in the previous chapter, it is noticeable that Arnold was still working at transforming the ethnicity of the English in the late 1860s. In 1866, taking issue with M'Elheran, Knox's disciple C. Carter Blake could still claim that 'the race-antagonism which exists between the so-called Celt and the Saxon at the present day, is as high as at any time during the period of history'.[34] This shows how ideas and attitudes do not change uniformally across the board, how old ideas take time to die, with residual and emergent notions jostling side by side. Even a single institution, such as *The Times*, was never consistent. Though *The Times* may have ridiculed Arnold's reaching out towards the Welsh, at moments, as we have seen, when it suited it, even *The Times* had been modifying its hard line Saxonism of the 1840s, if not always its anti-Irish rhetoric. An editorial of January 1847, commenting on Russell's Ireland Poor Relief measure, observed in a conciliatory way that

> The condition of Ireland is, directly, the condition of the British empire. No legislative union can tighten – no Utopian separation could dissolve – that intimate and close connexion between the two islands which has been formed by the hand of nature, and consolidated by the operations of time... Each year cements by closer fusion the twain branches of the Saxon and the Celtic stocks.[35]

This wilful fusion of 'stocks' suggests the alternative version of the argument that Arnold would make. Though Arnold does suggest that the Celt must change too, his emphasis falls on the transformation of the English. The strategy of *The Times* was to demand that the Celts mix themselves more – rather than enforce a greater separation such as the nationalists desired. Against Irish nationalism, interpreted in racial terms as a kind of racial consciousness, *The Times* would at times emphasize virtues of English mixture and suggest that their lack of mixture explained the problem of the Irish Celts. In 1857, ten years before Arnold's essay, it commented that 'The fact is, we are of a mulish breed, half Norman, half Saxon, and, as an Irishman would add, with several more halves from other races. The spirit of our numerous fathers is still in us.'[36] The evident reluctance here to include the Celts as an element in the English mixture remains indicative.

The continuing racial purity of the Celts in the European peripheries, romanticized by Renan and others, was thus contrasted with English mixture, to which it was suggested the Irish should properly conform. This argument in some degree contradicted the immigration scare voiced since Carlyle of the Irish swamping the Saxon English in the towns. The Welsh, by contrast, were already experiencing a huge inflow of immigrants into the Valleys. In the 1850s these issues were mediated by the experience of the Crimean War (1853–6) in which, as Tuthill Massy observed, the conflictual Celts and Saxons (English and French as well as Irish) suddenly found themselves confronted with the Slavo-Samartian Russian. In 1866 a reviewer of A. W. Kinglake's *History of the Invasion of the Crimea* noted that the Russians, who held 'the ambition of becoming the dominant race of the world', found themselves confronted with 'the two mighty branches of the Teuto-Celtic race'. The reviewer continued:

> That there is a national difference between the British and French is sufficiently certain, but this is a difference of degree rather than of kind. Both nations have the principal element, which is Celtic, in common. The romance of the extirpation of the ancient Britons by the Saxons is daily losing its authority as history. The bulk of the English people is Celt crossed with Saxon and other Teutonic invaders, who became the conquerors, not the extirpators, of the natives.[37]

Even before Arnold's essay, therefore, ethnologists were already announcing the demise of Teutonism. The English could now even be primarily Celts, as for Pike or Nicholas. Scientific racial theory, as Arnold was to claim, was indeed offering a new form of reconciliation, trying to bring Celt and Saxon together as one people.

The Arnolds and the Politics of the Church of England

As always with racial theory, refutation was only the spur to further invention. In the English case, given that the idea of Teutonic racial purity had always been a rather tenuous one, the complexity of the race was quickly adopted as its distinguishing characteristic: in the terms that Herbert Spencer was making acceptable, the English celebrated themselves as what might be termed a minor mixture, a mixture which had produced their own distinctiveness. Edwards' thesis, or its modification in Broca, meant that they did not have to worry about the degenerative effects of hybridity – by contrast, according to commentators such as Nicholas or J. W. Jackson, the English were able to inherit the best rather than the worst of their ancestors.[38] Arnold utilized the argument of the ethnologists that the English were essentially a racial mixture (though not a mixed race – he never advocated fusion) as a way of offering the basis for common political integration. In developing a more comprehensive identity for English culture, founded on a great dialectic, his model drew not only on Emerson, but showed a resemblance to those developed for the Anglican Church by Coleridge and, ironically, his father Thomas Arnold. These, in turn, were in some respects the effect of the campaign of Daniel O'Connell: the result of Catholic Emancipation in 1829 was to produce the reassessment of the role of the Church of England, which at that time had become more of a political than a religious institution, with little appeal beyond the upper ranks of English society.

Coleridge's *On the Constitution of Church and State, According to the Idea of Each*, published the year following emancipation, is widely acknowledged to have laid a new foundation for the Church of England and to have influenced not only Emerson, but also Thomas Arnold, F. D. Maurice and the Christian Socialists, Matthew Arnold, and many later cultural critics. As a model, it provided an early version of the idea which was later produced for the eventual resolution of the idea of English ethnicity. The basis of Coleridge's argument lay in the relation of the nation (defined as 'the Unity of the successive Generations of a People') to the state. The state itself, he argues, is at once made up of 'two antagonistic powers or opposite interests', those of 'PERMANENCE and of PROGRESSION', and of the 'two poles of the same magnet', the state and the national church.[39] Though Coleridge cites a conventional Saxonist history of the English constitution which he traces back to Alfred, he invokes no historical or other hierarchy between 'Goth and Celt', for he sees

Catholic emancipation very directly in terms of the enfranchisement of the Irish population so that they may become 'a component part of the united Common-weal'. According to Coleridge, it is the role of the state to provide containing and mediating channels that organize 'the free and permeative life and energy of the Nation'.[40] Coleridge thus proposes a dynamic model of the state which organizes the free energy of the nation through the dialectical ambivalence of its own institutions.

Thomas Arnold's *Principles of Church Reform*, published just three years later, was an enormously influential expansion and clarification of Coleridge's essay (it went into a fourth edition in the year of its publication, 1833), reprojected through the more nationalist eyes of Arnold's intellectual mentor, Baron Bunsen. Arnold's project was to heal the rifts that had been growing between the Church of England and the ever-stronger dissenting movement since the eighteenth century; Catholic emancipation had pushed it to a state of crisis. He develops Coleridge's argument about the relation of the state to the Church and nation in order to argue that the

> Church Establishment is essential to the well-being of the nation; that the existence of Dissent impairs the usefulness of an Establishment always, and now, from peculiar circumstances, threatens its destruction; that to extinguish Dissent by persecution being both wicked and impossible, there remains the true, but hitherto untried way, to extinguish it by comprehension; that different tribes should act together as it were in one army, and under one command, yet should each retain the arms and manner of fighting with which habit has made them most familiar.[41]

In the first place, therefore, Arnold advocates assimilation rather than extinction. Assimilation is achieved, however, not on the French or American model in which the many are required to conform to a common cultural template, but through 'comprehension', a tolerance, even encouragement, of diversity – allowing the 'different tribes' to fight in the ways and with the arms most familiar to them. Might it not be possible, Arnold asks, to constitute a Church thoroughly national, thoroughly united, thoroughly Christian, which should allow great varieties of opinion, and of ceremonies, and forms of worship, according to the various knowledge, and habits, and tempers of its members, while it truly held one common faith, and trusted in one common Saviour, and worshipped one common God? (pp. 28–9)

Much of the book is concerned with particular issues of reform in order to establish a national Church. The basis of Arnold's argument, however, is to invoke the common religious sentiments of the nation, beginning with the idea of the nation itself, over the theological differences of dissent: to make the Church's function as the Church of England more important than particular theological niceties, offering rather 'an earnest union in great matters, and a manly and delicate forbearance as to points of controversy' (p. 69):

> ...of all human ties, that to our country is the highest and most sacred: and *England*, to a true Englishman, ought to be dearer than the peculiar forms of *the Church of England*.
>
> For the sake, then, of our country, and to save her from the greatest possible evils, – from evils far worse than any loss of territory, or decline of trade, – from the sure moral and intellectual degradation which will accompany the unchristianizing of the nation, that is, the destroying of its national religious Establishment, is it too much to ask of good men, that they should consent to unite themselves to other good men, without requiring them to subscribe to their own opinions, or to conform to their own ceremonies? (pp. 28–9)

While Coleridge created the constitutional theology, Arnold invented the ideology of the national Church. Arnold, true to his Teutonic identifications, could not bring himself to include the Roman Catholics (that would happen in the 1830s and 1840s, in some degree, through the Oxford Movement); nevertheless his idea of an inclusive Church, primarily national and therefore tolerant of theological differences in pursuit of loyalty to the larger idea, was effectively disseminated through the English public school system which Arnold refounded, and achieved overwhelming success. So much so that, further supported by Matthew Arnold's friend and contemporary, A. P. Stanley, the leading liberal, broad-church theologian of his day, as the century developed many English men and women avoided crises of faith, of the kind that Tennyson related in *In Memoriam*, by identifying Church and nation, indeed by turning the nation into their Church and their religion.[42] The Church of England became in both senses the religion of England, and to some extent continues to fulfil this function today – a role which, arguably, goes back to Bede's *Ecclesiastical History* which sought to create a unified English Church and English people.[43] As John Wolffe observes, by the end of the nineteenth century many English people no longer separated their beliefs and loyalty to the Church from those to their country: 'Gothic architecture and choral evensong came to be valued as pillars of "Englishness" even by those sceptical of Christianity'.[44]

If anything could define what Matthew Arnold would have called 'the English genius', it might be that quality of 'an earnest union in great matters, and a manly and delicate forbearance as to points of controversy'. The tolerance of the Church of England, its inclusive model in which the individual's or minorities' own beliefs can be incorporated so long as he, she or they make some larger identification with the nation, in many ways provided the historical and ideological basis for its modern version, contemporary liberal multiculturalism. The acceptance of difference marked Britain out in the twentieth century from many other countries of Europe. This is often ascribed to the general tolerant qualities of the British people, which indeed is the case, but these attributes also reflect a long history of institutionalizing the ideology of tolerance, of which the Church of England remains a primary example. Thomas Arnold's essay points to the political theory behind this practice, which could be regarded as defining the centralist, consensual mode of British politics:

And the effect to be hoped for from assuming such a tone [of being 'comprehensive and conciliatory, rather than controversial'], would

be the bringing reasonable and moderate men to meet us, and to unite
with us; there would of course be always some violent spirits, who
would maintain their peculiar tenets without modification; but the
end of all wise government, whether in temporal matters or in
spiritual, is not to satisfy every body, which is impossible, but to
make the dissatisfied a powerless minority, by drawing away from
them that mass of curable discontent whose support can alone make
them dangerous. (pp. 32–3)

In *Culture and Anarchy*, Matthew Arnold, therefore, in some sense
merely reinterpreted his father's arguments, so as to make them
include not only the dissenters, but also the Catholics and Irish.
While Coleridge and Thomas Arnold were not addressing the question of race or racial difference explicitly, the models for the Church
and state that they developed were to prove well suited for adaptation
for subsequent forms of diversity, theological or otherwise, articulated within the nation.[45] Matthew Arnold, in his call for a new kind
of Englishman, and in his vision of an English ethnicity made up of
antithetical elements, was in many ways reworking the theologico-
political argument of his father. For Arnold, however, literature had
replaced religion as the true site of the free Church.

Kingsley

Even in the Saxonist camp, the shift of English identity from pure
Teuton to one of mixed allied races proved less problematic than
might have been expected. This was especially the case given that
there had always been an argument that although the English might
racially be Teuton, culturally they combined Teuton and Roman
characteristics. Many pre-eminent Saxonists had offered accounts
that could easily be adapted to a new recognition of the mixture of
English ethnicity, since many of them had always claimed that historically and culturally the heritage of the English was heterogeneous.
Even Charles Kingsley had already set up an argument that at one
level assimilates easily to that of Matthew Arnold, even if at another it

amounts to a Wagnerian rewriting of Thomas Arnold's 'Introductory Lecture'.

In some respects, Kingsley's *The Roman and Teuton* of 1864 could be said to have opened up a space for Arnold's *Culture and Anarchy* of 1869. Though presented according to a different historical argument, and seen through the lens of a staunch Saxonism, Kingsley argues that while racially Teuton – indeed, 'the only real Teutons left in the world' – the English are effectively the product of a cultural and historical mixture.[46] Thomas Arnold, it will be recalled, had made a similar argument, suggesting that English culture was a synthesis of Roman, Greek and Hebrew, but supplemented by the added factor which accounted for its greatness, namely the English race, derived from its German 'stock'. Kingsley simplifies Arnold to a synthesis of just the antithetical Roman and Teuton, which he portrays through the historical narrative of 'the human deluge' of the restless migratory Goths invading and finally subsuming the Roman empire. The effeminate Romans, Kingsley claims, were strengthened by 'the Gothic civilizer', the manly Teutons, in an overall argument which interprets the latter part of Roman history as a hybrid integration of Roman and Goth. The Roman clerisy produced the scholarly Christian inheritance, while the Goths brought 'order, justice, freedom, morality' and law. Law, Kingsley suggests, his eye always glancing towards the justification of the British Empire in his own day, was the key to Roman power.[47] Despite the cultural, legal and political intermixture between the Goths and Romans, the races, however, stayed resolutely apart:

> To amalgamate the two races would have been as impossible as to amalgamate English and Hindoos. The parallel is really tolerably exact. The Goth was very English; and the over-civilized, learned, false, profligate Roman was the very counterpart of the modern Brahmin.[48]

It is the English, untouched by the Celts in Kingsley's account, who then emerge combining the intellect of the Romans with the manliness of the Goths. While Kingsley sets this up as a historical account of the origins of the English race and their culture, his emphasis on the Teutonic purity of the race sits somewhat at odds with his account of the hybridism of the culture, achieved, he argues, through the work of the Roman clergy and scholar monks – 'delicate, nervous, imaginative, feminine characters' – among the Teutons. In individual cases, such as Theodoric or Dietrich, Kingsley even argues that 'the key to the man's character, indeed the very glory of it, is the long struggle within him, between the Teutonic and the Greek elements'.[49] The racial argument begins to ebb away even in Kingsley's own text as the racial conflict is internalized, while the account of the distinctiveness of English culture remains more or less the same – the synthesized culture does not depend on racial purity – indeed it transcends it to become part of the psychology of the national genius. In that respect, Kingsley's account actually facilitated the tendency to present the English as made up of two dialectical elements, whether German and Roman (or Greek), as in his case, or Celtic and Saxon, Greek and Hebrew, as in Arnold's, or Teuton and Roman again for the historian Sir Francis Palgrave, whose early Teutonism was, like Kingsley's, mediated in his later work by an insistence on the equal importance of the legacy of Imperial Rome.[50] Whatever the particularities of the elements, the emphasis returns again and again to the idea that the English are a synthetic product of different historical influences, conceptualized as a compound of racial and cultural origins always presented as a complementary antithesis of masculine and feminine qualities. Emerson went as far as suggesting that the English were actually hermaphroditic:

> When the war is over, the mask falls from the affectionate and domestic tastes, which make them women in kindness. This union of qualities is fabled in their national legend of *Beauty and the Beast*, or, long before, in the Greek legend of *Hermaphrodite*. The two sexes are co-present in the English mind.[51]

Perhaps it was an awareness of this quality that made Saxonists like Kingsley or Hughes insist so vigorously on the manly masculinity of the English and the need to renounce the feminine.

Though they would certainly have differed on the question of English hermaphrodism, Kingsley and Hughes were in agreement with Emerson in one respect, that is, they all included in their ideas of the English those who had spread themselves beyond the borders of England. On his death, Friedrich Max Müller wrote that 'Charles Kingsley will be missed in England, in the English colonies, in America, where he spent his last happy year; aye; wherever Saxon speech and Saxon thought is understood'.[52] In promoting Saxonism in America, Kingsley was always already expanding his account of the identity of the English to the English around the world.

The New English Dictionary

From the 1860s onwards, the profligacy of racial identities meant that having a particular racial origin became less essential for being English. The differences between the racial and the linguistic definitions of English ethnicity began to seem more porous, and it became harder to define the differences between them. Englishness became something inclusive, defined not in terms of autochthonous origins attached to a particular place, and only very generally in terms of origin. The English, by all accounts, were a largely immigrant race, as mixed as their language.

The inclusive, less overtly racialized identity of the English thereafter increasingly drew upon common cultural factors, above all the English language. For Arnold's new kind of Englishman, a new dictionary of the English language was developed, which would include all his composite elements. In June 1857 three members of the Philological Society began the project of a New English Dictionary – Chenevix Trench, Dean of Westminster (friend of Kemble and Tennyson, from an Irish family, and who, as Archbishop of Dublin, was required to preside over the Disestablishment of the Irish Church), Herbert Coleridge (the grandson of S. T. Coleridge, philologist and author of an essay on King Arthur), and Frederick Furnivall (irascible textual editor, egalitarian Christian Socialist,

172

friend of Maurice, Kingsley and Hughes).[53] The principle of this dictionary was not to be selective, exclusive or hierarchical, but rather to be inclusive. It was to be an inventory, not a standard, eliminating only words obsolete by 1150, the end of Old English. Chenevix Trench explicitly contrasted its function with that of the French *Dictionnaire de l'Académie française*. A dictionary, he wrote, should record all words:

> let their claim to belong to our book-language to be the humblest, and [the lexicographer] is bound to record them, to throw wide with an impartial hospitality his doors to them as to all other. A Dictionary is an historical monument, the history of a nation contemplated from one point of view.[54]

Chenevix Trench here uses, as Matthew Arnold was to do, the metaphor of the open door: the impartial hospitality which the dictionary offers the whole of the nation and its language means that its function is less that of an imperial vehicle, as has been recently claimed, than imperial in the sense of universal.[55] The fact that the New English Dictionary was inclusive, rather than exclusive on the *Académie Française* model, meant that it allowed a potentially endless range of varieties. Significantly, the national project was quickly extended by 1860 to include North America (Americans were allocated the eighteenth century to read; after 1925 the dictionary was partly edited in Chicago by William Craigie). The inclusive project of the New English Dictionary, that became the Oxford English Dictionary, was in some sense a first moment, or monument, in the history of the alliance between the UK and the USA that would form later in the century, founded on the basis of the language which they shared in common.

Immigration, Emigration

Arnold's essay on Celtic literature marked a turning point for the idea of English ethnicity – the comprehensiveness of its thesis, and Arnold's own literary authority, meant that, together with

Culture and Anarchy, it has been one of the most enduring cultural essays of the nineteenth century. Its argument, appealing to racial science not to create but to reconcile racial difference, offered what might be called a Broad Church account of English ethnicity. As with the Church of England, the appeal of Arnold's account was that he did not try to produce an exact doctrine or definition, vulnerable like Aryanism or Teutonism to technical or scholarly correction: rather, he offered a spectrum within which individuals could situate themselves according to their inclination and sense of themselves – so long, that is, as they were prepared to speak English. A Saxonist like Kingsley could still remain committed to Saxondom, while allowing for mixture at some level, while the hitherto excluded Celt could feel included if he or she wished. Another way of putting it would be to say that the enduring Saxon–Celt distinction was redefined as an internal division within the English rather than an external split between the English and a disavowed Welsh or Irish other. The elements continued, but worked their differences within the nation. After the Tractarian movement, the disestablishment of the Irish Church, the challenge to religion in general from science, even the identifications with Protestantism and Catholicism became less foundational (though as always, they could endure in particular situations – in Belfast or Glasgow, for example). As Home Rule for Ireland got closer, J. M. Robertson in *The Saxon and the Celt* (1897) definitively dismantled the ideological grounds for any lingering hostility towards the Celt. All those 'typical' English, who as a result of the great migrations of the nineteenth century were a bit of this and a bit of that, could be more comfortable with their identity. Meanwhile historians and ethnologists were free to continue to try to identify, as they did, the range of different peoples whom historically had arrived in Britain and left their particular ethnographic and cultural legacies.[56] In 1887 even *The Times* published an article in two parts entitled 'The British Race-Types of To-day'. Broadly indebted to Beddoe's *The Races of Britain* of two years earlier, it emphasized regional variations within a general account of racial heterogeneity. What was different was that, in stark contrast to the editorials of the 1840s, no value judgements about the worth or priority of the different races were given.[57]

The historical period of immigration up to the Conquest could also be connected to more recent immigration through the then still proud legacy of welcoming political exiles from Europe, and pointing to the benefits that historically had accrued from this practice. In 1897 the economic historian William Cunningham published *Alien Immigrants to England* (the first of whom are the Normans), in which he argued that over the centuries 'English sympathy for fugitive strangers had come to be deeply rooted and widely spread'. With recent Jewish immigration to Britain in mind, he concluded:

> The isolation of our country and the character of our people have been so marked, that we have been able to receive all sorts of strangers from abroad and to assimilate them; for they have not remained as separate elements, or only for a brief period, as the duration of cities and communities goes: they have been absorbed into our national life.[58]

Cunningham was attempting to bolster a dying liberal tradition. By the end of the century, Jewish immigration had taken over from Irish immigration as the major inward flow. Those less liberally minded than Cunningham – English aristocrats such as Lord Alfred Douglas, or Anglophiles such as Henry James – transferred the sentiments of racial hostility that once might have taken the form of anti-Celtism into anti-Semitism. Jewish immigration had to be distinguished from Irish or English. In 1878 even George Eliot complained when writing about the Jews that it would be 'a calamity to the English . . . to undergo a premature fusion with immigrants of alien blood'.[59] In 1905 the government passed the Aliens Act, the first immigration legislation in Britain, which marked the beginning of the end of Britain's long and noble history of being an open place of refuge for refugees and political exiles from Europe. The Aliens Act was primarily directed against the large numbers of Russian and

East European Jews who had been settling in great numbers in the East End of London.

By contrast with those 'undesirables' flowing in, the English themselves had been flowing out of England for centuries. It was Emerson who stressed how recognizable English populations could now be found all over the world. Where *English Traits* differs most from Arnold is that Emerson elaborates the qualities of the English not just in terms of England, but as a global 'population of English descent and language'. For Emerson, it is there that the power of the race becomes fully evident, although the rate of contemporary emigration causes anxiety: 'The spawning force of the race has sufficed to the colonization of great parts of the world; yet it remains to be seen whether they can make good the exodus of millions from Great Britain, amounting, in 1852, to more than a thousand a day' (p. 26). London becomes the heart of a population exodus, pumping the English out to the furthest parts of the world, but so powerfully that Emerson wonders whether it can sustain this 'spawning' vigour. At the same time, as Emerson's own visits to London testify, this movement was sustained by an imaginative power that drew the distant English populations back in, even if, when they arrived, their experience was one of a global imaginary, a dynamic centre whose primary impetus was to project its population outwards once more.

Chapter 6

'A Vaster England':
The Anglo-Saxon

Those who pride themselves on the unsullied racial purity and invincible character of the Conventional Briton, will receive a severe shock on reading De Foe's *True-blooded Englishman*, or, indeed, on becoming acquainted with the history of England. The British islands have been invaded and conquered so frequently, that their present inhabitants must be considered as either the most mongrel of races, or a mélange of distinct races, according as we incline to the hypothesis of amalgamation, or the reverse.... when we attempt to ascertain the true racial cognomen of the English, we are deafened by a Babel of conflicting scientific voices proceeding from anthropologists, ethnographers, philologists, historians, etc. There is wisdom in a multitude of counsellors; but –

"Who shall decide when doctors disagree?"

What are we English? Does any one know? Are we British, or Gaels, or Teutons, or Cymri, or Romans, or Belgians, or Saxons, or Angles, or Danes, or Norse, or Jutes, or Frisians, or Scandinavians, or Normans? Are we an amalgamation, or are all these types found tolerably pure on our soil? We had got it so comfortably settled that we were a Germanic, or Teutonic, or Saxon people.[1]

So, the year after Arnold's essay, the *Anthropological Review* with uncharacteristic good humour marked the waning of an ideology of Englishness and its ethnicity of the early nineteenth century: that the

English were essentially Saxon, that what was special about England's culture was its Saxon inheritance – identified with political stability, freedom and Protestantism – with Celts, that is in effect almost all those who were not Saxon, being regarded as inessential minorities bereft of cultural capital. We have seen how while the Irish nationalists of the 1840s were initially criticized for emphasizing their Irishness, they were soon characterized in ethnic terms as enfeebled Catholic Celts and contrasted to the energetic, self-reliant and resourceful Saxon, whose taxes were being plundered to send them famine relief. To a large extent all these oppositional categories – Saxon, English, Protestant, and Celt, Irish, Catholic – became interchangeable. The extreme version of this antagonistic view was found in the columns of *The Times* or the pages of Knox's *The Races of Men*. From the 1820s onwards, however, even before the apex of Saxon supremacism, the so-called Celts had started to fight back: by demanding Catholic emancipation, by countering English Saxonism with Welsh and Irish nationalism, by arguing against the extremism of the Saxonists, by asserting the value of Celtic people and their cultures, and by using the new techniques of racial anthropology to demonstrate that the English population was itself mixed in its ethnic characteristics and often not even very Saxon. Racial science was invoked to show that the Saxon fantasy was unsustainable. Matthew Arnold brought all these currents together to propose that the solution for the political problem of Ireland was to acknowledge and integrate Celtic elements within English culture, to include Celts within any account of English ethnicity, and so create a new more humane, cultured Englishman in the process. At the very least, the Celtic element could supply what the boorish English had always lacked, and could mediate the Englishman's hypermasculine John Bullishness.

> Verily nothing is sacred in these revolutionary days. Our scientific, our theological faiths are rudely attacked. Ruthless writers, like Mr Matthew Arnold, Mr Pike, and others will no longer permit us to believe ourselves an Anglo-Saxon race. Those who think the

English Saxons, depict the Anglo-Saxon as everything that is good. The opposite school think him everything that is bad. Mr William Maccall has written a lively sketch of 'The Fabulous Anglo-Saxon'. After depicting the exaggerated praises heaped on this being, he observes, he tried to discover who the Anglo-Saxon was, and he is 'compelled to avow that the Anglo-Saxon is a wholly fabulous personage; or that if he exists or has existed, he has always been a dunce, a dupe, driveller, and a drudge'.[2]

'But let us leave the dead to bury their dead, and let us who are alive go on unto perfection': like William Maccall, Arnold intuited the fact that by the late 1860s a vulnerable Saxonism, with its idea of the English as an unmixed race, was already on the wane as a national ideology of Englishness, even if some stalwart historians, such as J. R. Green, would carry on regardless into the 1880s.[3] By the time of Sidney Whitman's *Teuton Studies* (1895) the Teuton spirit had become entirely German.[4] Since it was the racial science of ethnographers such as Beddoe that proved how ethnically mixed the population was, refuting the primordial category of the Teuton, interest in representing the English according to the category of the pure Aryan race never got going in the way that it would in Germany or Sweden. Something altogether different occurred.

The new idea of English ethnicity as something heterogeneous meant that it could be opened up to include a whole range of ethnicities whose identities stretched beyond England's natural or national borders, dissolving all sense of boundaries and limits. Rather than disintegrate in the face of these Celtic challenges, the idea of English ethnicity was simply reworked and redeployed. What is often taken to be a 'crisis' of Englishness at any particular time is generally a sign that it is in the process of refashioning itself. In this case, what occurred was that the Saxon was transformed into the Anglo-Saxon. Over the next few decades, Arnold's idea of an inclusive English ethnicity was opened out, so as to include the English diaspora beyond. No longer defined solely by their historical and ethnic origins, the English were now recast as a transnational brotherhood united by race and language. They became a globalized race. The ideological basis for this had already been mapped out by Kingsley: his *Westward Ho!* (1855) ends with a new generation of adventurer-heroes 'who from that time forth sailed out to colonise another and a vaster England'.[5] Though Kingsley himself may have believed in a divine Teutonic mission, the 'new English' were no longer just Teutons.

The Saxon Becomes the Anglo-Saxon

> With respect to the term 'Anglo-Saxon', in its modern political application, it is ethnographically incorrect, though morally true. . . .
> In the course of these enquiries, we shall therefore consider all who acted under the devouring tendencies which the Anglo-Norman dynasty elicited, as designated by that same term of 'Anglo-Saxon'. All differences and distinctions of race merge in that general character, best exemplified by the People and States who glory loudest in claiming it – the Anglo-Saxon republics of the New World.
> Sir Francis Palgrave, *History of Normandy and of England* (1851, 1857)[6]

The change in the construction of English ethnicity was marked by the tendency to replace the word 'Saxon' by 'Anglo-Saxon' as the generic ethnic or racial term for the English. Anglo-Saxon was a more general category, which could imply both a mixed race and also a race beyond England, while still invoking a common racial and cultural origin in the Anglo-Saxons. Prior to the 1840s, the word was generally only used historically, to describe the old English language, or the English Saxons before the Conquest. According to the OED, the word 'Anglo-Saxon' for people, rather than language, was originally used in the ninth and tenth centuries to describe the English Saxons, as opposed to the old Saxons who had remained on the Continent, or the Angles who had come from Schleswig-Holstein. Revived in the sixteenth century by Camden, the term 'Anglo-Saxon' was sometimes used to describe all forms of old English and the people who spoke that language before the Norman Conquest. It was not until the 1840s that 'Anglo-Saxon' came to be used more widely for the English in general (OED records the first use of 'Anglo-Saxon race' in 1832) and those of Anglo-Saxon descent, anywhere in the world. Mackintosh, in his ethnological survey of 1866, is clearly aware of this wider modern meaning when he comments that 'The term *Anglo-Saxon* has little or no meaning in the present state of English anthropology, unless it be strictly limited to a combination of the Saxon and Anglian types'.[7] As the 'Saxon' identity of the English was challenged, so the term 'Anglo-Saxon', more user-friendly if less precise than alternatives such as 'Celto-Teutonic', began to be adopted. Its lack of specificity in strict ethnological terms was entirely useful. 'No race is so capable of honest work and so desirous of honest labour as the Anglo-Saxon', declared *The Times* confidently in 1848.[8] With the rise of modern nationalisms, the English as a Saxon race were replaced by the English as an Anglo-Saxon race.

'Anglo-Saxon' was sometimes used to mean 'Saxon', as opposed to 'Celt', but it was also used to suggest a modified Saxon, anglicized by the Celt, or potentially by any other early random ancestor. While its 'Anglo' connoted English as opposed to the Germanic 'Saxon', the compound made vague reference to the idea that the English were a mixed race and nation ethnically. It was, possibly, the first hyphenated identity – but whereas modern hyphenated identities tend to be associated with the psychic and social travails of Du Bois' 'double consciousness', the hyphenation of the Anglo-Saxon was designed, as Arnold suggests, precisely to reconcile and harmonize the warring factions of Saxon and Celt. The term, however, was not simply invented as a way of reconciling ethnic differences within England, or even within the United Kingdom. It was originally used predominantly in North America, and introduced into English precisely to describe the English abroad, the diasporic population. 'Anglo-Saxon' referred to indeterminate English people, of any kind, in any place. And so too, Englishness was reinvented for Anglo-Saxons around the world, deliberately designed for those who were out of place.[9]

At the end of the 1830s, while the English were still talking about themselves as Saxons, those of English 'stock' abroad, particularly in

North America, began to be described by the English themselves as Anglo-Saxons. The first context in which this occurred with significant impact on the public arena was in British North America (later to be known as Canada), when the French-speaking colonies made their first moves for independence. The Durham Report of 1839 had formulated the Canadian problem in terms of a war of two races, Anglo-Saxon and French. The employment of the word 'Anglo-Saxon' to describe those of English descent was initially a predominantly North American usage, or used in a North American context, as was the use of 'Anglo-Saxon' as a synonym for plain, unvarnished English.[10] This is certainly borne out by evidence from *The Times*, where the word 'Anglo-Saxon' begins to appear from 1839 onwards, largely in relation to discussions of the situation in British North America ('It is assumed by Lord Durham...that the difference between the races of French and Anglo-Saxon origin is *altogether incurable*').[11] In 1842, as discussions of the Durham Report in terms of a conflict of French and Anglo-Saxon races continued, we find the word also being used in the context of the struggle between Mexico and the new Republic of Texas, reported in terms of war between the Mexicans and the Anglo-Saxons.[12] By 1844 the term is being used in an article on the report of the Poor Law Commissioners in a way that anticipates Emerson's description of the 'spawning' race:

> The Anglo-Saxon race is naturally multiplying and spreading. It is always producing the physical materials of new empires and is not less fertile in the virtues and capacities necessary to found and govern them. It yearly throws off swarms of men and families of heroes. The stimulus of enterprise is deep in its nature. Without an effort, it scans the world; and without that miserable foppery of ambition which wastes the energies of other nations, it quietly marks for its own the riches of every unoccupied shore. Its natural advantages develope [*sic*] and assist its tendency. Here, then, is such an opportunity of peaceful colonisation as the world has not yet seen. The results must be great, and may be good. We cannot help breaking our narrow limits and overspreading the world.[13]

The Times was in fact critical of coerced pauper emigration, declaring that it was not much better than penal emigration, but it still endorsed the idea of colonization as endemic to the nature of the Anglo-Saxon race: 'We cannot help breaking our narrow limits and overspreading the world'. Racial consciousness of Saxon England was giving way to a perception of the global context of Anglo-Saxondom: after the Durham Report, the term 'Anglo-Saxon' appeared more and more frequently. While Knox continued to distinguish between the Saxon in England and the 'Anglo-Saxon republic' of the United States, in its 1852 riposte to John M'Elheran, *The Times* uses the terms 'Saxon' and 'Anglo-Saxon' almost synonymously, implicitly suggesting a more inclusive ethnic identity from which Celtic Ireland would not be excluded.[14]

Ideas about English ethnicity were affected by the impact of a succession of such events outside Britain: the Canadian rebellion of 1838 and the Durham Report of 1839, the 1848 revolutions in Europe, the Crimean War of 1854–6, the Indian 'Mutiny' of 1857, the American Civil War of 1861–5, and from the 1860s onwards, the attitudes and political activism of the Irish diaspora. All of these in different ways involved questions of race or nationality. We have seen how the Crimea produced the first political reconciliation of Saxons with Celts after the Napoleonic wars as Britain and France fought together against the Russians. The awareness of races and nationalities outside Europe, alternative 'others' against whom the English might define themselves, was heightened by rebellions such as the Indian Mutiny, many accounts of which were racialized in lurid terms. The American Civil War may in the short term have alienated Britain and the US, but in the longer term it created a new sense of 'the Anglo-Saxon' and the possibility of a political or quasi-spiritual federation between Anglo-Saxon peoples. Its immediate impact in Britain, however, was to highlight the North's commitment to the federal system. Commentators pointed to the marked contrast between the resolve of the North's fight to prevent the dismemberment of the Union and the contemporary Liberal English sentiment that the Empire should be allowed to break up.

The Anglo-Saxon

One of the most telling indications of the arrival of the term 'Anglo-Saxon' as the preferred racial description of what might be called the unmarked diasporic English (as opposed to the earlier local form of the Saxon) occurred with the establishment of the *Anglo-Saxon Magazine* in 1849 – a journal addressed to, and concerned with, Anglo-Saxons around the world. In retrospect, the *Anglo-Saxon* was somewhat premature, and might have survived much longer than it did had it been published twenty years later when its message would have been accorded a more enthusiastic reception.[15] Its chief editor was the poet Martin F. Tupper, friend of Gladstone, author of the in-its-time celebrated *Proverbial Philosophy*, whose enthusiasm for things American was to produce a wildly successful American tour in 1851 which included a dinner at the White House and the publication in Philadelphia of a compilation of proverbs entitled *The Proverbialist and Poet*, which, as the *Dictionary of National Biography* puts it, 'consisted almost exclusively of elevating quotations from Tupper, Solomon, and Shakespeare'.[16] Very different from Kemble's emphasis on English Saxonism in *The Saxons in England*, which appeared in the same year, the *Anglo-Saxon* was intended to operate as the organ of a new globalized racial consciousness and raise a 'pride of race' for Anglo-Saxons around the world, wherever they might be. Its opening introductory 'Address to Anglo-Saxons' describes the race as grown from the same trunk (oak, naturally), but now scattered all over the world accomplishing its greater destiny: 'This we believe to be the *Destiny*, the *Mission*, of the Anglo-Saxons'. However, the journal adds, 'in order to accomplish this Destiny, to fulfil this Mission, we must first become *united* in some things at least, if not in all. We must have some *Rallying Point*'. Divisions of religion and political institutions must be by-passed for a larger union between Anglo-Saxons everywhere:

And there is one Field upon which we may all meet as Brothers, one Platform upon which we may teach without confusion, one *Bond of*

Union which can embrace all our Race, – *our Mother Language* – the *'kindly English Tongue.'*

The whole Earth may be called the *Father-land* of the Anglo-Saxon. He is a native of every clime – a messenger of heaven to every corner of the Planet.

The aim of the *Anglo-Saxon Magazine* was to enshrine Anglo-Saxon knowledge and history. This would soon be supplemented, it was announced, by an Anglo-Saxon Club in London. The 'Address' concludes with an Anglo-Saxon map of the world, which, it is decreed, 'every man whose thoughts and words are English, whether Briton or American, Indian or Australian', should place before him. He will then feel a 'pride of race' as he contemplates the fact that almost a quarter of the surface of the globe, coloured a suitable pink, 'is already under the influence of the Anglo-Saxon genius' (figure 6.1).[17] Just in case the Anglo-Saxon reader might miss the significance of the diaspora, a second map makes the point in a graphically brighter form (figure 6.2).

The most interesting feature of these maps is who gets included: the whole of North America, as well as Malaya and India (notice how little the Anglo-Saxon has penetrated Africa at this point). The Anglo-Saxon fraternity here is broad enough to include anyone who speaks English, and subscribes to an interest in the kind of English cultural topics which the magazine then featured in its issues: the King Alfred Jubilee, 'the Present Condition and Progress of the Anglo-Saxon Race' (a long article which draws liberally from Robert Knox's lectures on the Saxon in the *Medical Times*), Anglo-Saxon Ladies, emigration, a series on English colonies, and Anglo-Saxon literature. The line of connection between global Anglo-Saxons is always drawn back to their Saxon origins, most notably in two illustrations. The first depicts an Anglo-Saxon chieftain having just arrived on the shores of England beneath the cliffs of Dover in AD 449. The second shows his nineteenth-century equivalent 1,400 years later, now standing in the tropics beside a map of Sarawak (figure 6.3).

Figure 6.1
'The Anglo-Saxon Map', Prospectus, *Anglo-Saxon Magazine*, 1849, between pages
18 and 19. Courtesy of the Bodleian Library, University of Oxford.

All this confidence in the Anglo-Saxon comes directly after 1848,
but the editors are as concerned as Kemble to distinguish their project
from anything resembling the 1848 revolutions:

> ...this Rage for *Nationalities* is a very different thing from Pride of
> Race or Breed – especially the Pride of an Anglo-Saxon, whose
> country is circumscribed by no arbitrary boundaries, whose Home is
> independent of any form of Empire, Monarchy, or Republic. It is the
> pride of the eagle that ranges from North Pole to the South – not
> limited to some petty district, not confined by country or climate.[18]

Already here the Anglo-Saxon is being promoted as a global creature,
his home 'independent' of any country or climate, as expansive in

186

his universalism as the imperial eagle itself. For the next hundred years this sentiment would be developed and repeated again and again.

The *Anglo-Saxon Magazine* did not survive long enough to establish its projected worldwide English readership. In *The Pedigree of the English People*, the Celtophile Nicholas revels in its failure.[19] He assumes, however, that it was but a propagandist organ for Saxonism, missing the point that this new contemporary Anglo-Saxonism was, in a different way, also proposing a composite identity for the English. The new consciousness of the 'Anglo-Saxon race' as a global diaspora, of which Tupper's journal was the first significant marker, was to increase steadily for the rest of the century. As the illustrations of the Anglo-Saxon chieftain suggest, this conception had everything to do with the British Empire. If the Saxon had been the man of England, the Anglo-Saxon was the man of Englands everywhere.

The Anglo-Saxon Empire

When people talk about the British Empire in the twenty-first century, they tend to assume that it operated as a single imperial unit, of which British India functioned as the jewel, and that the Empire disintegrated because British government was forced to decolonize after the Second World War. In fact, with the exception of India and Ireland (the latter a somewhat different case since it was constitutionally part of the United Kingdom), the most substantial territories of the British Empire – Canada, South Africa, Australia and New Zealand – were given independence from the mid–nineteenth century onwards quite voluntarily, sometimes even in the face of opposition from the local colonial population. By 1910 they were self-governing dominions (Canada 1867; Australia 1901; New Zealand 1907; South Africa 1910), independent except for certain inter-Empire matters (the most contentious one was that they were not allowed to set their own immigration laws with respect to other parts of the Empire). It was precisely because so much of the Empire was independent, that India, with its paternalistic government,

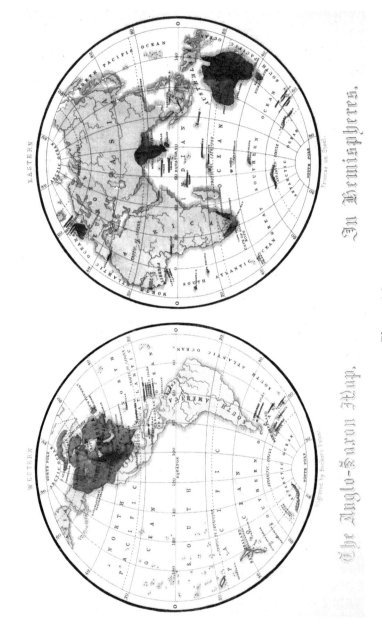

Figure 6.2

'The Anglo-Saxon Map', *Anglo-Saxon Magazine*, vol. 2, no. 5, 1849, between pages 108 and 109. Courtesy of the Bodleian Library, University of Oxford.

Figure 6.3

'An Anglo Saxon Chieftain, AD 449 and AD 1849', *Anglo-Saxon Magazine*, vol. 1, no. 2, 1849, between pages 100 and 101. Courtesy of the Bodleian Library, University of Oxford.

became the dominant part of what might be called the Third British Empire. While the dominions became independent, in the last quarter of the nineteenth century the Empire was expanded to include much of Africa, and this shifted the balance of the whole system.

The distrust of imperialism during the reign of Louis Napoleon (1852–70) that had been so marked in Britain seemed to turn round in 1871 with the defeat of France in the Franco-Prussian war, the culmination of the rise of Prussia after the Austro-German war of 1866. The year 1871 was perhaps the final moment which drew any surviving latter-day Teutonists towards a more anglicized Anglo-Saxonism. It also coincided with the emergence of a new British imperialism. This is often dated to Disraeli's purchase of the Suez Canal shares in 1875, or to his Crystal Palace speech three years earlier, in which he, who had formerly characterized the colonies as the millstone round the country's neck, effectively announced the upholding of the Empire as one of the objectives of the Conservative Party, while criticizing the Liberals for trying 'to effect the disinte-gration of the empire of England'. Although in practice Disraeli's major interest in terms of imperial foreign policy was directed towards India, the terms of his speech were consistent with his characteriza-tion of the Empire here as English. Disraeli argued that the liberal attempts to effect the disintegration of the Empire had failed

> through the sympathy of the Colonies with the Mother Country. They have decided that the Empire shall not be destroyed, and in my opinion no minister in this country will do his duty who neglects any oppor-tunity of reconstructing as much as possible our Colonial Empire, and of responding to those distant sympathies which may become the source of incalculable strength and happiness to this land.[20]

Disraeli, always more of an opportunist than an originator, was clearly alert to shifts in sentiment that were taking place, particularly about race, and the refashioning of the Empire as a confederation of the English. Catherine Hall has argued that social relations within Britain were determined by the Empire from 1830 to the mid-1860s.[21] From the 1860s onwards, colonial consciousness itself became a part of a self-image of the English who no longer saw themselves in possession of a circumscribed domestic space. The delocalizing of Englishness into the Empire meant that its boundaries dissolved. 'England' had no inside or outside. It was everywhere. By the time of Rupert Brooke, there would even be an 'English heaven'.

Contemporary popular interest in, and awareness of, the Empire was predominantly focused on the Colonial Empire, in part because the Colonial Empire was connected to one of the major issues of nineteenth-century British society: emigration. This was either because people were personally involved in emigration at the level of themselves or their own families, or, among the upper echelons, because colonization was widely regarded as the best solution to what was deemed to be the social problem of overpopulation. Anxiety about population growth initiated by Thomas Malthus's *Principles of Population* (1798) was augmented by the boom and slump phenomena of capitalism, which meant that for recurrent periods, large numbers of workers were unemployed. In 1843, during the Chartist disturbances, Carlyle called for a State Emigration service. For the most part, however, with the exception of Wakefield's New Zealand colonization scheme, migration, whether internal or external, was organized by the people themselves (or their landlords) and the government was not involved.[22] At times, this produced a concern that too many people were leaving the country, particularly as the vast bulk of them went not to British colonies but to the United States, which was not then seen as an ally or friendly power.[23] At its worst, emigration seemed an exodus: a mass defection of millions of people from the state.[24] It was only gradually, from the 1830s onwards, with the writings and campaigns of Horton, Napier, Wakefield, Buller and others, that economists and colonial secretaries began to link the issue of emigration with the Empire, and try to coordinate the questions of overpopulation and spontaneous emigration with colonization. In 1847 *The Times* put it simply: why not turn all these emigrants into colonists? 'Let the emigrant cease to feel that he is forsaking his country, and all that he holds dear. Make Canada a country of England. Steam has brought it closer than Scotland

at the era of the Union.'[25] The appearance of Fenians in the US and
Australia in the 1860s meant that politicians in Britain also began
to worry seriously about the possible effect of the colonies (and
the US) becoming full of English-hating Irish. Already in 1847, in
the context of a discussion of transportation to Australia, *The Times*
had raised the spectre of a colony bent on a Frankenstinian revenge
on its creator:

> ...should a great piratical confederacy spring from the south and
> spread over the oceans, the archipelagos, and the labyrinths which
> those islands so entirely command; – should the fair peninsulas of Asia,
> of Africa and South America be threatened by a new form of Anglo-
> Saxon audacity and ambition, returning upward from the farthest
> south, the horrors of the northern hordes and the fall of Rome
> might then be repeated, and England herself might in process of
> ages fall by the hands of her own outcast offspring.[26]

The remedy for this alarming spectre was first to end transportation
and, secondly, as we have seen, in response to the Fenian threat, to
try, belatedly, to include the Irish among the Anglo-Saxons. While
the Americans were encouraged to consider themselves Anglo-
Saxons too, attempts were made to reroute emigration to the British
colonies. Although anglophile Americans were relatively easy to
persuade, the Irish abroad were decidedly uninterested, and enthusiasts of Anglo-Saxon federation such as Charles Dilke and, above all,
James Anthony Froude, found a hostile reception awaiting them
among Irish emigrants when they visited North America.

Interest in the Empire in relation to colonization was also the result
of a major change in the ideology of empire which resulted from the
Repeal of the Corn Laws in 1846. The advent of free trade meant that
much of the economic advantage of colonies, which had been based
on a mercantilist system providing commercial monopolies, disappeared. This situation produced a low point for the British Empire,
which Liberals and even Conservatives such as Disraeli began to
consider more and more as a financial burden. The colonies required

a global system of military and naval protection, involving Britain in wars almost every year, and yet seemed to be offering little in return. The precedent of the American colonies meant that they could not be taxed. This situation came to a head in 1858–9, when Canada imposed 20 per cent import tariffs on British goods, while still expecting that Britain would bear the cost of its defence; this became a serious issue with the advent of the American Civil War in 1861. After Gladstone, champion of liberalism and liberty, was appointed Colonial Secretary in 1845, it became an accepted and oft-repeated observation that the break-up of the Empire was simply a matter of time – a sentiment still strong enough in 1870 for the Earl of Carnarvon to ask in the House of Lords whether it was official government policy.

In 1862–3 Goldwin Smith, Regius Professor of Modern History at Oxford, published a series of letters in the *Daily News*, which were then collected into a book called *The Empire*. Smith's essays represented the most sustained critique of the colonies and the colonial system since Adam Smith's *The Wealth of Nations* of 1776 and Jeremy Bentham's 'Emancipate Your Colonies!' of 1793. Ever after, Goldwin Smith was associated with Cobden and Bright under the tag, 'Little Englanders', that is, politicians who argued against the territorial expansion of the Empire, and for its gradual dissolution.[27] This may have been true for Cobden and Bright, but in Smith's case the characterization of 'little England' worked both ways. In his 1953 novel, *In the Castle of My Skin*, George Lamming remarks that the island of Barbados was known for many years as 'Little England'.[28] 'Little England' was also an informal name for various territories of the Empire. In defining the term 'empire' in the book's Preface, Smith points to the radical discrepancy between its different parts:

> In the case of our Empire this definition will embrace a motley mass of British colonies, conquered colonies of other European nations, conquered territories in India, military and maritime stations, and protectorates.[29]

Smith's argument against empire was formulated at the time of the Trent Affair of 1861, when Britain and the Unionist Northern United States came very close to war, which in turn highlighted the vulnerable position of Canada. His reasoning was based on empire's cost and risk: should not the question of colonial expenditure, he argued, be accompanied by discussion of the question of colonial emancipation? He did not, however, advocate decolonization in terms of simply cutting formal ties, for it was accompanied by the argument that much of the Empire in fact constituted a series of little Englands around the world. There was no need to have a formal imperial structure, when more fundamental informal ties would keep the colonies bound to the 'mother country'.

> That connection with the Colonies, which is really a part of our greatness – the connexion of blood, sympathy, and ideas – will not be affected by political separation. And when our Colonies are nations, something in the nature of a great Anglo-Saxon federation may, in substance if not in form, spontaneously arise out of affinity and mutual affection.[30]

Smith distinguished between settlement colonies and dependencies, the latter including the West Indies, Gibraltar and India. With regard to India, at that time the only major non-settler colony, he remarked that 'the crucial question probably is, whether the English can convert India from a dependency into a Colony'. If not, he adds, then 'the days of our dominion are numbered'. Although Smith's suggestions received an immediate fighting riposte from *The Times*, he was able to produce figures derived from trade or emigration records to argue that though the Empire might be dismembered, England would still be 'the heart and centre of a great confederacy of states belonging to her own race'.[31] Smith thus trumped Gladstone's anti-imperialism by arguing that the dismemberment of Empire would not really be a dismemberment at all, since in a different way the colonies would survive as part of the body of a single race dispersed over the world, continuously pumped out from the heart of

England. As often in this period, the progressive argument (here anti-colonialism) invoked race as its new coordinate. Smith effectively broke up the Empire into territories of racial identity (colonies) and difference (dependencies), and argued that union with the former would survive political emancipation and lead to a new kind of empire: an Anglo-Saxon federation.

Smith was not the first to suggest some kind of Anglo-Saxon federation held together by a common racial identity, but he was the first to propose it as a specific ideology of empire. This new way of thinking was doubtless partly responsible for the striking change in the attitude towards empire that developed by the end of the decade. By 1871, the *Spectator* was suggesting that 'England's best alliance would be the free confederation of the English race in every part of the world. Change "English' for 'Anglo-Saxon", and in that sentence lies the policy of the future.'[32]

Chapter 7
'England Round the World'

'England Round the World': Dilke

In 1869 the possibility of a worldwide confederation of Anglo-Saxons was reorientated by the Liberal politician Charles Wentworth Dilke in his book *Greater Britain*. The idea of English culture and language increasingly dominating the globe drew freely on contemporary theories of Aryan expansion derived from comparative philology. The Aryans, as Max Müller had recently characterized them, were instinctively impelled by their racial drives to migrate ever further westwards, following the star of empire, 'ever pushing with burning energy towards the setting sun', as Dilke himself put it, echoing Bishop Berkeley.[1] However, as in Kingsley's *Westward Ho!*, this colonizing drive was defined as English, not Aryan.

In 1866–7, while still in his early twenties, Dilke had set off to travel round the world. What was particular about his journey was that he only visited English-speaking countries. The effect on Dilke was to produce an acute sense of pride in a common culture of the English whom he found dispersed all over the planet. He called this 'Greater Britain' on the analogy of Great Britain, but at the same time made it quite clear that he identified Greater Britain with England. He wrote:

> In 1866 and 1867, I followed England round the world: everywhere I was in English-speaking, or in English-governed lands. If I remarked

that climate, soil, manners of life, that mixture with other peoples had modified the blood, I saw, too, that in essentials the race was always one.

The idea which in all the length of my travels has been at once my fellow and my guide – a key wherewith to unlock the hidden things of strange new lands – is a conception, however imperfect, of the grandeur of our race, already girdling the earth, which it is destined, perhaps, eventually to overspread. (p. vii)

Dilke's ideas come quite close to those of Tupper in the *Anglo-Saxon*, but what makes them particularly powerful for a practically minded English reader is that in this case he has actually 'followed England round the world' and seen with his own eyes the 'grandeur' of the race. The English who are now girdling the earth – the same metaphor that Henry James would later use for the 'English-speaking territories of the globe' – may have 'modified the blood' through the influence of climate and mixture with other races, but 'in essentials' the race is 'always one'. Despite his overt racialism, Dilke's attitude is pragmatic: race, here, is not being applied in any technical sense: it has, rather, become a general category, loosely combining 'blood' and culture to produce an international transnational identity. Some degree of racial mixture is seen as the norm, not the aberration. Like Tupper, Dilke is relatively relaxed about the question of race in strict racial terms, with the result that even India is envisaged as belonging to the greater Englands beyond the seas. What is more important is that 'the race' remains moulded together, through a commonality of institutions and of language:

In America, the peoples of the world are being fused together, but they are run into an English mould: Alfred's laws and Chaucer's tongue are theirs whether they would or no. There are men who say that Britain in her age will claim the glory of having planted greater Englands across the seas. They fail to perceive that she has done more than found plantations of her own – that she has imposed her institutions upon the offshoots of Germany, of Ireland, of Scandinavia, and of Spain. Through America, England is speaking to the world.

> Sketches of Saxondom may be of interest even upon humbler grounds: the development of the England of Elizabeth is to be found, not in the Britain of Victoria, but in half the habitable globe. If two small islands are by courtesy styled "Great," America, Australia, India, must form a "Greater" Britain. (pp. vii–viii)

Dilke was the first to claim the appearance of what Niall Fergusson has called 'Anglobalization', on his journey along, as he put it, 'the Anglo-Saxon highway round the globe' (p. 189).[2] His *Greater Britain* was the first book about the British Empire to characterize it from a racial and cultural perspective, and the first to propose an idea that became ever stronger during the course of the nineteenth century: of an English brotherhood spread around the world, sharing the same language and institutions, making up Englands beyond England. For Dilke, the ultimate aim of this process was to achieve the 'universal dominion of the English people' (p. 564). Dilke's global perspective – signalled by the gold globe on the spine of his book (figure 7.1) – was to give ideas about English ethnicity a radically new orientation.

Instead of a painstaking inquiry into English origins from the past, Dilke wrote of what they had come to be in the present. What struck him was what he called 'the grandeur' of the race, that the English

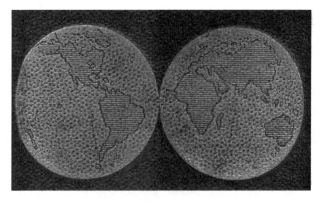

Figure 7.1
Sir Charles Wentworth Dilke, *Greater Britain* (1868) (spine).

198

had now spread out into a global diaspora. Englishness had become for him what Raymond Williams would call 'a structure of feeling'. This meant that the English were no longer attached to nation, even to England itself: 'That which raises us above the provincialism of citizenship of little England', he opined, 'is our citizenship of the greater Saxondom which includes all that is best and wisest in the world' (p. 390).

As his talk of citizenship might suggest, Dilke was himself a republican. For him, as for the editors of the *Anglo-Saxon Magazine*, the greatest example of 'the greater Saxondom' was the USA. However, Dilke arrived in the United States at the end of the Civil War, a time not propitious for British–American relations. In addition to the arguments about the Trent incident, Dilke's visit coincided with the Fenian invasions of Canada, one of which he witnessed. His republican enthusiasm for the US was therefore somewhat tempered by his fear of its potential Irish domination, and his awareness that five million Irish had emigrated there in coercive circumstances that made England their enemy, not their natural friend. After a chapter discussing the threat of the Fenians, he ends however by declaring somewhat optimistically that the son of a Fenian becomes 'the normal gaunt American, quick of thought, but slow of speech, whom we have begun to recognise as the latest product of the Saxon race'. Mindful of the fact that the bulk of English emigrants also went to the States, Dilke finds himself able to claim of the US that 'she must fuse together all the races that settle within her borders, and the fusion must now be in an English mould' (pp. 218–19). For Dilke, oblivious to ethnological niceties about hybridity, all the races fuse into one, and that one is English. Does this mean that he saw the Anglo-Saxons merging with the newly emancipated slaves? That possibility clearly gives him little cause for concern – Dilke followed Knox in his belief in the 'antipathy everywhere exhibited by the English to coloured races' (p. 182). In 1863 the American James L. Bryce had justified this particular English characteristic in the following way: 'The immeasurable contempt and prejudice against the inferior race, which characterize all branches of the English race,

whether the British masters ruling Hindoo servants, or English landlords with Irish Kelts, or Anglo-Americans among Indian tribes, or
Southern slaveholders toward slaves, or "Yankees" toward negroes, is
an unfortunate but legitimate inheritance from Teutonic ancestors.'[3]

Still sharing a common racial and cultural inheritance, the USA,
for Dilke, paradoxically remains England's best 'colony'. This is
because it is in the US that the Englishman becomes most English:

> After all, there is not in America a greater wonder than the English-
> man himself, for it is to this continent that you must come to find him
> in full possession of his powers. Two hundred and fifty millions of
> people speak or are ruled by those who speak the English tongue, and
> inhabit a third of the habitable globe; but, at the present rate of
> increase, in sixty years there will be two hundred and fifty millions
> of Englishmen dwelling in the United States alone.

For the liberal Dilke, the progressive American becomes the fulfilment of the Englishman, and as the country expands he envisages a
time when the US may take over as the – still definitively 'English' –
global centre of a Greater Britain.

> America is becoming, not English merely, but world-embracing in the
> variety of its type; and, as the English element has given language and
> history to that land, America offers the English race the moral direct-
> orship of the globe, by ruling mankind through Saxon institutions and
> the English tongue. Through America, England is speaking to the
> world. (pp. 223–4)

While he was largely responsible for inventing the idea of the
English as a shared culture of Anglo-Saxons around the globe, this
quotation makes it clear that Dilke's racialism was relatively old fash-
ioned. In some respects his ideas come close to those of Knox, another
radical republican, whose *Races of Men* had recently been reissued in a
second edition.[4] Like Knox, Dilke tends to use the term 'English' or
'Saxon' for the race, and 'Anglo-Saxon' for the diaspora (the book's
index, on the other hand, often merges the two). While in the US, as

elsewhere, he remains haunted by Knox's idiosyncratic claim that the Saxon is not a successful emigrant outside its own climes, and even suggests, following Knox, that in general only native peoples survive, assimilating the ever weakening invaders. Knox had claimed that the population growth in the US which so astonished Malthus was only sustained by continuing fresh immigration and that all exotic populations would eventually be absorbed into indigenous ones.[5] Latham had in turn cited several pages from Knox in a discussion of the issue in his *Man and His Migrations* of 1851.[6] The question of race and 'acclimation', Knox had emphasized more recently in *The Lancet* in 1859, was a question on whose solution 'depends the existence of what some are pleased to call "the Colonial Empire of Britain"'.[7] Again and again, therefore, Dilke returns to the question that troubles him as he travels, that of the long-term survival of English emigrants:

> Hitherto it has been nature's rule, that the race that peopled a country in the earliest historic days should people it to the end of time. The American problem is this: Does the law, in a modified shape, hold good, in spite of the destruction of the native population? Is it true that the negroes, now that they are free, are commencing slowly to die out? That the new Englanders are dying fast, and their places being supplied by immigrants? Can the English in America, in the long run, survive the common fate of all migrating races? Is it true that, if the American settlers continue to exist, it will be at the price of being no longer English, but Red Indian? It is certain that the English families long in the land have the features of the extirpated race. . . . Are we English in turn to degenerate abroad, under pressure of a great natural law forbidding change? It is easy to say that the English in Old England are not a native but an immigrant race; that they show no symptoms of decline. There, however, the change was slight, the distance short, the difference of climate small.[8]

Similarly, when in Australia he remarks, 'Looming in the distance, we still, however, see the American problem of whether the Englishman can live out of England. Can he thrive except where mist and damp preserve the juices of his frame? . . . In Australia and

America – hot and dry – the type has already changed. Will it eventually disappear?' (pp. 383–4).

Dilke's comment here already implicitly contains his solution to this pressing question. If 'the type has already changed', then it suggests that climate and racial mixture have modified the race. Though his anxieties continued, in the face of the evidence before his eyes, therefore, Dilke concludes positively by modifying Knox's model of unalterable races to an idea of the English developing through racial fusion with proximate races, and so becoming a new, dynamic race, a trope already anticipated in the progressive evolutionism of Lyell, echoed by Tennyson in *In Memoriam* (1850), and later to be championed by Galton and Spencer. As Pike argued in 1866, Darwin's *Origin of Species* (1859) had already begun to modify the racial ideas of this period – even if its emphasis on favoured races, racial struggle, and extermination, was ostensibly made only with respect to animals. Darwin's work not only gave a new prestige to a certain form of scientific analysis of race, language and history, but also sustained the arguments of both opposing camps in the domain of race: on the one hand, his arguments could be used to strengthen the thesis of polygenesis; on the other hand, he brought back into view Lyell's emphasis on the creation of new species and the extinction of old – a mechanism which Lyell had himself illustrated in human terms: 'let the mortality of the population of a large country represent the successive extinction of species, and the births of new individuals the introduction of new species'.[9] Lyell's resignation to the 'certain doom' and 'speedy extermination of the Indians of North America and the savages of New Holland' came in as a handy complement to the idea of the English as a race that was not only a historical product but one still advancing and developing in a global context of what Spencer would characterize as 'the survival of the fittest'.[10] With the *realpolitik* of Lyell and Knox, Dilke himself openly admitted that English colonization was achieved through the 'extirpation' of other 'cheaper' races ('the Anglo-Saxon', he remarked proudly, 'is the only extirpating race on earth').[11]

At the point where scientific and cultural ethnography appeared to have demonstrated that the English taken as a whole were a mixture of different 'proximate' races, Darwin and Spencer's work allowed the development of an evolutionary paradigm not of degeneration but of a transcendent identity according to which the English had evolved by means of a special destiny into a more advanced race set above all others. The identity of the English as a result became as much prospective as retrospective. It was thus relatively easy for Arnold's literary, gendered and often metaphorical account of the polarities of Englishness to be developed into a new cultural–racial model of the English as a race in the process of formation, emerging as different varieties of the Anglo-Saxon type in different parts of the globe, a paradigm that was conveniently close to Prichard's 'scientifically' discredited but still appealing idea that racial intermixture could produce 'an entirely new and intermediate stock'.[12] While the scientists and philologists argued, as Freeman would see so clearly, popular ideas of transnational forms of belonging emerged that developed their own agendas. Dilke's new global perspective encouraged a way of characterizing the English so that the Celt–Saxon division through which they were formerly defined was shifted to a question of their difference from other more distant races. The idea of varieties of English populations developing around the world allowed the liberal Dilke to by-pass the antimonies of the Celt–Saxon dichotomy altogether. As with Anglo-Saxons in North America, 'Celt' and 'Saxon' disappeared under the wider umbrella of being 'English'. So, in 1901, Kipling would relate that Kim was 'English', even though he turns out to be Irish.

Like Smith, Dilke distinguishes clearly between settlement colonies (such as North America, New Zealand and Australia) and India, which he concludes is not available for European colonization. At the same time, he raises the question that would so concern John Seeley, namely that whereas England identifies its own national character with liberty, and whereas the English colonies are governed on the basis of freedom ('the map of the world will show that freedom exists only in the homes of the English race'), India is run as a form of 'imperialism', even if, in his account, it amounted to a 'well-administered despotism'. Dilke, who uses the term 'imperialism' in its original, disparaging sense, laments that 'England in the East is not the England that we know'. His long-term view is that 'if freedom be good in one country it is good in all', which means that in the end the English will have to leave the sub-continent, the England that remains unrecognizable.[13] It was for this reason that, since Dilke was an enthusiast for Greater Britain on racial and cultural grounds, he remained unenthusiastic with respect to Britain's tropical exploitation colonies (a sentiment significantly increased by his pathological fear of the banana). Elsewhere, the impression Dilke gives his reader as he travels is one of repeatedly encountering England overseas – English people, English language, English architecture, English churches and English institutions, transported and replicated around the world. Dilke thus gives a global perspective to the British Empire, which he interprets primarily in terms of its Englishness. Following Smith, he argues that the links would be stronger if, like the US and Britain, the colonies were independent from each other. 'With the more enlightened thinkers of England, separation from the colonies has for many years been a favourite idea', he remarks, adding: 'After all, the strongest of the arguments in favour of separation is the somewhat paradoxical one that it would bring us a step nearer to the virtual confederation of the English race' (pp. 390–1).

Though his warnings about the dangers of the banana went entirely unheeded, so far as we can tell, Dilke's book was otherwise extraordinarily influential. It went through many reprintings and editions, a second, more imperially minded version, *Problems of Greater Britain* (1890), and inspired poetic and even childrens' versions.[14] The book's popularity in the colonies is still attested to today by the availability of second-hand copies on the Internet, many of which are to be found for sale in bookshops in Australia, New Zealand, South Africa, Canada and the US. Dilke's role in the dissemination of the idea of an English empire is nicely brought out through an inscription on the half-title page of a copy of the eighth edition (1894) of *Greater Britain* now in Hong Kong University Library (figure 7.2).

Here, Cades has inscribed his Christmas present to his father – a copy of *Greater Britain* – with three extracts. The first is from

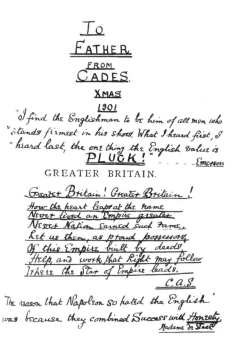

To
FATHER
FROM
CADES.
XMAS
1901

"I find the Englishman to be him of all men who
"stands firmest in his shoes. What I heard first, I
" heard last, the one thing the English value is
PLUCK!" - - - - Emerson

GREATER BRITAIN.

Greater Britain! Greater Britain!
How the heart leaps at the name
Never lived an Empire greater
Never Nation earned such fame.
Let us then, as proud possessors
Of this Empire built by deeds
Help, and work that Right may follow
Where the Star of Empire leads.
C.A.S

The reason that Napoleon so hated the English
was because they combined Success with Honesty,
Madame De Stael

Figure 7.2

Inscription on the half-title page of a copy of Sir Charles Wentworth Dilke's
Greater Britain, 8th edn. (1894). Reproduced courtesy of Hong Kong
University Library.

Emerson's *English Traits* (1856) – 'the one thing the English value is PLUCK!', an accurate characterization of what became the most favoured personal attribute for those such as Baden Powell who identified with the British Empire. The second consists of an enthusiastic poetic eulogy to following the 'star of empire' of 'Greater Britain', signed by C.A.S.

> Greater Britain! Greater Britain!
> How the heart leaps at the name
> Never leaped an empire greater
> Never nation earned such fame.

Let us then, as proud possessors,
Of this empire built by deeds,
Help, and work, that light may follow
Where the star of empire leads.

C.A.S. was in fact Cades himself, whose full name was Cades Alfred Middleton Smith, an engineer and commercial entrepreneur who in 1912 went out to be the first Taikoo Professor of Engineering at the newly founded Hong Kong University.[15] He concludes his inscription with a version of Madame de Staël's anglophile praise for English honesty ('The English particularly annoy him [Bonaparte], because they have found a way to combine success with honesty, which Napoleon would prefer people to think impossible').[16] This inscription not only brings together two of the period's most significant texts about the English, Emerson and Dilke, but it also makes the larger point: Englishness above all involves not just race as such but above all a set of values – here, pluck (Kingsley's favourite quality) and honesty. The inscribed book itself testifies to the material dissemination of such an idea of Englishness: it was not just an ideology to be found in books, it was also a practice, carried out to the colonies and beyond. As Eric Richards has observed in his exhaustive study of migration from the British Isles, 'the British became a global people in the late nineteenth century. It was an extraordinary open world in which British capital, trade, and their accompanying personnel reached into practically every country in the world.' Or as Marx and Engels had memorably described the British bourgeoisie in 1848: they 'nestle everywhere, settle everywhere, establish connections everywhere'.[17]

The instant success of Dilke's book seems to have marked a new awareness of this extraordinary phenomenon: instead of perpetually contrasting Celt with Saxon, the new Anglo-Saxon turned outwards, and now saw himself as a global brand. This consciousness was prompted not just by a change in sentiment, but also by changes in technology. The first voyage round the earth (Magellan's) had been completed in 1521, entirely by ship. What was new about Dilke's voyage round the world was that he went not by hot air, as did the Englishman Phileas Fogg in Jules Verne's novel (which Dilke preceded by five years), but by steam – either by boat or train, across sea and land, on commercial carriers. Dilke's account suggests the ease with which it was possible for him to travel round the world, in the first great age of passenger steam ships. By 1861 Brunel's *SS Great Britain*, driven by its innovative screw propeller which replaced the paddle wheel, had already taken the first English cricket team to tour Australia (they won the series).[18] The 1860s ushered in a new era of international travel that brought the development of regular links between Britain and the colonies which could be used by travellers and emigrants alike. The globalization of Englishness was no doubt also helped immeasurably by the fact that the first successful transatlantic telegraph was completed in July of the same year as Dilke began his tour (1866), establishing a direct link 'between the two kindred nations, dwelling on the opposite shores of the same great sea, nations of the same blood, speaking the same language'; within a few years, almost the whole of the British Empire would be in instant global communication with itself.[19]

Ruskin and Rhodes

The development of new technology allowed the practical as well as imaginative coalescence of Anglo-Saxons around the globe, Anglo-Saxons who, to the English at least, could all be regarded as English. The new technology of globalization would also be emphasized by John Ruskin in his inaugural lecture at Oxford in February 1870. In a passage which he would later describe as 'the most pregnant and essential' of all his teachings, Ruskin proclaimed to yet another assembled crowd of Oxford undergraduates not only that the Anglo-Saxon race had a higher destiny, but that it had a duty to colonize the territories of the earth:

> There is a destiny now possible to us – the highest ever set before a
> nation to be accepted or refused. We are still undegenerate in race;

207

a race mingled of the best northern blood. We are not yet dissolute in temper, but still have the firmness to govern, and the grace to obey. . . . Within the last few years we have had the laws of natural science opened to us with a rapidity which has been blinding by its brightness; and means of transit and communication given to us, which have made but one kingdom of the habitable globe. One Kingdom; – but who is to be its king? . . . it must be – it *is* with us, now, "Reign or Die." . . .

And this is what she [this country] must either do, or perish: she must found colonies as fast and as far as she is able, formed of her most energetic and worthiest men; – seizing every piece of fruitful waste ground she can set her foot on, and there teaching these her colonists that their chief virtue is to be fidelity to their country, and that their first aim is to be to advance the power of England by land and sea: and that, though they live on a distant plot of ground, they are no more to consider themselves therefore disfranchised from their native land, than the sailors of her fleets do, because they float on distant waves. So that literally, these colonies must be fastened fleets.[20]

Ruskin strategically combines a reference to England's 'mingled' but undegenerate race with an invocation of the new forms of technology that 'have made but one kingdom of the habitable globe'. His imperialist evocation of a global community of English colonies as 'fastened fleets' advancing the power of England is notable for its reassurance that, however far from England they may actually be, they will never be disenfranchised from their native land. Ruskin here lays the ground for Rupert Brooke's sentiment that if he should die, 'there's some corner of a foreign field / That is for ever England'. Less sentimentally, the new technology makes it possible for the English diaspora to remain united, while also facilitating a whole new era of land seizure for colonial settlements. Ruskin's call found at least one sympathetic ear among the students in his audience: Cecil Rhodes.

Rhodes' 'Confession of faith', written four years later, shows the clear influence of Ruskin's injunction. With Ruskin and Rhodes, the anti-colonial arguments of Goldwin Smith and Dilke, who wanted to abandon the Empire and establish a confederacy of Anglo-Saxons, were turned into a programme for colonization and control of the world by Anglo-Saxons. Rhodes wrote:

> I contend that we are the first race in the world and that the more of the world we inhabit the better it is for the human race. I contend that every acre added to our territory means the birth of more of the English race who otherwise would not be brought into existence.[21]

While Rhodes was most interested in imperial expansion in order 'to make the world English', he remained committed to the notion of an imperial federation, a global political affiliation of independent English-speaking people (he gave Parnell £10,000 on the understanding that Ireland would retain its dominion status after Home Rule).[22] He continued this even after his death in 1902, when in his will he established the Rhodes scholarships, whereby potential suitably 'manly' leaders of the Anglo-Saxon world would all come to study at Oxford University. After being drawn in to Oxford from the remotest colonies, the Rhodes scholars would then flow back out again in the systolic rhythm of the globalized English. Rhodes left the most scholarships to the United States, in the hope that their time in Oxford would gradually lead the American elite to seek to heal what by that stage had come to be seen as the tragic flaw of the split in Anglo-Saxondom.[23] The scholarships were to bring about 'the recovery of the United States for the making the Anglo-Saxon race but one Empire. What a dream! but yet it is probable. It is possible.'[24] The outcome of his dream, and his scholarships, Rhodes claimed, would be world peace – because the whole world would be absorbed into the Anglo-Saxon empire (Rhodes was even prepared to consent to the absorption of the British Empire into the American Union to achieve this dream).[25]

'To us England will be wherever English people are found': John Seeley

From this time on, the new idea of a contemporary globalized English ethnicity would become more and more involved in grandiose imperial dreams of the future. Even though the project had originally been anti-imperialist, it would eventually become tainted by its identification with imperialism itself. The two most influential theorists of this universal Englishness that was turned into a form of imperialism were, once again, historians: John Seeley and J. A. Froude.

Dilke's book was experiential, the product of a journey round the world in which he actually encountered city after city, community after community. Though he had planned a journey round the British Empire, he had not anticipated the argument that he was to make about it. The effect of his remarkably timely book was also to produce a reorientation of historical perspectives, and to produce a new kind of historical argument. Whereas to date English historians had looked back to the past to explain the present, they had in general not questioned the perspective of their starting point, which was a concern with English affairs, focused on parliament and dynasties. Although Kemble and others had written on institutions rather than politicians or monarchs, their own local perspective remained the same. In 1883 Seeley published a course of lectures that he had given in Cambridge called *The Expansion of England* (it was reprinted nine times by the Jubilee year of 1897) and which was to become, as the Bolshevik Karl Radek was later to put it irreverently, 'a sort of Koran for British imperialism'.[26] Here, for the first time, Dilke's new global perspective of empire registered an impact on historical thinking. Instead of putting England at the centre and treating the colonies as peripheries, Seeley wrote his history starting from the perspective of Dilke's Greater Britain. All European history since the time of Columbus and Vasco da Gama, he argued, has been determined by its relation to the new worlds that were found in that era. In the same way, anticipating Salman Rushdie's observation that 'the problem with the English is that their history happened overseas', Seeley suggests that 'the history of England is not in England but in America and Asia' (p. 10). He complains that historians write

as if the England of which histories are written were the island so-called, and not the political union named after the island, which is quite capable of expanding so as to cover half the globe. To us England will be wherever English people are found, and we shall look for its history in whatever places witness the occurrences most important to Englishmen. (p. 141)

And so, as 'England is expanding into Greater Britain, English history will be wherever this expansion is taking place'. For Seeley as for Dilke, Greater Britain is still England.

Seeley's most famous remark in the lectures, 'we seem, as it were, to have conquered and peopled half the world in a fit of absence of mind' (p. 10), was meant to highlight how the English empire had been created by English adventurers and settlers, not by the deliberate imperialist design of politicians. The emphasis on an absence of mind also served as a comment on the way in which the people of England had not readjusted their sense of themselves to include the populations of Canada and Australia. They displayed very little interest, he claimed, in the second Empire: ' "What matters," we have said, "its vastness or its rapid growth? It does not grow for us" ' (p. 17). The key question was who counted as 'one of us'. Canada, Australia, South Africa and the West Indies meant that there were 'ten millions of Englishmen who live outside the British Islands. The latter are of our own blood and are therefore united with us by the strongest tie.' The people of the Indian empire, by contrast, Seeley says, echoing Lord Lyndhurst's remark on the Irish, 'are of alien race and religion, and are bound to us only by the tie of conquest' (p. 13). India's alienness, however, serves only to emphasize how far the Colonial empire, according to Seeley, was little less than England itself. Nothing illustrates the opening out of notions of English ethnicity better than the global extension of Englishness to be found in *The Expansion of England*.

Seeley astutely ascribes the liberal indifference to the colonies between 1840 and 1870 as an effect of the ever-increasing commitment to free trade. However, he argues that this is because people are still thinking according to an old model, in which the British Empire is regarded as a 'possession', like a landed estate, which should produce an income. None of the colonies produce a direct income, he concedes, but that is because they are not really part of an empire at all:

> Greater Britain is not a mere empire, though we often call it so. Its union is of the more vital kind. It is united by blood and religion. . . . our Empire is not an Empire at all in the ordinary sense of the word. It does not consist of a congeries of nations held together by force, but in the main of one nation, as much as if it were no Empire but an ordinary state. (p. 60)

The British Empire is Greater Britain, which in turn is simply an expansion of England. Logically, this ought to mean that Canada and Australia should be considered no differently from the English counties of Kent and Cornwall. Here, Seeley's emphasis that 'England' is not the 'island so-called', but 'the political union named after the island, which is quite capable of expanding so as to cover half the globe', isolates the core of what has happened to the idea of England, the English and Englishness. England names simultaneously the island and the Greater Britain beyond; the English, the people of England and English people everywhere. Seeley pushes the implications of this logic remorselessly:

> If the colonies are not, in the old phrase, possessions of England, then they must be a part of England; and we must adopt this view in earnest. We must cease altogether to say that England is an island off the north-western coast of Europe. . . . We must cease to think that emigrants, when they go to colonies, leave England or are lost to England. We must cease to think that the history of England is the history of the parliament that sits at Westminster. . . . When we have accustomed ourselves to contemplate the whole Empire together and call it all England, we shall see that here too is a United States. Here too is a great homogeneous people, one in blood, language, religion and laws, but dispersed over a boundless space. (p. 184)

Seeley thus transforms England from a tiny island off the coast of Europe into a limitless people dispersed over boundless space. Again and again he insists on this almost metaphysical expansion of the meaning and boundaries of England and the English. The word 'England' is no longer attached to the particular place called England: it is a global federation of the English diaspora, held together by a racial and cultural bond, 'an extension of the English nationality' and the 'English race', defined in the loosest terms as a community of 'blood'. In practice, England has expanded to become a vast global state, an empire without borders or ends, dissolving time and space. But what holds it together?

Greater England, as Seeley sometimes calls it, is united by a common race, religion, language and institutions. Though India may be alien in blood, a Greater Britain can achieve 'ethnological unity' on the same principle as heterogeneous England can make up a common nationality of the whole country:

> If in these islands we feel ourselves for all purposes one nation, though in Wales, in Scotland and in Ireland there is Celtic blood, and Celtic languages utterly unintelligible to us are still spoken, so in the Empire a good many French and Dutch and a good many Caffres and Maories may be admitted without marring the ethnological unity of the whole. (p. 59)

This ethnic diversity can constitute a whole because the enormous distances which prevented the nation's unity in the past are now dissolved by modern science, electricity and steam. Technology enables a commonality of racial and cultural unity:

> ... distance has now no longer the important influence that it had on political relations.
>
> In the last century there could be no Greater Britain in the true sense of the word, because of the distance between the mother-country and its colonies and between the colonies themselves. This impediment exists no longer. Science has given to the political organism a new circulation, which is steam, and a new nervous system, which is electricity.
>
> What we call our Empire ... is not properly, if we exclude India from consideration, an Empire at all ... it is a vast English nation, only

a nation so widely dispersed that before the age of steam and electricity its strong natural bonds of race and religion seemed practically dissolved by distance. (pp. 86–9)

The more persuasive Seeley's thesis became, the less Englishness was about England – it was rather about a world outside England as such, 'a vast English nation' so widely dispersed that it relied on modern technology to hold it together. All that was now lacking for this 'vast English nation', Seeley argued, was a constitutional framework, which ought to follow the solution already successfully instituted by the United States, namely federalism.

From this time on, the idea of a Britannic Federation would be actively canvassed by advocates of Greater Britain.[27] Its greatest devotee was Freeman, who had written the first part of a *History of Federal Government from the Foundation of the Achaian League to the Disruption of the United States* in 1863.[28] In 1886 he published a volume of lectures entitled *Greater Greece and Greater Britain, and, George Washington, The Expander of England,* with an Appendix on 'Imperial Federation'. Towards the end of his lecture on Washington, Freeman asks 'What is England?' and answers:

The old Teutonic name speaks for itself; it is the land of the English, the land of the English wherever they may dwell. Wherever the men of England settle, there springs to life a new England. There was a day when Massachusetts was not England; there was an earlier day when Kent itself was not England. The elder and the younger land, the land beyond the sea and the land beyond the Ocean, have been made England by the same process. Men went forth from the First England to found a second, and from the second England to found a third. In our onward march we passed from the European island to the American mainland. In each case there was a making of England, an expansion of England.... In each case the newer England became the greater.[29]

Freeman's enthusiasm for the idea of England as a global repetition effect links back to Maine's argument about the way in which philology had allowed people remote from each other to claim

214

'community of descent'. For while philologists had come to deny the link between race and language, in practice, as both Maine and Freeman recognized, to see this only from the perspective of the linguists missed the point. What Freeman appreciated was that the popular sense of a link between language and race had become the basis of new transnational identities that were giving rise to pan-Germanism and pan-Slavism – and could, therefore, equally provide the basis for a confederation of the English, an expanded 'England', around the world.[30] Language and linguistic affinity, as he had argued in his essay 'Language and Race' (1877), had become the foundation of a new popular politics – whatever the philologists, or indeed the anthropologists, might now be saying.

Froude

No consideration of an expanded England would be complete without J. A. Froude, not the last but the greatest of the theorists of a global Englishness. His *Oceana, or England and Her Colonies* (1886) envisaged not an empire of Oceana ('the English race do not like to be parts of an empire') but 'a "commonwealth" of Oceana held together by common blood, common interest, and a common pride'.[31] Froude is often described as the popularizer of Carlyle: he himself suggested that he never claimed to go beyond the ideas of his master. His difficulties with high Anglican theology (Froude shares, no doubt for him uncomfortably, and perhaps vice versa, the distinction in the nineteenth century with Salman Rushdie in the twentieth of having his novel publicly burnt in England on religious grounds) led him to look for broader forms of identification, or an alternative religion, and he eventually found this in a certain idea of England and its future, in particular its role as the centre of a larger empire of Englishness. While taking an interest in the British Empire generally, as a matter of pride, his overt racialism meant that his interest was largely focused on those parts of the Empire that were settlement colonies: he called these 'other Englands'.

Like Carlyle before him, Froude was not particularly interested in
refining the concept of race as a biological category – he alluded to it,
when it suited him, merely to reinforce his prejudices, which were
unsophisticated.[32] Of the morality of the inhabitants of the West Indies
he remarked that 'there is sin, but it is the sin of animals, without shame,
because there is no sense of doing wrong'.[33] While the prolific population of the West Indies gave Froude cause for anxiety, in other
colonies he assumed that native peoples were dying out.[34] Froude
was most interested in the Anglo-Saxon, ascribing his positive qualities
as stemming not so much from his zoological stock, as from his historical development, in particular from what was for Froude the key
moment of history since the time of Christ: the Reformation. It was
nevertheless certain 'innate' qualities of the Anglo-Saxon, being freedom-loving, resourceful, etc., which were responsible for the Reformation, with the result that in a wonderfully ambiguous circular
argument he argued that it was also Protestantism in turn which
encouraged the Anglo-Saxon qualities of resourcefulness, self-reliance
and honesty. For Froude, the key racial, cultural and political division
lay between the Protestant Anglo-Saxon nations and the Catholic
Celtic ones. From his accounts, it is impossible to tell which part of
the combination was responsible for the other – their relationship is that
of the mobius strip. Importantly, Froude seems to suggest that those
who shared the same history could take on Anglo-Saxon qualities – he
did not worry too much, therefore, about the particular racial mix of
Britain, except in the case of the Irish, because they had remained
Catholic. While he was prone to make racist remarks about the Irish,
Froude also encouraged the movement away from an identity of the
English focused on racial origins towards one based on a less specific
racial identity of a shared language, culture, history and religion. Like
many of his contemporaries, Froude considered that the sterling qualities of the Anglo-Saxon were under threat, not so much from the Celts
any longer, as from industrialization. Following Tacitus, he identified
Anglo-Saxons with the countryside, and saw the development of
England's vast cities, with their crowded slums, as essentially threaten-
ing the country with degeneration, both of body and spirit.

Froude's most original intervention came in a widely noticed review entitled 'England's Forgotten Worthies', which was published in the *Westminster Review* in 1853. In this essay on Hakluyt's *Voyages*, which he calls 'the Prose Epic of the modern English nation', Froude elaborated a central myth of the Victorian age which identified the English not only with their Saxon forbears, but also with the resourceful English of the incipiently Protestant Elizabethan age. These Englishmen – Richard Hawkins, Sir Walter Raleigh, Lord Thomas Howard and Sir Richard Grenville – were portrayed as adventurers of the globe, harrying the great Catholic power of the world, their heroism defined as exemplifying the greatest qualities of the English in the epic formation of the nation.

Froude best exemplifies a central argument of British imperial ideology, for which, contrary to the analysis of Marx and Lenin, imperialism was in some sense not the product of capitalism, but a form of resistance to it. Imperialism would save the nation from the degeneration produced by city life. *Laisser-faire* liberals saw the Empire as essentially a market for goods, in which case there was no particular need for it to remain an empire as such. By contrast, Froude developed a theory of empire which appealed to the English middle classes who then, as now, despised commercialism, offering to them a grander aim and object for contemplation, something that the individual could identify with without distinguishing it from the religion that had created it – a vast England which transcended ordinary England in almost religious terms. Froude specifically sets this argument up in political as opposed to economic terms: economically, the emigrant would become a potential consumer of British goods wherever he or she went. But what Froude focuses on is something rather different. Those who have emigrated to the colonies 'are Englishmen like ourselves'.[35] The Empire is an empire of Englishness, a vast interconnected world community whose social imaginary Froude attempted to delineate and consolidate.[36]

Paradoxically, though by no means untypically as we have seen, Froude developed his idea of an English empire from his experience of the Irish. His attitude towards the Irish was itself

217

contradictory – the same man who could call them 'squalid apes' could also write that the Irish were 'still among the most interesting of peoples'.[37] It was largely his comments on the Irish that led John Mackinnon Robertson, who was born on the Arran isles, to characterize *Oceana* in 1897 as 'painful proof of the extent to which literary faculty can be turned to evil purposes'.[38] Like Carlyle, Froude blamed Irish unrest on British government policies towards Ireland as much as on the Irish themselves. The problem with Ireland, he observed in 1841, citing the popular adage of the (Irish born) Duke of Wellington, was that 'Ireland was a half conquered country. We should have to conquer it altogether or to let it go.'[39] It was his experience of going to America in 1872 to defend his ideas about Ireland that led Froude to realize the extent of the antagonism towards England that Irish Americans felt. He then worried that while emigration was utilized as the common rationale for an overcrowded population in times of economic downturn, England was exporting its own people to a country where they would be encouraged to take on another national identity, which was politically dominated by the Irish. By 1870, about 4 million British subjects had emigrated to the US in the previous 25 years, from a total population of about 26 million. Whereas the English went to America and became Americans, the Irish, Froude noticed, never lost their loyalty to their homeland. Moreover, unlike those who went elsewhere, the Irish who emigrated to America were 'our bitterest enemies'.[40] Froude's idea was to encourage the same kind of loyalty for English emigrants as he encountered in the Irish abroad. He found inspiration for this idea of English empire in the resolute spirit displayed by Northern Unionists in the American Civil War, determined to maintain the country as one people ('Earnestly desirous I was and always had been to see a united Oceana – united as closely as the American States are united') (p. 91). If instead of going to the US, Froude argued, Englishmen and women could be encouraged to go to Canada, New Zealand and Australia, then instead of shedding their nationality, they could be encouraged to keep it, and England would in effect be expanded:

where their well-being would be our well-being, their brains and
arms our brains and arms, every acre which they could reclaim from
the wilderness so much added to English soil, and themselves and their
families fresh additions to our national stability.[41]

The result would be the development of a federation, or family of
nations, all of which would see themselves specifically as English.
Froude's Englishness was thus transportable, and best developed
outside England itself. So it was that the fear of the spectre of Irish
nationalism developing around the world inspired Froude with the
idea of an international identity for the English.

And so Froude transported himself, to have a look first hand. In
1884, the year after the publication of Seeley's *The Expansion of
England*, he set off with his son on a tour comparable to Dilke's,
following the never setting sun around the English empire round
the world. He sailed from South Africa to Australia, to New Zealand,
and then to San Francisco. Despite his imperial interests, he declined
the chance to visit Canada, on the grounds that it was too cold. His
book *Oceana* is a combination of travel accounts of his journey with
observations on the Englishness (or not) of the inhabitants, his fre-
quent encounters with what Froude assures his reader was the universal desire to remain part of the British Empire, and constant
reflections on how a federated empire might be organized. Froude's
thesis is always bound up with the issue of migration: following
Seeley's metaphor of acorn and oak, the greater Britain, for Froude,
involves the branches of the original tree flourishing abroad, scooping
up the undesirable excess of population which produces the crowded
cities of England. The life of those who leave is imagined in terms of
the inhabitants transposing and transfiguring themselves from the
crowded cities to the healthy countryside where the emigrants revert
to a vigorous Saxon or Elizabethan yeoman stock. The colonies are
not now receptacles for the surplus impoverished population, nor
for convicted criminals. They are a means through which the
English race can regenerate itself. In the face of inevitable 'physical
decrepitude' (p. 9) and degeneration in the cities, it can save itself

from the effects of capitalism. Eventually, these invigorating sentiments would be brought home to England in the Boy Scouts and
Girl Guides movements, and in less organized ways, in late nineteenth-century naturism or in the novels of D. H. Lawrence. With
Froude, the colonies become the repository of Tory anti-capitalist
sentiment, offering health for the English, 'where the race might for
ages renew its mighty youth' (p. 10), for the lost yeoman class, and
ultimately, for the impoverished aristocracy themselves (Kenya, with
its profusion of game, would be a popular destination). These ideas
found their apogee in the novels of Rider Haggard, where a certain
kind of aristocratic and yeoman English masculinity is pursued and
renewed in the wilds of Africa and Latin America, far from an
England ravaged by late nineteenth-century feminism.

After Froude, Englishness abroad came increasingly to represent an
Englishness not sustainable any more within England itself, a lost
identity that had to be recreated in the colonies. The English colonists became more English than the English – more patriotic, more
healthy, in cities 'where children grow who seem once more to
understand what was meant by "merry England"':

> Amidst the uncertainties which are gathering round us at home . . . it is
> something to have seen with our own eyes that there are other
> Englands beside the old one, where the race is thriving with all its
> ancient characteristics. (p. 17)

The true England flourishes anew in other Englands. England itself is
no longer properly the real England, which has moved elsewhere.
Here Froude initiates the nostalgic idealizing tradition which would
henceforth represent England as lost, departed, an absent centre
ineluctably vanished into the past – a contemporary example of
which would be Roger Scruton's *England: An Elegy*. The object of
Scruton's elegy is encapsulated in his brilliant portrait of his teacher,
Mr Chapman:

> The fact that England had, during his absence, changed beyond
> recognition, only enhanced its holy ambience in his memory. England

for him was no longer a real place, but a consecrated isle in the lake of forgetting, where the God of the English still strode through an imaginary Eden, admiring His works.[42]

This element of nostalgia for a lost England, an England now disappeared but which could be refound and recreated in the other Englands around the world, was central to the ways in which Froude gives an emotional charge to his vision of the empire where England can perhaps be rediscovered. England is now best imagined abroad, or imagined from abroad.

The imaginary relocation of England from the past to the elsewhere is Froude's particular and powerful individual trope. In terms of its global perspective per se, Froude's book, like much of his work, is not particularly original. Conceptually, *Oceana* is a reworking of Dilke's *Greater Britain* on the basis of Seeley's *Expansion of England*. Froude, however, invokes Sir James Harrington's *The Commonwealth of Oceana* of 1656 to claim that his Elizabethan predecessor had prophesied that the English race would disperse over the whole globe. By tracing his imperial vision back to Harrington's utopian sketch of a perfect commonwealth, Froude gives the impression that the present is the fulfilment of a destiny or plan that goes back to the heroic Elizabethan times, when England first became England. The millions of Anglo-Saxons now spread over the vast continents of North America and Australasia have exceeded Harrington's wildest dreams.

Yet the vision is but half accomplished. The people have gone out, they have settled, they have cultivated the land, they have multiplied. . . . Harrington contemplated that Oceana would be a single commonwealth embraced in the arms of Neptune, and the spell which can unite all these communities into one has not yet been discovered. (p. 2)

Froude's *Oceana* is, at a political level, the pursuit for the secret of that spell. The problem that Froude confronts puts, as it were, Knox with Seeley: since the love of liberty is intrinsic to the Anglo-Saxon, what

221

is the spell that will dissolve the rule that 'one free people cannot govern another free people'? What magic spell, Froude insistently asks, can bring all these colonies together in a more formal way? The popular sentiment, he keeps repeating, is there, and everywhere he goes he keeps reassuring the reader that it was just like England. In Adelaide, he speaks of 'the pure English that was spoken there. They do not raise the voice at the end of a sentence, as the Americans do, as if with a challenge to differ from them.' 'It was busy England over again, set free from limitations of space. There were the same faces, the same voices, the same shops and names on them.' 'We were 12,000 miles from England; yet we were in England still, and England at its best.' When he arrives in Melbourne, Froude sees the suburban villas 'all the more reminding one of England', 'it was English life all over again', 'they were as English as ourselves'. He goes to a pantomime: 'The audience was English to the heart.... It was English without a difference.' In Victoria he remarks, 'again, I felt how entirely English it all was.... In thought and manners, as in speech and pronunciation, they are pure English and nothing else.' In Sydney, we are told, 'The Australians speak all pure English as it is taught in schools.... it showed how English they yet were.'[43] And so on, round the Anglo-Saxon countries dispersed over the globe, which the new technology now so easily and effectively links together.

By contrast with the politicians and their colonial policies, or indifference to the colonies, which he criticizes remorselessly, Froude argues, as Seeley does, that 'the people of England have made the colonies. The people at home and the people in the colonies are one people. The feeling of identity is perhaps stronger in the colonies than at home' (p. 14). Just as the empire was created through the spirit of the Elizabethan adventurers, and emigration initiated by the people themselves, so it is the people themselves who now continue to hold it together:

An 'empire' of Oceana there cannot be. The English race do not like to be parts of an empire. But a 'commonwealth' of Oceana held

222

together by common blood, common interest, and a common pride
in the great position which unity can secure – such a commonwealth
as this may grow of itself if politicians can be induced to leave it alone.
(p. 12)

Two problems follow from this identification with popular sentiment, a trope which was central to Saxonism. The first question is
how can any more formalized union emerge, a commonwealth such
as Harrington envisaged, even in the naturalistic Burkean organic
form which Froude evokes, if he wants to exclude the politicians?
The second is that though the people may have made the colonies,
the fact remains that the bulk of English emigrants do not emigrate to
them, but go to the United States instead:

> Four fifths of the English and Scotch and Irish who annually leave our
> shores to find new homes become citizens of the United States. Can
> no effort be made in connection with the Colonial Governments to
> direct at least part of this fertilising stream into our own dominions?
> (p. 223)

The only solution to this is to turn back to the despised politicians,
to whom Froude has a certain degree of access. As his Australian
critics pointed out, Froude generally moved in the highest social and
diplomatic circles during his tour, for the most part meeting the
grandees of the most anglophile social strata. Socially, and in his
writing, 'the people' whom he eulogized in fact always remain
remote from him. In its own terms, the problem with *Oceana* is
that it denies its own claims in its mode of address: 'They *are* a part
of us', Froude affirms enthusiastically to his reader. Yet for all his
claims about the complete identity of the English abroad with those
'at home', he indicates clearly here that in his mind he is still
addressing an exclusively domestic English audience, even while he
argues that those on the periphery are no different from them.
Despite their Englishness, the English in the colonies remain separated – they remain a 'they'. He does seem to contemplate an
Australian or New Zealand reader as part of his audience. He does

223

not say, on the logic of Catherine's declaration about Heathcliff in *Wuthering Heights*, 'you *are* a part of us' – or, as the more gentle, tolerant and inclusive Ford Madox Ford would later say of the English diaspora, 'All these fellows *are* "ourselves"'.[44] The colonies will save the soul of the English, of over-industrialized England, but only by 'our' going out to 'them'. The identity of the English everywhere is thus implicitly refused. At some level, they remain, in Jean Rhys's words, 'horrid colonials'. The text tells us this, even while it argues otherwise.

Oceana was extraordinarily successful – it was already into a fifth edition the year of its publication. Just twelve months later the indefatigable Froude produced a sequel with *The English in the West Indies, or the Bow of Ulysses* (1887).[45] *Oceana* had been written in the context of the death of Gordon in Khartoum and an associated atmosphere of imperial disintegration, though while he was there, Froude took much comfort in the fact that Australia had just volunteered to participate in the British Sudan campaign (Suakin, 1884–91), which Froude considered 'a practical demonstration in favour of Imperial unity'. By the time of *The English in the West Indies*, on the other hand, general sentiments seemed to have moved towards imperial enthusiasm: there had been Queen Victoria's Golden Jubilee, Gladstone had resigned over Ireland, and the first Colonial conference and exhibition had been held in London. Froude now writes more confidently about the Empire, which he sees as no longer under threat of being disbanded from the centre, and perhaps therefore he speaks more frankly. He distinguishes between the countries which he had included in Oceana, the federation of 'people of the same race and character, drawn together by equality and liberty', and those colonies which are predominantly populated by 'people of different races and different characters, who have quarrelled for centuries'. Now that the countries of Oceana have been given self-government of their own affairs, 'the result of the wide extension of the suffrage throughout the Empire has been to show that being one the British people everywhere intend to remain one. With the same blood, the same language, the same habits, the same traditions, they do not mean to be shattered into dishonoured fragments.' This 'centripetal power' holds them together, and seems to lead inevitably towards imperial federation. Froude argues that it would be easy enough to give Home Rule to all the colonies were 'the population of our colonies as homogeneous as in Australia' (as he considers). But then he adds: 'When we think of India, when we think of Ireland, prudence tells us to hesitate.'[46] India, Ireland or the West Indies, if given half the chance, he suspects, would immediately move out of the imperial orbit. Unlike Smith, Froude finds this unpalatable, and advocates the generic two-state solution for the Empire: of liberty for the Anglo-Saxon colonies, and a paternalist autocratic rule for the rest.

'And what should they know of England who only England know?'

Notwithstanding these contradictions, with Dilke, Seeley and Froude the idea of English ethnicity was effectively globalized, moved out from the centre to absorb the remotest colonial peripheries. To judge how far the populations of the colonial empire themselves accepted the idea about being English would require another volume. The American adoption of a racial and imperial Anglo-Saxonism has been well documented.[47] Elsewhere, few of those brought up in the twentieth century in the countries of Froude's *Oceana* could claim never to have experienced the pull of some relation to Englishness. Emerson put it more dramatically and more globally, claiming that England has 'stamped the knowledge, activity, and power of mankind with its impress. Those who resist it do not feel it or obey it less. The Russian in his snows is aiming to be English. The Turk and Chinese also are making awkward efforts to be English.'[48] You can find this in the oddest places – like the Union Jack that still forms part of the flag of Hawaii (it is also there, of course, on the flags of Australia and New Zealand). Those most attracted to the idea of English ethnicity were typically the Anglophile upper classes, or those aspiring to be part of them, those espousing conservative politics, or just those anglophiles, such as Samuel Hawthorne, filled with a 'yearning for England'. Many of the writers who expressed anglophile sentiments, such as the Australian poets Adam Lindsey Gordon or Douglas Sladen, were originally emigrants from England. But others were not. Current nationalist sentiments mean that in the old settler colonies, as the old dependencies, anglophile writers tend to be downplayed in the literary canon.[49] Enough writing remains, however, as evidence of the extent to which Englishness or pan-Anglicanism successfully created an identity for those of English descent elsewhere: a form of long-distance nationalism, were it not for the fact that England itself had been spread out everywhere. Diasporic transnationalism might describe the phenomenon more accurately. The sentiments are enthusiastically illustrated in the following poem by Sladen, first published in *Australian Lyrics* in Melbourne in 1883, which nicely encapsulates many of the feelings, and cultural icons, that we have encountered. In 1888 Sladen republished it as the epigraph to *Australian Ballads and Rhymes*:

> This little volume
> Inspired by Life in the Greater Britain
> Under the Southern Cross,
> Is Dedicated
>
> TO THE ENGLISH OF THREE CONTINENTS
>
> We are all children of the men who fought at Crecy,
>   We were all Englishmen when Shakespeare wrote:
> We are all Englishmen, compatriots *in esse*,
>   Though called Australians, Yankees, and what not.
>
> We are all English, and the centuries will find us
>   Living in homes with old familiar names
> Of towns in England, or her battles, to remind us
>   That we, who now are pilgrims, have our claims
>
> To those whom Westminster entombs in antique glory,
>   To Devonshire's sea-kings and Chaucer's Tales,

226

To Wiclif's Bible and the proud Armada story,
  Alfred the Great and him who conquered Wales.

We are all Englishmen, and one in our devotion,
  Whether the York we have be old or new;
And English if Boston o'erlooks the German Ocean,
  Or has the broad Atlantic in her view.

We are all Englishmen, though the new Melbourne poses
  Upon Port Phillip as a southern queen,
And the old Melbourne in sweet Derbyshire still dozes –
  A fit handmaiden for a rustic scene.

We are all Englishmen, wedded in one great union
  Of blood and language, history and song;
We are all English, and will cherish our communion
  In face of all the world the world's life long.[50]

Sladen shows that his preoccupation here, as with Goldwin Smith, was more with 'healing the schism in the Anglo–Saxon race', that is, affiliating with the United States, than worrying about potentially alien parts of the Empire such as India.[51] All the English, wherever they may be, according to Sladen, share a common history, language and literature.

English literature, as literary historians have shown, had been developed as a subject for schools and universities in the colonies long before it was ever taught in England.[52] It is odd that Froude, the devotee and biographer of Carlyle, does not invoke the potential role of literature as an agent of cultural and political cohesion in the Empire, especially given that the latter had already suggested its secret power. In 1841, in *On Heroes and Hero Worship*, Carlyle had claimed that the English would prefer to give up the Indian Empire before Shakespeare. The reason for this, he suggested, was that Shakespeare 'apart from spiritualities' was 'a real, marketable, tangibly useful possession':

> England, before long, this Island of ours, will hold but a small fraction
> of the English: in America, in New Holland, east and west to the very

Antipodes, there will be a Saxondom covering great spaces of the Globe. And now, what is it that can keep all these together into virtually one Nation, so that they do not fall out and fight, but live at peace, in brotherlike intercourse, helping one another? This is justly regarded as the greatest practical problem, the thing all manner of sovereignties and governments are here to accomplish: what is it that will accomplish this? Acts of Parliament, administrative prime-ministers cannot. America is parted from us, so far as Parliament could part it. Call it not fantastic, for there is much reality in it: Here, I say, is an English King, whom no time or chance, Parliament or combin-ation of Parliaments, can dethrone! This King Shakspeare, does not he shine, in crowned sovereignty, over us all, as the noblest, gentlest, yet strongest of rallying-signs; indestructible; really more valuable in that point of view than any other means or appliance whatsoever? We can fancy him as radiant aloft over all the Nations of Englishmen, a thousand years hence. From Paramatta, from New York, whereso-ever, under what sort of Parish-Constable soever, English men and women are, they will say to one another: 'Yes, this Shakspeare is ours; we produced him, we speak and think by him; we are of one blood and kind with him'.[53]

The creation of a global Shakespeare cult in the nineteenth century – in which he became more of a deity than a king – was indeed to follow.[54] In terms of the Empire, however, though Carlyle would never have thought of it, and neither Sladen nor Froude mentions it, there was one even more popular activity which Froude could not but have encountered, which might just have answered to that magic spell, that added X factor for which he searched so earnestly, and which in fact broke through all imperial divisions: sport, and more specifically, cricket – the game with which we began in *Tom Brown's Schooldays*, here graphically shown marking the reach of the global English, from the distant Tropics to the Cumbrian hills (or quite possibly some green hills far away that to an English eye look remarkably like the Cumbrian hills) (figure 7.3).[55]

In 1891 Rudyard Kipling published 'The English Flag', a poem which automatically assumes, as in this illustration, that the English

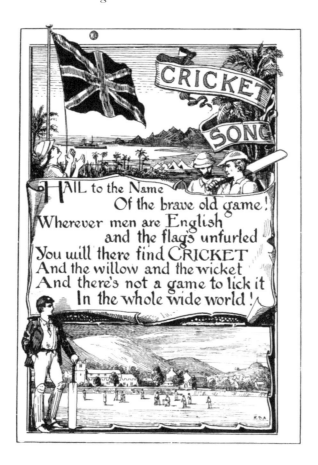

Figure 7.3
From *Sedbergh School Songs*, written and illustrated by R. St John Ainslie (Leeds: Richard Jackson, 1896), page 56.

flag is the Union Jack.[56] The poem's most famous line, 'And what should they know of England who only England know?', neatly characterizes the sense of the existence of an expanded England: that by this time 'England' is much more than just England, and that you cannot even know 'England' if you only know England. The shift from the idea of English ethnicity between the two halves of the nineteenth century can be effectively illustrated by contrasting the 'Teutomaniac' views of Thomas Arnold in 1842, which we encountered in chapter 1, with those of Kipling just over fifty year later in 1896. The paradigm has in a sense been turned inside out: whereas, for Arnold, England was one component in a much vaster Teutonic civilization, for Kipling, the real England had become that vaster civilization, encountered all over the globe.

Chapter 8

Englishness: England and Nowhere

So it was that during the course of the nineteenth century, English-ness was translated from the national identity of the English living in England into a diasporic identity beyond any geographical boundaries which included all the English who had now emigrated all over the globe. 'England' was no longer attached to a particular place, but rather to imaginative identifications such as the countryside, Shakespeare or sport – an England that could always be recreated elsewhere, so long, in the words of Seeley, as 'Englishmen in all parts of the world still remembered that they were of one blood and one religion, that they had one history and one language and literature'.[1] The word 'England' itself became a synonym that could be used equally to describe the country England, Great Britain and Greater Britain (so even today, England and English are often used instead of Britain and British).

The dream of the nineteenth century was that the great global diaspora – including the United States – would one day be united in a 'Britannic Confederation' of Anglo-Saxons – a dream dear not only to Rhodes, Freeman or Froude but also to Arthur Conan Doyle, who dedicated his novel *The White Company* (1891) thus:

TO THE HOPE OF THE FUTURE
TO THE HOPE OF THE FUTURE
THE REUNION OF THE ENGLISH-SPEAKING RACES
THIS LITTLE CHRONICLE
OF OUR COMMON ANCESTRY IS INSCRIBED[2]

Although this reunion was never to come to pass, it nevertheless remains the case that – as the Nazis were keen to point out – since that time the 'English' nations have always fought on the same side in major wars, and the continued power of this bond goes some way to explaining Britain's ambivalence towards a non-English speaking Europe, as well as the imagined sense of a 'special relationship' with the USA. And as Dilke had dreamed, English has indeed become the dominant global language.

Though a few improbable forms of English nationalism (morris dancing, pageants) were invented at home by folk enthusiasts, by the end of the nineteenth century Englishness was defined less as a set of internal cultural characteristics attached to a particular place, than as a transportable set of values which could be transplanted, translated and recreated anywhere on the globe, embodying the institutions and social values of Anglo-Saxon culture: language, literature, law, liberty, justice, order, morality and Protestant Anglican religion.[3] As J. H. Curle, a Scottish mining engineer who spent his life travelling the colonial world, put it in 1912, in entirely predictable but noticeably abstract terms:

> The character of the British remains humanity's best asset. This 'character' has little to do with brains or morals. It is built of respect for the law, the strongly developed sense of justice, liberty, and fair play, a fairly high standard in money matters, and good common sense.... We have balance, and because of it have been called to rule over half the world.[4]

As it was assumed and adopted into the discourse of imperialism, Englishness was transformed into an ethnicity unlike any other; because it was no single ethnicity but an amalgamation of many, it became a cosmopolitan ethnicity that comprised the transcendence of individual ethnicity or nation, just as 'English' was used as a general category that designated more than the particularity of the people and culture of the territory of England. This imperial (in the sense of universal) identity led not only to an increasing emphasis on the idea of a 'Greater Britain' of English-speaking Anglo-Saxons, but eventually also to the imperial (in the political sense) idea that the Englishman was in some sense above any narrow ethnicity or race of the kind observable in other countries – he was, as *The Times* had argued in 1852, a 'born cosmopolite', free of the 'follies of nationality'. The Englishman was therefore suited to rule all races. The Englishman was 'reserved' in more senses than one. As the self-created perfect Englishman T. S. Eliot was to put it in 1948, the Englishman identifies 'his own interests with a tendency to obliterate local and racial distinctions'.[5] In this mode, the Englishman operated with regard to race in the same way as John Barrell has argued that the English gentleman operated with regard to class: disdaining a local nationalism, and thus above all interests, he was particularly fitted to represent and rule all interests.[6]

British imperialism, in turn, justified itself not so much through the French concept of the *mission civilisatrice*, but rather through the argument that its particular power, responsibility and burden was the creation of global order and the administration of an impartial justice, based on a belief in a fundamental English decency: *Pax Britannica*. The particular ethnic characteristics of the English, whose ethnicity was now subsumed into the unmarked ethnicity of the Anglo-Saxon, made them uniquely qualified for this role. Though a comprehensive account such as Houston Stewart Chamberlain's *Die Grundlagen des neunzehnten Jahrhunderts* (*The Foundations of the Nineteenth Century*) (1899), which elaborated an interdisciplinary analysis of a pan-German identity, was fortunately never written for the English, a distinctive nexus of ideas about Englishness as an ethnicity was developed across different disciplines and practices so as to create the dominant cultural imperial frame-work.[7] With Rhodes, with Baden Powell, with Kipling's Five Nations, with the poetry of Austin, Henley and Newbolt, with Milner's 'Kindergarten' and the Round Table group, with the

'empire and commerce' imperialism of the Liberal Party under
Chamberlain at the end of the century, the originally anti-imperial
ideas of a pan-Anglican community were turned into the official ideology of empire, a Greater Britain possessing a common imperial
identity that was at once racial and linguistic, cultural and institutional.[8] Emerson's 'spawning vigour' of emigration was turned into
Kipling's invocation to 'send forth the best ye breed'. The argument
for the dismemberment of empire had been refashioned into a new
kind of imperialist dream signalled in Conan Doyle's dedication: a
union of English-speaking peoples, a federation governed by an
imperial parliament in London (or even elsewhere). The dream
began in the 1870s; by 1884 the Imperial Federation League was
established and the first Colonial Conference was held in London
three years later. The federal system allowed for colonial nationalism
while offering a different political formation from the modern world-
system of sovereign nation-states initiated by the League of Nations
in 1919. The idea was discussed at length from Froude's time
onwards, and seemed almost possible with the establishment of the
Union of South Africa in 1910. Although the Statute of Westminster
of 1931 declared the legislatures of the dominions to be of equal
status to that of the United Kingdom, the Imperial Conference
of 1923 had already marked the end of attempts to establish
the 'imperial commonwealth' first envisaged by Lord Rosebery in
Adelaide in 1884, the year after Seeley's book was published.[9]
Nevertheless, as Paul Rich argues, 'the Commonwealth concept by
the late 1930s had effectively pre-empted the more radical critics of
imperialism on the left who had hoped optimistically at the end of the
First World War that the edifice of empire would be abolished
completely'.[10] The federal initiative survived in a different form in
the British Commonwealth of Nations, now the Commonwealth.
Today, it comprises a third of the world's nations and population,
though it often remains split, just as the Empire was, between the
'old' and the 'new' Commonwealth. The many Commonwealth
organizations include cultural institutions such as the Association
for Commonwealth Literature and Language Studies (with nine

chapters, including one in the USA) and the English-Speaking Union (ESU). The ESU was founded in 1918 to promote 'international understanding and friendship through the use of the English language'. The first US branch was established two years later (there are now 74). By 2006, there were branches of the ESU in over fifty countries: the map of the ESU on its website looks like an expanded version of the British Empire, still coloured red. A more recent idea, which almost reverts to Smith, Dilke and Rhodes' ideas of a specifically English global federation, has been the concept of the 'Anglosphere'.[11]

The rapprochement between Britain and the United States, which developed on the basis of an Anglo-Saxon axis in the early twentieth century, has never really been broken since. Winston Churchill, author of the strategically titled *History of the English-Speaking Peoples*, invented the idea of a 'special relationship' between the US and Britain.[12] It doesn't, of course, exist – except that informally, the English-speaking countries in general operate in consort with each other, and consider that their interests have much in common. At a political level, the lingering power of informal Anglo-Saxonism remains strong. It can't be just a coincidence that the three countries of the international community which invaded Iraq were the US, the UK and Australia. Such is the power of the English world that even former colonies that were never fully a part of the English-speaking cohort, such as India, having taken a lot of trouble to get rid of the yoke of British colonialism, now simply affiliate themselves – to another branch of the Anglo-Saxon family.

The eventual identification of Englishness and imperialism meant that, from the beginning of the twentieth century, the critique of imperialism and the Englishness with which it was identified were developed in tandem – by figures as diverse as J. A. Hobson, D. H. Lawrence, Virginia Woolf, George Orwell, Noel Coward, E. P. Thompson and Raymond Williams. So in 1939 the communist Jack Lindsay asked, '*England, Our England*, what is it?' and suggested that for most ordinary English people, it was not 'ours'.[13] More recently, traditional Englishness has often been critiqued in the name of a new 'British' multicultural identity which posits itself against an imagined homogeneous traditional Englishness very far from the ethnic diversity and diasporic culture that was actually emphasized in the nineteenth century. It is at this point that we can put a finger on the secret of the curious emptiness of Englishness so remarked on in recent decades. It was never really here, it was always there, delocalized, somewhere else: by the end of the nineteenth century, England had been etherized, so that England and the English were spread across the boundless space of the globe, held together by the filiations of a vaguely defined Anglo-Saxon ethnicity, common language, institutions and values. Even within England itself, identity in terms of origins and attachment to place had long since been dissolved, so that the situation was no different for those who had never gone abroad. Millions of English and Irish people were migrants, without ever having left the British Isles.

II

While England, in its guise as 'Englandland', appears to foreigners as a country so full of centuries of history, many English people know nothing of their ancestors beyond their grandparents – hence the other side of England, which manifests itself as a permanent youth culture. Ask English people where they come from, and many will hesitate. They will often tell you they don't know quite how to reply to that question, that they don't feel that they are 'from' anywhere in particular. They were born in one place, in London, lived some of their childhood somewhere else, in Devon, after which the family moved to Cornwall. They then went to university in York, and now work in Birmingham. No one in their family still lives in Devon or Cornwall and they know nobody there. Before them, their parents have lived similarly migratory lives, moving from the countryside to the city, from rural to city slum, then gradually working their way upwards towards the suburbs, often carefully discarding the memories, and evidence, of their impoverished past in the process. Ask them where their grandparents came from, and they will say, 'well two of my grandparents were Irish, I think, one came from Scotland, and one from somewhere in Lancashire'. There will also be aunts and uncles, or great aunts and uncles, who at some point went off to North America, or Australia, or South America, whom they never knew, and with whom the family has lost touch, with a few others 'lost in the war'. People will often talk about this aspect of their families as if it were a problem specific to them, rather than recognizing that this pattern is probably more common than any other for English people. If the English were classified as a 'mixed race' by nineteenth-century ethnologists, in terms of the ethnographic mixture resulting from the history of different peoples who had migrated to England in the distant past, for most English people, mobility and mixture are also very much a reality of their own families and their own experience. The new unlocalized English identity of the nineteenth century was developed not just for the English diaspora, but for people whose domestic migrations were often as uprooting and dislocating as those who ventured far over the seas.

We have seen how the effect of all the work concerned with the relations between culture, ethnicity and race in late eighteenth and nineteenth-century Britain meant that, from the 1850s onwards, the division of the population of the British Isles into the two races of Saxons and Celts, with the former regarded as the legitimate inhabitants and the latter as some indigenous population who should be got rid of, gradually gave way to an acceptance that the population of Britain was irreducibly mixed in what would today be called ethnic terms. The reaction against the hitherto dominant representation of English people and culture as predominantly Germanic (Teutonic or Saxon), that produced a construction of English ethnicity as a mixture of races, opened Englishness out to a more comprehensive identity, which could involve other peoples, religions and cultures, as they moved in, out and about. Englishness became an incorporative identity: its global reach meant that it offered an identification for many who responded to the push-pull rhythm of its circulating dynamic: among writers, for example, Henry James, Katherine Mansfield and many another American and colonial – as well as

237

émigré intellectuals, such as Joseph Conrad, Ludwig Wittgenstein, Bronislaw Malinowski, Lewis Namier, Karl Popper, Isaiah Berlin, Ernst Gombrich, Nicolaus Pevsner, Ernst Gellner, Geoffrey Elton and George Steiner, that extraordinary group which, as Perry Anderson pointed out, became the replacement for the English intelligentsia of the nineteenth century.[14] The great anglophile himself, T. S. Eliot, caught the impossible paradox of a delocalized England perfectly in the *Four Quartets*: 'the intersection of the timeless moment / Is England and nowhere. Never and always'.[15] In the twentieth century, it was not only Anglo-Saxon Americans, colonials and émigrés who came to the imperial centre that was both England and nowhere. Much twentieth-century Commonwealth or postcolonial literature (particularly Caribbean literature) was written in London. And although Commonwealth or postcolonial writers are usually treated as a separate tradition from the Modernists in a kind of literary apartheid, it was the same magnetic power that drew in the likes of Nirad Chaudhuri, V. S. Naipaul and Jean Rhys to the metropolitan centre. From his childhood in Bengal, Chaudhuri describes the imperial aura of Englishness very exactly:

> What I have written about Shillong leads me naturally to speak of another intangible and exotic element in the ecology of our lives. To us it was absent and yet real, as Shillong was, but its power was immensely greater, for while our conception of Shillong soon reached the perimeter which bounded it, our idea of this other thing never struck against barriers from which it had to recoil. In the end this came to be very much like the sky above our head, without, however, the sky's frightening attribute of vast and eternal silence, for it was always speaking to us in a friendly language in the knowledge of which we were improving from day to day. Perhaps I need not formally proclaim that this was England as we defined and understood it, that is to say, with Scotland, Ireland, and Wales merged in it, and Europe conceived as its corona.[16]

Absent yet real: what Chaudhuri does not yet here include in the story of his preoccupation with a timeless England under an English heaven is that Englishness often came to function as a coded term for whiteness, for the invisible norm against which all other ethnicities were measured and defined, though even at the end of the nineteenth century it was not uniformally racialized, particularly in the hetero-geneous metropolitan centres. What was often unexpected was that non-white people would also respond to the idea of Englishness and be able to negotiate their own identifications despite residual racialism. They have often succeeded, modifying its surface particula-rities while continuing its fundamental forms.

Though now generally identified with its transformation into imperial ideology, there is another way in which such ideas of delocalized Englishness continue to operate as part of the social consensus within Britain today which relates to this kind of experi-ence. The fact that Englishness in the nineteenth century was detached from immovable fixities such as birth, place or even a definable race (however then conceived) made an immense differ-ence to English society in the centuries that have followed. It could be argued that the continuing tradition of flexibility and comprehen-sion has been a major reason why, since the mid-twentieth century, immigration has, relatively speaking, been so successful in Britain compared to other countries in Europe. In the English case, what is astonishing but unmistakable is that the cultural apparatus developed for the English diaspora of the colonial settler empire was successfully translated and reincorporated into a modern ideology of a tolerant multiracial society. Unexpectedly, therefore, it was a relatively con-servative English liberal tradition that pioneered a particular version of Englishness, in which the nation was no longer conceived solely within the national space, and where those who constituted the nation were at least potentially broadly conceived to include an ethnic diversity always open to further inclusion. England and the English have always involved a syncretic community of minorities, then as now. There can always be one more. This is the synthetic secret of English society, not to make it the top nation as Pike argued, but one whose tolerant liberalism is actively inclusive, self-critical and, in what is probably now yesterday's parlance, multicultural (a concept invented in another 'English' settler colony, Canada). English liberalism has been the subject of stringent critique, but it is a marker of its formation that it has very often generated that critique from within, and has actively sought to overcome its own shortcomings. In the twentieth century, the particular construction of Englishness meant that it was responsive to the very different conditions that ensued after the Second World War, and able successfully to negotiate changing conditions, changing peoples. Some will want to challenge this view, many with good reasons, but the testimony in support of it comes in strange ways: take, for example, the Sangatte refugee camp, which sprung up in Northern France at the entrance to the Channel Tunnel. What was astonishing about this was that the camp was full of international migrants who were already within 'fortress Europe', though often still in various forms of illegality. Why though did they want to come to England? Because they thought that in England they would encounter a comparatively greater tolerance and positive reception than elsewhere in Europe, a willingness to accept immigrants of different cultures and religions, to assimilate them to its values without requiring them to destroy their particular cultural identities, to regard them, and to encourage them to regard themselves, as part of the same society. Sangatte was in fact closed down at the insistence of the British government, but looking at it rather differently, it is a strange and bizarre testimony that it came to exist there in the first place – that so many people from all over the world wanted to cross the Channel to live within England's hospitable shores.

The English tolerance of the difference of others within a broad social consensus goes back, perhaps unexpectedly, to the question posed by Thomas Arnold, only outdated in its masculine bias: 'is it too much to ask of good men that they should consent to unite themselves to other good men, without requiring them to subscribe to their own opinions, or to conform to their own ceremonies?' In the nineteenth century, the liberal and even not-so-liberal English were proud that England welcomed refugees, asylum seekers, exiles and immigrants. Today, others still regard it as a comparatively gentle,

240

compassionate and inclusive society, in which, as Ford Madox Hueffer put it (before he anglicized himself into Ford Madox Ford), very different sorts of people 'tolerantly and pleasantly may live together'.[17] The liberal achievement of the nineteenth century was that the ethnicity of Englishness was transformed from a Saxonist doctrine of racial singularity and exclusivity, to become just that.

Notes

Preface

1   W. Lloyd Warner and Paul S. Hunt, *The Social Life of a Modern Community*, Yankee City Series vol. 1 (New Haven: Yale University Press, 1941) 212.

2   Interestingly, the second edition of the OED (1989) still defines 'ethnic' in terms of race ('a group of people differentiated from the rest of the community by racial origins or cultural background'); UNESCO, *The Concept of Race: Results of an Inquiry* (Paris: UNESCO, 1951).

Introduction: Exodus

1   Recent works not cited in subsequent notes include Antony Easthope, *Englishness and National Culture* (London: Routledge, 1999); Judy Giles and Tim Middleton, *Writing Englishness 1800–1950* (London: Routledge, 1995); Jeremy Paxman, *The English* (London: Michael Joseph, 1998); Julian Wolfreys, *Being English: Narratives, Idioms, and Performances of National Identity from Coleridge to Trollope* (Albany: State University of New York Press, 1994).

2   Benedict Anderson, *The Spectre of Comparisons: Nationalism, Southeast Asia, and the World* (London: Verso, 1998).

3   Rupert Brooke, 'The Soldier', *1914 & Other Poems* (London: Sidgwick and Jackson, 1915) 15.

4   Oscar Wilde, *De Profundis* (1905; London: Methuen, 1922) 71–2.

5   Oscar Wilde, 'The Importance of Being Earnest', in *The Works of Oscar Wilde*, vol. 5 (New York: Lamb, 1909) 303.

6   Henry James, *English Hours* (Boston: Houghton Mifflin, 1905) 36.

7   Ibid, 13.

8   Ibid, 37.

9   Although this may suggest an interestingly risqué analogy between the British Empire and women's underwear, Henry James was hardly the person to propose it: the modern girdle was not invented until 1910 by the French designer Paul Poiret.

10 Ralph Waldo Emerson, *English Traits and Representative Men* (London: Oxford University Press, 1923) 10.

11 James, *English Hours*, 37.

12 Ian Watson, 'Victorian England, Colonialism and the Ideology of *Tom Brown's Schooldays*', *Zeitschrift für Anglistik und Amerikanistik* 29:2 (1981): 117–18.

13 Thomas Hughes, *Tom Brown's Schooldays*, ed. F. Sidgwick (London: Sidgwick and Jackson, 1913) 16. Further references will be placed in the text.

14 Eric Richards, *Britannia's Children: Emigration from England, Scotland, Wales and Ireland since 1600* (London: Hambledon and London, 2004).

15 Emerson, *English Traits and Representative Men*, 29.

Chapter 1   Saxonism

1   Ford Madox Hueffer [Ford], *England and the English* (New York: McClure, Phillips, 1907) 259. Cf. Krishnan Kumar, 'English or British', in *The Making of English National Identity* (Cambridge: Cambridge University Press, 2003) 1–17.

2   Linda Colley, *Britons: Forging the Nation, 1707–1837* (New Haven: Yale University Press, 1992) 120–32.

3   As late as 1895, for example, G. A. Henty, in *Wulf the Saxon: A Story of the Norman Conquest*, was writing of 'that admixture of Saxon, Danish, and British races which had come to be known under the general name of English' (London: Blackie and Sons, 1895) v.

4   John Beddoe, *The Races of Britain: A Contribution to the Anthropology of Western Europe* (Bristol: Arrowsmith, 1885); William Z. Ripley, *The Races of Europe: A Sociological Study* (London: Kegan Paul, Trench, Trubner, 1900).

5   William Z. Ripley, *Selected Bibliography of the Anthropology and Ethnography of Europe* (New York: D. Appleton, 1899).

6   Felipe Fernández-Armesto, ed., *The Times Guide to the Peoples of Europe* (London: Times Books, 1994).

7   David Miles, *The Tribes of Britain* (London: Weidenfeld and Nicolson, 2005); Brian Sykes, *The Blood of the Isles* (London: Bantam Press, 2006).

8   Luke Owen Pike, *The English and Their Origin: A Prologue to Authentic English History* (London: Longmans, Green, 1866) 15.

9   Not including those titles followed by the dates of particular historical periods, the Bodleian Library catalogue lists 411 entries for 'History of England', 26 for

'History of Britain', and 3 for 'History of the United Kingdom'. A notable addition to the latter would be Goldwin Smith's slightly differently titled *The United Kingdom: A Political History* (London: Macmillan, 1899).

10 Hugh A. MacDougal, *Racial Myth in English History: Trojans, Teutons, and Anglo-Saxons* (Hanover: University Press of New England, 1982).

11 Stephanie L. Barczewski, *Myth and National Identity in Nineteenth Century Britain: The Legends of King Arthur and Robin Hood* (Oxford: Oxford University Press, 2000).

12 Alfred, King of England, *The Proverbs of Alfred: Re-edited from the Manuscripts*, by the Rev. Walter W. Skeat (Oxford: Clarendon Press, 1907) 2. For Alfred's forms of national life in the eighteenth century, see Kathleen Wilson, *The Island Race: Englishness, Empire and Gender in the Eighteenth Century* (London: Routledge, 2003).

13 Velma Bourgeois Richmond, 'Historical Novels to Teach Anglo-Saxonism', in *Anglo-Saxonism and the Construction of Social Identity*, ed. Allen J. Frantzen and John D. Niles (Gainesville: University Press of Florida, 1997) 183–7.

14 'The Caucasian race has thus, in all ages, and in all varieties of condition in which the different branches of it have been placed, evinced the same great characteristics, marking the existence of some innate and constant constitutional superiority; and yet, in the different branches, subordinate differences appear.... Among these branches, we, Anglo-Saxons ourselves, claim for the Anglo-Saxons the superiority over all the others.' Jacob Abbott, *History of King Alfred of England* (New York: Harper Bros, 1877) 39.

15 Daniel Defoe, 'The True-Born Englishman', lines 334–47, in *Daniel Defoe*, ed. J. T. Boulton (London: Batsford, 1965) 63–4.

16 W. C. Sellar and R. J. Yeatman, *1066 and All That* (New York: E. P. Dutton, 1931) 5–6.

17 'This active general [Hengist]...carried devastation into the most remote corners of Britain; and being chiefly anxious to spread the terror of his arms, he spared neither age, nor sex, nor condition, wherever he marched with his victorious forces. The private and public edifices of the Britons were reduced to ashes: The priests were slaughtered on the altars by those idolatrous ravagers: The bishops and nobility shared the fate of the vulgar: The people, flying to the mountains and deserts, were intercepted and butchered in heaps.... Thus was established, after a violent contest of near a hundred and fifty years, the Heptarchy, or seven Saxon kingdoms, in Britain; and the whole southern part of the island, except Wales and Cornwall [sic], had totally changed its inhabitants, language, customs, and political institutions.... Hence there have been found in history few conquests more ruinous than that of the Saxons; and few revolutions more violent than that which they introduced.' David Hume, *History of England* (London: Printed for A. Millar, 1773) 33–6. On Hume's *History*, see R. J. Smith, *The Gothic Bequest: Medieval Institutions in British*

Thought, 1688–1863 (Cambridge: Cambridge University Press, 1987) 76–83; for eighteenth-century Saxon radicalism, 98–113.

18 E. A. Freeman, *William the Conqueror* (London: Macmillan, 1888) 3.

19 Ian Baucom, *Out of Place* (Princeton: Princeton University Press, 1999).

20 Christopher Hill, 'The Norman Yoke', in *Democracy and the Labour Movement*, ed. J. Saville (London: Lawrence and Wishart, 1954). For the popularity of the Norman Yoke thesis with Southerners after the American Civil War, who made an analogy between the postbellum South and post-Conquest England, see Gregory A. Van-Hoosier-Cary, 'Anglo-Saxon Studies in the Postbellum South', in *Anglo-Saxonism and the Construction of Social Identity*, ed. Allen J. Frantzen and John D. Niles (Gainesville: University Press of Florida, 1997) 157–72.

21 E. A. Freeman, *The History of the Norman Conquest of England: Its Causes and Its Results*, 6 vols. (Oxford: Clarendon Press, 1867).

22 Reginald Horsman, *Race and Manifest Destiny: The Origins of American Racial Anglo-Saxonism* (Cambridge, MA: Harvard University Press, 1981).

23 Tom Paulin, *The Day-Star of Liberty: William Hazlitt's Radical Style* (London: Faber and Faber, 1998) viii, notes Hazlitt's preference for a nativist, 'muscular', plain-speaking 'old English' style.

24 Stuart Gilbert, *An Historical Dissertation concerning the Antiquity of the English Constitution* (Edinburgh: A. Kincaid and J. Brill, 1768) iv, title page.

25 Cornelieus Tacitus, *The Germania of Tacitus with ethnological dissertations and notes by R. G. Latham* (London: Taylor, Walton and Maberly, 1851). Latham's book is discussed at length by Charles Kingsley in *The Roman and the Teuton: A Series of Lectures delivered before the University of Cambridge*, in *The Works of Charles Kingsley*, vol. 10 (London: Macmillan, 1884) 47–57.

26 H. Trevor Colbourn, *The Lamp of Experience: Whig History and the Intellectual Origins of the American Revolution* (Chapel Hill: Published for the Institute of Early American History and Culture at Williamsburg, Va., by University of North Carolina Press, 1965); J. R. Hall, 'Mid-Nineteenth Century American Anglo-Saxonism', in *Anglo-Saxonism and the Construction of Social Identity*, ed. Allen J. Frantzen and John D. Niles (Gainsville: University Press of Florida, 1997) 133.

27 Francis A. March, 'Is There an Anglo-Saxon Language?', *Transactions of the American Philological Association*, 3 (1872) 97.

28 Sharon Turner, *The History of the Anglo-Saxons, Comprising the History of England from the Earliest Period to the Norman Conquest* (1799–1805; London: Longman, Hurst, Rees, Orme and Brown, 1823).

29 Richard Marggraf Turley, 'Nationalism and the Reception of Jacob Grimm's *Deutsche Grammatik* by English-speaking Audiences', *German Life and Letters* 54:3 (2001): 234–52.

30 E. A. Freeman, 'Race and Language', *Historical Essays*, 3rd ser. (London: Macmillan, 1879) 173–230.

31 Thomas Arnold, *Introductory Lectures on Modern History, Delivered in Lent Term, MDCCCXLII with the Inaugural Lecture, Delivered in December MDCCCXLI*, ed. Henry Reed (New York: Appleton, 1847) 45–6.

32 Thomas Carlyle, *Chartism*, in *Sartor Resartus. Lectures on Heroes. Chartism. Past and Present. With the author's latest corrections* (London: Chapman and Hall, 1888) 45. Further references will be cited in the text.

33 John Macculloch, *The Highlands and Western Isles of Scotland, in Letters to Sir Walter Scott*, vol. 4 (London: Longman, Hurst, Rees, Orme, Brown, and Green, 1824) 294.

34 Robert Crawford, *Devolving English Literature* (Oxford: Oxford University Press, 1992).

35 Colin Kidd, *Subverting Scotland's Past: Scottish Whig Historians and the Creation of an Anglo-British Identity, 1689–c.1830* (Cambridge: Cambridge University Press, 1993); 'Teutonist Ethnology and Scottish Nationalist Inhibition, 1780–1880', *Scottish Historical Review* 74.1.197 (1995): 45–68; William Ferguson, *The Identity of the Scottish Nation* (Edinburgh: Edinburgh University Press, 1998).

36 Thomas Carlyle, 'The Nigger Question', in *Critical and Miscellaneous Essays: Collected and Republished*, vol. 7 (1849; London: Chapman and Hall, 1869) 107.

37 Maike Oergel, 'The Redeeming Teuton: Nineteenth-century Notions of the "Germanic" in England and Germany', in *Imagining Nations*, ed. Geoffrey Cubitt (Manchester: Manchester University Press, 1998) 75–91.

38 Thomas Babington Macaulay, *The History of England from the Accession of James II*, 5 vols (London: Longman, Brown, Green, and Longmans, 1849–61); Sir Francis Palgrave, *History of the Anglo-Saxons* (London: John Murray, 1831); *The Rise and Progress of the English Commonwealth* (London: John Murray, 1832); *The History of Normandy and of England* (London: J. W. Parker and Son, 1851–64), in *The Collected Historical Works of Sir Francis Palgrave*, 10 vols (Cambridge: Cambridge University Press, 1919). Cf. Roger Smith, 'European Nationality, Race, and Commonwealth in the Writings of Sir Francis Palgrave, 1788–1861', in *Medieval Europeans*, ed. Alfred P. Smyth (Basingstoke: Macmillan, 1998) 233–53.

39 Palgrave, *Collected Historical Works*, vol. 9, 440. Limitation of space prevent me from being able to do full justice here to the complexity of Palgrave's work.

40 Benjamin Disraeli, *Tancred, or the New Crusade*, Bradenham edition vol. 10 (1847; London: Peter Davis, 1927) 153.

41 Edward Bulwer-Lytton, *Harold: The Last of the Saxon Kings* 3 vols (London: R. Bentley, 1848).

42 John Mitchell Kemble, *The Saxons in England* (London: Longman, Brown, Green, and Longmans, 1849) iii. Further references will be cited in the text.

43 William Stubbs, *Constitutional History of England in its Origin and Development* (Oxford: Clarendon Press, 1874–8); John Richard Green, *A Short History of the*

English People (London: Macmillan, 1874), *The Making of England* (London: Macmillan, 1881); Freeman, *History of the Norman Conquest*.

44 Amédée Thierry, *L'Histoire des Gaulois, depuis les temps les plus reculés jusqu'à l'entière soumission de la Gaule à la domination romaine*, 3 vols (Paris: A. Sautelet, 1828).

45 Freeman, *William the Conqueror*, 198.

46 Samuel Taylor Coleridge, *Marginalia* vol. 1, ed. George Whalley (London: Routledge and Kegan Paul, 1980) 170.

47 Horsman, *Race and Manifest Destiny*, 394. Adaptations of Scott, in plays and children's books particularly, were widespread – see Richmond, 'Historical Novels to Teach Anglo-Saxonism', 178.

48 Michael Banton, *Racial Theories* (Cambridge: Cambridge University Press, 1987) 13; John Sutherland, *The Life of Walter Scott: A Critical Biography* (Oxford: Blackwell, 1995) 229; Andrew Sanders, 'Utter Indifference? The Anglo-Saxons in the Nineteenth Century Novel', in *Literary Appropriations of the Anglo-Saxons from the Thirteenth to the Twentieth Century*, ed. Donald Scragg and Carole Weinberg (Cambridge: Cambridge University Press, 2000) 157–62.

49 Sir Walter Scott, *Ivanhoe*, ed. Ian Duncan (Oxford: Oxford University Press) 27.

50 Kemble, *The Saxons in England*, 21.

Chapter 2 'New Theory of Race: Saxon v. Celt'

1 Richard Hernstein and Charles Murray, *The Bell Curve* (New York: Free Press, 1994); D. Posthuma et al., 'Genetic Contributions to Human Brain Morphology and Intelligence', *Journal of Neuroscience*, October 4, 2006, 26 (40):10235–42.

2 Sir Francis Galton, *English Men of Science: Their Nature and Nurture* (London: Macmillan, 1874).

3 For programmes going on till the 1970s in Canada and Sweden, see Gunnar Broberg and Nils Roll-Hansen, eds, *Eugenics and the Welfare State: Sterilization Policy in Denmark, Sweden, Norway and Finland* (East Lansing: Michigan State University Press, 1996).

4 Stephen G. Alter, *Darwinism and the Linguistic Image* (Baltimore: Johns Hopkins University Press, 1999) 31–2.

5 Sir Francis Palgrave, 'The Conquest and the Conqueror', in *The Collected Historical Works of Sir Francis Palgrave* (Cambridge: Cambridge University Press, 1919), vol. 9, 435 (my emphasis). Even today, you can find the term 'nation' being used for ethnic groups (for example, 'first nations').

6 For the paradoxical logics of nineteenth-century racial theories, see Robert J. C. Young, *Colonial Desire: Hybridity in Theory, Culture and Race* (London: Routledge, 1995).

7   J. S. Mill, *The Collected Works of John Stuart Mill*, ed. J. M. Robson, 33 vols (London: Routledge and Kegan Paul, 1963–91) 23, 397.

8   Peter Mandler, *The English National Character: The History of an Idea from Edmund Burke to Tony Blair* (New Haven: Yale University Press, 2007). Further references will be cited in the text.

9   Mill, 'Of Ethology, or the Science of the Formation of Character', in *A System of Logic, Collected Works*, vol. 8, 861–74.

10 Walter Bagehot, *Physics and Politics* (London: Henry S. King, 1872) 63.

11 George W. Stocking, 'French Anthropology in 1800', *Isis* 55:2, no. 180 (1964) 146.

12 Cf. Silvia Sebastiani, 'Race and National Characters in Eighteenth-Century Scotland: The Polygenetic Discourses of Kames and Pinkerton', *Cromohs*, 8 (2003) 1–14.

13 Robert Chambers, *Vestiges of the Natural History of Creation* (Edinburgh: John Churchill, 1844) 307.

14 James Anthony Froude, *The English in the West Indies, or the Bow of Ulysses* (1888, London: Longmans, Green, 1909) 87.

15 On race and civilization, see Robert J. C. Young, 'Culture and the History of Difference', in *Colonial Desire*, 29–53.

16 Cf. J. Kenny, 'A Question of Blood, Race, and Politics', *Journal of the History of Medicine and Allied Sciences* 61 (2006): 456–91.

17 E. A. Freeman, *Historical Essays*, 3rd ser. (London: Macmillan, 1879) 191.

18 Thomas Arnold, *Introductory Lectures on Modern History, Delivered in Lent Term, MDCCCXLII with the Inaugural Lecture, Delivered in December MDCCCXLI*, ed. Henry Reed (New York: Appleton, 1847) 45.

19 Sophie Gilmartin, *Ancestry and Narrative in Nineteenth-Century British Literature: Blood Relations from Edgeworth to Hardy* (Cambridge: Cambridge University Press, 1998).

20 Thomas Babington Macaulay, *The History of England from the Accession of James II* (London: Longman, Brown, Green, and Longmans, 1849–61), vol. 1, 23–4; vol. 3, 143.

21 Fiona Stafford, *The Last of the Race: The Growth of a Myth from Milton to Darwin* (Oxford: Clarendon Press, 1994).

22 Thomas Nicholas, *The Pedigree of the English People: An Argument, Historical and Scientific, on the Formation and Growth of the Nation; tracing race-admixture in Britain from the earliest times, with especial reference to the incorporation of the Celtic aborigines* (London: Longmans, Green, Reader, 1868).

23 Cited in Harriet Ritvo, *The Animal Estate: The English and Other Creatures in the Victorian Age* (Cambridge, MA: Harvard University Press, 1987) 67.

24 Cf. Alan Macfarlane, *The Savage Wars of Peace* (Oxford: Blackwell, 1997).

25 Charles Darwin, *Darwin's Notebooks on Transmutation of Species*, ed. Gavin de Beer, *Bulletin of the British Museum* (Natural History): Historical Series, vol. 1 (London: British Museum, 1960) 55; Francis Galton, *Hereditary Genius: An Inquiry into its Laws and Consequences* (London: Macmillan, 1869); *Inquiries into Human Faculty and its Development* (London: Macmillan, 1883).

26 On the ideology of the 'mother tongue', see Christopher Hutton, *Linguistics and the Third Reich: Mother-Tongue Fascism, Race and the Science of Language* (London: Routledge, 1999).

27 J. F. Blumenbach, *The Anthropological Treatises of Johann Friedrich Blumenbach*, ed. and trans. T. Bendyshe (1775–95; London: Anthropological Society, 1865).

28 James Cowles Prichard, *The Eastern Origin of the Celtic Nations Proved by a Comparison of Their Dialects with the Sanskrit, Greek, Latin, and Teutonic Languages: Forming a Supplement to Researches into the Physical History of Mankind* (London: J. and A. Arch, 1831) 8.

29 James Cowles Prichard, *Researches into the Physical History of Man*, ed. George W. Stocking (1813; Chicago: University of Chicago Press, 1973).

30 Sir Henry Sumner Maine, *Dissertations on Early Law and Custom* (London: John Murray, 1883) 1.

31 Franz Bopp, *Über das Conjugationssystem der Sanskritsprache in Vergleichung mit Jenem der Griechischen, Lateinischen, Persischen und Germanischen Sprachen* (Frankfurt am Main: Andreäischen, 1816); Hans Aarsleff, *The Study of Language in England, 1780–1860* (Princeton: Princeton University Press, 1967) 133–61; Thomas Preston Peardon, *The Transition in English Historical Writing 1760–1830* (New York: Columbia University Press, 1933).

32 Friedrich von Schlegel, 'On the Indian Language, Literature and Philosophy [*sic*]', in *Aesthetic and Miscellaneous Works*, trans. E. J. Millington (London: George Bell and Sons, 1900) 439.

33 Thomas R. Trautmann, *Aryans and British India* (Berkeley: University of California Press, 1997).

34 Henry Lonsdale, *A Sketch of the Life and Writings of Robert Knox the Anatomist* (London: Macmillan, 1870) 380, cited in Reginald Horsman, *Race and Manifest Destiny: The Origins of American Racial Anglo-Saxonism* (Cambridge, MA: Harvard University Press, 1981) 404. On Disraeli's racial views, see David L. Dinkin, 'The Racial and Political Ideas of Benjamin Disraeli', M.Sc. thesis (University of Bristol, 1981); L. J. Rather, *Reading Wagner: A Study in the History of Ideas* (Baton Rouge: Louisiana State University Press, 1990).

35 Christopher Hutton, 'Race and Language: Ties of "Blood and Speech": Fictive Identity and Empire in the Writings of Henry Maine and Edward Freeman', *Interventions: International Journal of Postcolonial Studies* 2:1 (2000): 52–72.

36 Ernest Renan, *Histoire générale et système comparé des langues sémitiques. Histoire générale des langues sémitiques* (Paris: Benjamin Duprat, 1855). Cf. J. W. Jackson,

'The Aryan and the Semite', *Anthropological Review* 7:27 (1869): 333–65; Ivan Hannaford, *Race: The History of an Idea in the West* (Baltimore: Johns Hopkins University Press, 1996) 253.

37   F. Max Müller, 'Ethnology v. Phonology', in Baron C. C. J. Bunsen, *Outlines of the Philosophy of Universal History* (London: Longman, Brown, Green, and Longmans 1854) 349.

38   John MacCulloch, *The Highlands and Western Isles of Scotland, in Letters to Sir Walter Scott*, vol. 4 (London: Longman, Hurst, Rees, Orme, Brown, and Green, 1824) 263–4.

39   For example, A. H. Sayce, 'Language and Race', *Journal of the Anthropological Institute of Great Britain and Ireland* 5 (1876): 212–21.

40   Robert J. C. Young, 'Race and Language in the Two Saussures', *Philosophies of Race and Ethnicity*, ed. Peter Osborne and Stella Sandford (London: Continuum Books, 2002) 63–78, 183–5.

41   J. Fau, *The Anatomy of the External Forms of Man*, ed. with additions by Robert Knox, MD (London: Hyppolyte Bailliere, 1849) xi. On Knox's links to the phrenologists, and to Walker in particular, see Evelleen Richards, 'The "Moral Anatomy" of Robert Knox: The Interplay Between Biological and Social Thought in Victorian Scientific Naturalism', *Journal of the History of Biology* 22:3 (1989): 392.

42   Alexander Walker, *Physiognomy Founded in Physiology, and Applied to Various Countries, Professions, and Individuals* (London: Smith, Elder, 1834). Charles Bell's *Essays on the Anatomy of Expression in Painting* (London: Longman, Hurst, Rees, and Orme, 1806) reached its seventh edition by 1877. Robert Knox, *A Manual of Artistic Anatomy: For the Use of Sculptors, Painters and Amateurs* (London: Henry Renshaw, 1852), *Great Artists and Great Anatomists: A Biographical and Philosophical Study* (London: J. Van Voorst, 1852).

43   Francis Galton, *Inquiries into the Human Faculty* (London: Macmillan, 1883). On physiognomy, see Mary Cowling, *The Artist as Anthropologist: The Representation of Type and Character in Victorian Art* (Cambridge: Cambridge University Press, 1989), and Lucy Hartley, *Physiognomy and the Meaning of Expression in Nineteenth Century Culture* (Cambridge: Cambridge University Press, 2001).

44   George Jabet, *Notes on Noses* (London: Richard Bentley, 1852) 4, 120.

45   'Physiognomy', *Anthropological Review* 6:21 (1868): 137–54.

46   George Combe, *The Phrenologist's Own Book: A Practical Treatise on Phrenology; with directions for examining heads, and a description of the requisite instruments* (Philadelphia: Kay and Troutman, 1849) 9.

47   Frances E. Kingsley, ed., *Charles Kingsley: His Letters and Memories of His Life* (London: Macmillan, 1904) 175.

48   Roberto Romani, *National Character and Public Spirit in Britain and France, 1750–1914* (Cambridge: Cambridge University Press, 2002) 217.

49 George Combe, *A System of Phrenology*, vol. 1, 5th edn (Edinburgh: Maclachlan, Stewart, 1843) 34–5.

50 Joseph Vimont, *Traité de phrénologie humaine et comparée: accompagné d'un magnifique atlas in-folio de 120 planches*, 5 vols (Paris: J. Ballière, 1832–5).

51 Samuel George Morton, *Crania Americana; Or, A Comparative View of the Skulls of Various Aboriginal Nations of North and South America: To which is Prefixed an Essay on the Varieties of the Human Species* (London: Simpkin, Marshall, 1839).

52 George Combe, appendix, 'Phrenological Remarks on the Relation between the Natural Talents and Dispositions of Nations, and the Development of their Brains', in Morton, *Crania Americana*, 271, 274.

53 Combe, *A System of Phrenology*, vol. 2, 359–61.

54 For the popular continuance of books on phrenology and physiognomy, see, for example, Henry Shipman Drayton, *Indications of Character in the Head and Face* (New York: Fowler and Wells, 1881). On the history of phrenology, see John Van Wyhe, *Phrenology and the Origins of Victorian Scientific Naturalism* (Aldershot: Ashgate, 2004).

55 William Z. Ripley, *The Races of Europe: A Sociological Study* (London: Kegan Paul, Trench, Trubner, 1900) 304–5 (first published in New York in 1899).

56 Anon, *New Exegesis of Shakespeare, Interpretation of his Principal Characters and Plays, on the Principle of Races* (Edinburgh: A. & C. Black, 1859); John William Jackson, *Ethnology and Phrenology as an Aid to the Historian* (London: Trübner, 1863).

57 Romani, *National Character and Public Spirit in Britain and France*; Mandler, *The English National Character*.

58 Immanuel Kant, *Anthropology from a Pragmatic Point of View*, trans. Mary J. Gregor (The Hague: Nijhoff, 1974) 175–82.

59 Hyppolite Taine offered a different and more popular direction with respect to national character. While classifying the English into various types, he then distinguished these by different psychological characteristics (*Notes sur l'Angleterre*, Paris: Hachette, 1871). On foreign Anglophiles, see Ian Buruma, *Voltaire's Coconuts, or Anglomania in Europe* (London: Weindenfeld and Nicolson, 1999).

60 On Chenevix, see Roger Cooter, *The Cultural Meaning of Popular Science: Phrenology and the Organization of Consent in Nineteenth-Century Britain* (Cambridge: Cambridge University Press, 1984) 57–9.

61 Richard Chenevix, *An Essay Upon National Character, Being an Inquiry into some of the Principal Causes which Contribute to Form and Modify the Characters of Nations in the State of Civilisation* (London: James Duncan, 1832) vol. 1, 12–13.

62 Edward Bulwer Lytton, *England and the English*, 2 vols (London: Richard Bentley, 1833); J. S. Mill, 'The English National Character', 1834, *Collected*

Works, vol. 23, 722. Cf. Stefan Collini, 'Anglo-Saxon Attitudes', in *Absent Minds: Intellectuals in Britain* (Oxford: Oxford University Press, 2006) 69–89.

63   Mill, *Collected Works*, vol. 20, 236.
64   Mill, *Collected Works*, vol. 17, 1563. Buckle was poised to make a major statement on the English in his *History of Civilization in England* (London: John W. Parker, 1857–61), but despite completing two volumes, he unfortunately died before he reached the topic of England itself.
65   Mill, *Collected Works*, vol. 24, 973. The best analysis of Mill's relation to Empire is Uday Singh Mehta's *Liberalism and Empire: A Study in Nineteenth-Century British Liberal Thought* (Chicago: University of Chicago Press, 1999). For a defence of Mill's attitudes to race, of the 'they didn't really mean it' school, see Georgios Varouxakis, *Mill on Nationality* (New York: Routledge, 2002).
66   Charles H. Pearson, *National Life and Character: A Forecast* (London: Macmillan, 1893).
67   Anon., 'Colonisation', *Phrenological Journal* 11, n.s.1 (1838): 258.

Chapter 3   Moral and Philosophical Anatomy

1   Robert Knox, *The Races of Men. A Fragment* (London: H. Renshaw, 1850). Further references will be cited in the text.
2   Henry Lonsdale, *A Sketch of the Life and Writing of Robert Knox* (London: Macmillan, 1870) 130, 157; A. W. Beasley, 'The Other Brother: A Brief Account of the Life and Times of Frederick John Knox LRCSEd', *J.R.Coll. Surg.Edinb.*, 46 (2001): 119–23.
3   Obituary of Robert Knox, *Annals of Military and Naval Surgery, and Tropical Medicine and Hygiene* 1 (1863): 367. According to Edward Mussey Hartwell, of Johns Hopkins University, in Knox's day 'many of the early American physicians and anatomists studied at Edinburgh; where, early in this century, there were several extramural private schools of anatomy. Of these, that of Dr Robert Knox was the most famous and frequented. In the winter of 1828–9, he had a class of 505: the largest in Europe.' 'The Study of Anatomy, Historically and Legally Considered', *Journal of Social Science* 13 (1881) 61.
4   Lonsdale, *Life of Robert Knox*, 330.
5   I. Maclaren, 'Robert Knox MD, FRCSEd, FRSEd 1791–1862: The First Conservator of the College Museum', *Journal of the Royal College of Surgeons* 45 (2000): 392–7. Cf. Robert Knox, 'Anatomical Museums: Their Objects and Present Condition', *The Medical Times: A Journal of English and Foreign Medicine, and Miscellany of Medical Affairs* 14 (1846) 307–9, 327–8.

6 Lonsdale, *Life of Robert Knox*, 196; M. H. Kaufman, 'Frederick Knox, Younger Brother and Assistant of Dr Robert Knox: His Contribution to "Knox's Catalogues"', *J.R.Coll.Surg.Edinb.*, 46 (2001): 44–56.

7 Robert Knox, *Memoirs: Chiefly Anatomical and Physiological, read at various times to the Royal Society in Edinburgh, the Medico-Chirurgical, and other societies* (Edinburgh: Rickard, 1837).

8 Rev. of A Manual of Human Anatomy, by Robert Knox, *Medical Times and Gazette: A Journal of Medical Science, Literature, Criticism, and News*, NS, 6, old series, 27 (1853) 121.

9 Knox, 'Slavonian Race', *The Medical Times* 19 (1848) 121; Royal Manchester Institution, 'The Races of Men', by Robert Knox, M.D., F.R.S.E. – ref. M6/1/70/73, date: 26 February–15 March 1847.

10 Robert Knox, 'Lectures on the Races of Men', *The Medical Times* 18 (1848): 97–9, 117–20, 133–4, 147–8, 163–5, 199–201, 231–3, 263–4, 283–5, 299–301, 315–16, 331–2, 365–6; 19 (1848–9): 1–3, 17–18, 33–4, 49–50, 69–70, 121–3, 141–2, 175, 191–3, 247–8, 315–16. The lectures on 'The Races of Men' followed on an earlier lectures series, 'Lectures on the Physiological Anatomy, the Special Physiognomy of Man, and on the Anatomy of Tissues, Morbid and Healthy', which Knox had published in 1845 (*The Medical Times* 12 (1845) 7–9, 21–2, 33–4, 55–7, 74–5, 136–7, 156–7, 239–40, 264–8, 285–6, 299). A considerable part of these lectures had been devoted to distinguishing the races through cranial measurements of various kinds.

11 Westmacott was the son of Sir Richard Westmacott, RA, Britain's most successful official sculptor, who was widely involved in creating public victory monuments in London and elsewhere after the Napoleonic Wars. He illustrated other books by Knox (*A Manual of Artistic Anatomy*, 1852; *Human Anatomy*, 1853).

12 Anon., 'The Late Dr Robert Knox', *The Lancet* (1863): 1, 20.

13 C. Carter Blake, review of *The Life of Robert Knox, the Anatomist*, by Henry Lonsdale, *Journal of Anthropology* 1:3 (1871): 334.

14 Ibid., 336. In his account, Blake passes over the fact that Lyndhurst gave his speech in 1836, fourteen years before Knox published his book. Druitt's role in the story suggests a later date.

15 Robert Knox, *The Races of Men: A Philosophical Enquiry into the Influence of Race over the Destinies of Nations. With Supplementary Chapters* (London: H. Renshaw, 1862).

16 'The Origin of the *Anthropological Review* and its relation to the Anthropological Society', *Anthropological Review* 6:23 (1868): 431–42.

17 Anon., 'Knox on the Celtic Race', *Anthropological Review* 6:21 (1868): 191.

18 Blake, review of *The Life of Robert Knox*, 333.

19 Evelleen Richards, 'The "Moral Anatomy" of Robert Knox: The Interplay Between Biological and Social Thought in Victorian Scientific Naturalism', *Journal of the History of Biology* 22:3 (1989): 376, 410–35.

20 Charles Pickering, *Races of Man and Their Geographical Distribution* (Philadelphia: Printed by C. Sherman, 1848); Charles Hamilton Smith, *Natural History of the Human Species, its Typical Forms, Primaeval Distribution, Filiations, and Migrations* (Edinburgh: Lizars, 1848); W. F. Van Amringe, *An Investigation of the Theories of the Natural History of Man* (New York: Baker and Scribner, 1848); R. G. Latham, *The Natural History of the Varieties of Man* (London: Van Voorst, 1850), *The Ethnology of the British Colonies and Dependencies* (London: Van Voorst, 1851), *The Ethnology of the British Islands* (London: Van Voorst, 1852); Thomas Smyth, *The Unity of the Human Races* (Edinburgh: Johnstone and Hunter, 1851).

21 Léon Poliakov, *The Aryan Myth: A History of Racist and Nationalist Ideas in Europe*, trans. Edmund Howard (London: Chatto, Heinemann for Sussex University Press, 1974); Trautmann, *The Aryans and British India*.

22 'Of race, so far as it means an original and inherent difference in the way of superiority or inferiority between one aggregate of human beings and another, I know nothing.' R. G. Latham, *The Nationalities of Europe* (London: William H. Allen, 1863), vol. 1, vii; A. H. Sayce, *Introduction to the Science of Language* (London: Kegan Paul, 1880), vol. 2, 122.

23 D. W. Mackintosh, 'Comparative Anthropology of England and Wales', *Anthropological Review*, 4:12 (1866): 5.

24 Isaac Taylor, *The Origin of the Aryans: An Account of the Prehistoric Ethnology and Civilisation of Europe* (London: Walter Scott, 1889); Thomas H. Huxley, 'The Aryan Question and Pre-Historic Man' (1890), in *Man's Place in Nature and Other Anthropological Essays* (London: Macmillan, 1894) 276.

25 In his Presidential Address to the Royal Anthropological Institute of 1917, Sir Arthur Keith recalled how Knox, despite his eccentricities and contretemps with the Ethnological Society, was still playing an active part in the Society in 1860. The contrast he then makes with Latham is stark: 'One cannot forget the picture that the late Dr. John Beddoe draws of the old man about the year 1857 ... broken down, disappointed, and poor. He had seen the recognition, the honours, and the pensions pass to those who quietly climbed the rungs of the official ladder, while he was left in his dusty study, forgotten, neglected, and unrequited for his hard and studious labours.' Sir Arthur Keith, 'Presidential Address. How can the Institute best serve the needs of anthropology?' *Journal of the Royal Anthropological Institute of Great Britain and Ireland*, 47 (1917): 17, citing John Beddoe, *Memories of Eighty Years* (Bristol: Arrowsmith, 1910) 248. Thomas Gordon Hake's account of Latham gives an even less flattering picture: *Memoirs of Eighty Years* (London: Richard Bentley, 1892) 208–12. Against

Huxley, Peter Mandler, *The English National Character: The History of an Idea from Edmund Burke to Tony Blair* (New Haven: Yale University Press, 2007) claims that Latham was 'probably the most widely read ethnologist of this period' (p. 85), but gives no evidence of his being the most widely read aside from his oft-reprinted language textbook *The English Language* (1841). The claim certainly conflicts with the view of the DNB that 'his erudite writings remain indigestible despite their historical interest'.

26 For Knox's relation to Darwin, see Richards, 'The "Moral Anatomy" of Robert Knox', 375.

27 Charles Darwin, *The Descent of Man and Selection in Relation to Sex*, 2 vols. (London: John Murray, 1871) 23, 28; Stephen G. Alter, *Darwinism and the Linguistic Image* (Baltimore: Johns Hopkins University Press, 1999) 37. The Darwin Correspondence Online Database records that four of Darwin's correspondents draw his attention to various aspects of Knox's work.

28 Robert Knox, *Great Artists and Great Anatomists: A Biographical and Philosophical Study* (London: J. Van Voorst, 1852) 27. Knox's views on evolution are set out in his articles on Zoology and Palaeontology in the *Lancet*, 1855–6; see also Evelleen Richards, 'A Political Anatomy of Monsters, Hopeful and Otherwise: Teratogeny, Transcendentalism, and Evolutionary Theorizing', *Isis* 85:3 (1994): 377–411.

29 Charles Darwin, *The Origin of Species by means of Natural Selection, or the Preservation of the Favoured Races in the Struggle for Life* (London: John Murray, 1859) 434.

30 Lynn Nyhart, 'The Disciplinary Breakdown of German Morphology, 1870–1900', *Isis* 78 (1987): 365–89.

31 J. Fau, *The Anatomy of the External Forms of Man*, ed. with additions by Robert Knox, MD (London: Hyppolyte Bailliere, 1849) 312.

32 James Hunt, 'Introductory Address on Study of Anthropology', *Anthropological Review* 1:1 (1863): 1–20.

33 The most serious account of Knox's work remains Richards' 'The "Moral Anatomy" of Robert Knox', 373–436. See also Michael B. Biddis, 'The Politics of Anatomy: Dr Robert Knox and Victorian Racism', *Proc. Roy. Soc. Med.*, 69 (1976): 245–50.

34 Lambert Adolphe J. Quetelet, *A Treatise on Man and the Development of his Faculties*, trans. R. Knox (Edinburgh: William and Robert Chambers, 1842) 122–6.

35 Lewis P. Curtis, Jr., *Anglo-Saxons and Celts: A Study of Anti-Irish Prejudices in Victorian England* (Bridgeport: Conference on British Studies at the University of Bridgeport, 1968) 72, notes that even John Beddoe defines the Irish by their 'Africanoid' features.

36 Compare the differences between Knox's *The Races of Man* (1850) and Latham's *The Natural History of the Varieties of Man* (1850), reviewed together in the *Eclectic Review* n.s. 1 (1857): 586–604.

37 John Pinkerton, *A Dissertation on the Origin and Progress of the Scythians or Goths, Being an Introduction to the Ancient and Modern History of Europe* (London: John Nichols, 1787) 69.

38 Pinkerton, *A Dissertation*, 69; Knox, letter to *The Times*, cited by Richard Tuthill Massy, *Analytical Ethnology: The Mixed Tribes in Great Britain and Ireland, and the Political, Physical and Metaphysical Blunderings on the Celt and Saxon Exposed* (London: Balliere, 1855, repr. 1858) 230.

39 See, for example, [W. B. Donne], 'Austria and Hungary', *Edinburgh Review* 90: 181 (1849): 238.

40 Anon., 'Knox on the Celtic Race', *Anthropological Review* 6:21 (1868): 187.

41 Robert Knox, 'Some Observations on the Potato Disease', *The Medical Times* 13 (1846): 272–4.

42 Knox, *Races of Men*, 4–7, 16–17.

43 [Robert Knox], *The Greatest of Our Social Evils. Prostitution, as it now exists in London, Liverpool, Manchester, Glasgow, Edinburgh and Dublin. By a Physician* (London: H. Bailliere, 1857) 197. This book was a translation of works by Gustave Richelot and others, to which Knox, 'the English Editor', added extensive comments, as here.

44 Alan Lester, 'British Settler Discourse and the Circuits of Empire', *History Workshop Journal* 54 (2002): 25–48.

45 Lonsdale, *Life of Robert Knox*, 323.

46 Knox, *Races of Men*, 8. Disraeli's notorious 'all is race' remark in *Tancred* (1847) predates both journal and book versions of *The Races of Men* by at least a year. The language of *Coningsby* (1844) at times resembles that of Knox and Carlyle in its insistence on fact and natural law: 'Do you think that the quiet humdrum persecution of a decorous representative of an English university can crush those who have successively baffled the Pharaohs, Nebuchadnezzar, Rome, and the Feudal ages? The fact is, you cannot destroy a pure race of the Caucasian organisation. It is a physiological fact; a simple law of nature.... No penal laws, no physical torture, can effect that a superior race should be absorbed in an inferior, or be destroyed by it. The mixed persecuting races disappear; the pure persecuted race remains.' Benjamin Disraeli, *Coningsby, or the New Generation*, Bradenham edition vol. 7 (1844; London: Peter Davis, 1927) 263.

47 W. F. Edwards, *Des caractères physiologiques des races humaines, considérés dans leur rapports avec l'histoire, lettre à M. Amédée Thierry, auteur de l'histoire des Gaulois* (Paris: Jeune, 1829).

48 Cited by Claude Blanckaert, 'On the Origins of French Ethnology: William Edwards and the Doctrine of Race', in *Bones, Bodies, Behavior: Essays on*

Biological Anthropology, ed. George W. Stocking, Jr. (Madison: University of Wisconsin Press, 1988) 19.

49 Edward Long, *The History of Jamaica: Or, General Survey of the Antient and Modern State of that Island; with Reflections on its Situation, Settlements, Inhabitants, Climate, Products, Commerce, Laws, and Government*, vol. 2 (London: Lowndes, 1774) 336.

50 Edwards, *Des Caractères Physiologiques des Races Humaines*.

51 Thomas De Quincey, *Confessions of an English Opium-Eater, and Other Writings*, ed. G. Lindop (Oxford: Oxford University Press, 1985) 73. It was only the Mutiny that prompted the English to make serious attempts to understand the caste system.

52 For a detailed analysis of nineteenth-century theories of hybridity, see Robert J. C. Young, *Colonial Desire: Hybridity in Theory, Culture and Race* (London: Routledge, 1995).

53 Edwards, *Des Caractères Physiologiques*, 25–9. See also Alain F. Corcos, 'Colladon of Geneva, a Precursor of Mendel?' *Journal of Heredity* 59:6 (1968): 373–4. George Combe, *The Constitution of Man in Relation to External Objects* (London: Simpkin, Marshall, 1839) also cites Edwards' theory of hybridity and the Colladon mice experiment in Appendices V and VII (102, 105). According to the Advertisement, by this fourth edition (eighth impression) of the popular edition, Combe's book had sold almost 50,000 copies in the UK.

54 Robert Chambers, *Vestiges of the Natural History of Creation* (Edinburgh: John Churchill, 1844) 277; John Crawfurd, 'On the Classification of the Races of Man', *Transactions of the Ethnological Society of London* 1 (1861): 357.

55 Nott and Gliddon, in their *Types of Mankind*, the most influential work of American anthropology of the nineteenth century, cite Edwards' work as the authority for their thesis of the permanence of racial types. Josiah Nott and George R. Gliddon, *Types of Mankind: or, Ethnological Researches, Based upon the Ancient Monuments, Paintings, Sculptures, and Crania of Races, and upon Their Natural, Geographical, Philological, and Biblical History* (London: Trübner, 1854) 93.

56 It is worth noting that Darwin's discussion of hybridism in *The Origin of Species* and *The Descent of Man* did not really contradict the Edwards thesis, because he himself used the idea that there were different degrees of interfertility between different plants and animals. In his discussions of hybridity even Darwin allows analogous evidence from plants and animals, just as the raciologists did, and it was this that appeared to substantiate the distant and proximate races theory of humans. Darwin used this evidence to undermine the distinction between species and varieties. Others, however, invoked the notion of racial 'types' to avoid the problematic term 'species' altogether, and by characterizing types as distant or allied, utilized the idea of species difference, a difference and

distinction of kind rather than merely of degree, while circumventing the
problematic term. Darwin, *The Origin of Species*, 245–78; *The Descent of Man*,
vol. 1, 215–50.

57 Pierre Paul Broca, *On the Phenomena of Hybridity in the Genus Homo*, trans. C.
Carter Blake (1860; London: Anthropological Society, 1864).

58 Peter J. Bowler, *The Mendelian Revolution: The Emergence of Hereditarian Concepts
in Modern Science and Society* (Baltimore: Johns Hopkins University Press, 1989).

59 Sir Arthur Keith, *Nationality and Race* (1919), cited in Poliakov, *The Aryan
Myth*, 52.

60 Nicholas Pevsner, *The Englishness of English Art* (1956; Harmondsworth:
Penguin, 1964) 197.

61 Dagobert Frey, *Englisches Wesen in der bildenden Kunst* (Stuttgart: W.
Kohlhammer, 1942) 11–16. Although Pevsner claims that Frey is 'absolutely
free . . . from any Nazi bias' (p. 10), the latter's emphasis on the connection
between national character and aesthetic style had led him to be 'one of three
leading professors selected by the Nazi high command to validate Poland as a
"Teutonic land" deserving of German invasion and to rewrite Polish history
without Jewish involvement' (www.dictionaryofarthistorians.org/freyd.htm).
Frey was relieved of his post in 1945, but subsequently rehabilitated. On Frey,
see Max Weinreich, *Hitler's Professors: The Part of Scholarship in Germany's Crimes
Against the Jewish People* (New York: Yiddish Scientific Institute, 1946); on
Pevsner, see *Pevsner on Art and Architecture, The Radio Talks*, ed. Stephen
Games (London: Methuen, 2002) xxii–xxvii. Though not as late as Frey, in
1900 the American ethnologist William Ripley was still proclaiming the 'utter
irreconcilability of the Teutons and the so-called Celts' in Britain. William Z.
Ripley, *The Races of Europe: A Sociological Study* (London: Kegan Paul, Trench,
Trubner, 1900) 333.

62 Frey, *Englisches Wesen*, 443.

Chapter 4   *The Times* and Its Celtic Challengers

1 Robert Knox, *The Races of Men. A Fragment* (London: H. Renshaw, 1850) 22–3.

2 Emerson, *English Traits*, 155–6.

3 Leslie Williams, *Daniel O'Connell, the British Press, and the Irish Famine: Killing
Remarks*, ed. William H. A. Williams (Aldershot: Ashgate, 2003) 29.

4 Arthur Irwin Dasent, *John Thadeus Delane, editor of 'The Times': His Life and
Correspondence* (London: John Murray, 1908) vol. 1, 1–4.

5 The Dean of Canterbury [Henry Wace], 'John Thadeus Delane', *Cornhill
Magazine* 152 n.s. (1909): 95.

6   J. M. D. Olmsted, *François Magendie: Pioneer in Experimental Physiology and Scientific Medicine in XIX Century France* (New York: Schuman's, 1944).

7   George Webbe Dasent, *The Prose or [sic] Younger Edda, commonly ascribed to Snorri Sturluson* (London: William Pickering, 1842); on slavery, see Dasent, *Annals of an Eventful Life* (London: Hurst and Blackett, 1870) 1, 57–62. Dasent's translations went on to play a major role in the popularization of Norse literature in Britain.

8   Wace, 'John Thadeus Delane', 93.

9   Williams, '*The Times*, O'Connell and Repeal', in *Daniel O'Connell, the British Press, and the Irish Famine*, 25–46.

10 *The Times*, 6 June 1843: 4.

11 *The Times*, 3 October 1844: 4.

12 *The Spirit of the Nation. Ballads and Songs by the Writers of 'The Nation,' with Music* (Dublin: James Duffy, 1846).

13 *The Times*, 3 January 1844: 4.

14 *The Times*, 31 March 1847: 4.

15 Gwyneth Tyson Roberts, *The Language of the Blue Books: The Perfect Instrument of Empire* (Cardiff: University of Wales Press, 1998).

16 Foster's reports were subsequently collected as *Letters on the Condition of the People of Ireland. Repr. with additions from The Times* (London: Chapman and Hall, 1846; reprinted 1847); Williams, *Daniel O'Connell, the British Press and the Irish Famine*, 102–3.

17 *The Times*, 28 August 1845: 5.

18 *The Times*, 9 October 1847: 4; 15 October 1847: 5. Delane himself, however, organized a collection from *The Times*.

19 *The Times*, 12 December 1848: 4.

20 Mill, *Collected Works*, vol. 24, 981.

21 *The Times*, 12 December 1848: 4.

22 *The Times*, 2 December 1848: 5.

23 *The Times*, 30 October 1846: 4.

24 *The Times*, 12 January 1849: 4.

25 Charles Darwin, *The Descent of Man* (1871; London: John Murray, 1901) 544–5.

26 *The Times*, 31 March 1847: 4.

27 *The Times*, 12 December 1848: 4.

28 Roberto Romani, *National Character and Public Spirit in Britain and France, 1750–1914* (Cambridge: Cambridge University Press, 2002) 224–7.

29 Thomas Babington Macaulay, *The History of England from the Accession of James II* (London: Longman, Brown, Green, and Longmans, 1849–61), vol. 2, 118–19.

30 Linda Colley, *Britons: Forging the Nation, 1707–1837* (New Haven: Yale University Press, 1992).

31 L. Perry Curtis, *Anglo-Saxons and Celts: A Study of Anti-Irish Prejudices in Victorian England* (Bridgeport: Conference On British Studies at University of Bridgeport, 1968); *Apes and Angels: The Irishman in Victorian Caricature* (Newton Abbot: David and Charles, 1971). Curtis has been criticized for generalizing too broadly, ignoring the variety of English attitudes to the Irish, and, above all, overemphasizing the role of race. So Roy Foster, in *Paddy and Mr Punch*, concludes that 'It remains doubtful whether the generalizations of simple racial prejudice against the Irish really apply': R. F. Foster, *Paddy and Mr Punch: Connections in Irish and English History* (London: Allen Lane, 1993) 193. Revisionist historians of the 'they didn't really mean it' school generally cite what Foster describes as Sheridan Gilley's 'brilliant critique of the Curtis thesis'. Gilley, however, is in fact concerned to deny the parallel suggested by contemporary commentators, which Curtis emphasizes, between the situations of the slaves in the United States and the Irish in Britain. Gilley does this by arguing that the cases were simply not comparable, on the unexpected grounds that one racialism was based on truth while the other was invented: 'The most obvious of these differences stem from objective differences of race. Unlike Anglo-Saxons and Celts, Caucasians and Negroes are in fact different races. ... there is a difference between a real physical distinction between races and one largely contrived': Sheridan Gilley, 'English Attitudes to the Irish in England, 1780–1900', in Colin Holmes, ed., *Immigrants and Minorities in British Society* (London: Allen and Unwin 1978) 90–1. In order to disprove English anti-Irish racism, Gilley goes on to suggest that some Anglo-Saxons even found Celtic women 'remarkably attractive' – something that he finds unimaginable with regard to attitudes towards African-American women: 'Though gentleman prefer blondes, it has never been disputed that Celts might be beautiful by looking Celtic, whereas white racism was of such ferocity that the idea that "black is beautiful" is one which Negroes find difficult to accept even now' (p. 92). As for the Irish, if Englishmen such as Froude thought the Irish 'more like tribes of squalid apes than human beings', then Gilley comments helpfully that 'perhaps this was no more than they seemed' (p. 99). This 'brilliant' critique of racialism in anti-Irish prejudice is not one to which some would wish to put their name. Roberto Romani provides the most balanced recent account: 'British Views on Irish National Character, 1800–1846', in *National Character and Public Spirit in Britain and France*, 201–27.

32 James Cowles Prichard, *The Eastern Origin of the Celtic Nations Proved by a Comparison of Their Dialects with the Sanskrit, Greek, Latin, and Teutonic Languages: Forming a Supplement to Researches into the Physical History of Mankind* (London: Sherwood, Gilbert and Piper, 1831); *The Eastern Origin of the Celtic Nations Proved by a Comparison of Their Dialects with the Sanskrit, Greek, Latin,*

and Teutonic Languages: Forming a Supplement to Researches into the Physical History of Mankind, ed. R. G. Latham (London: Houlston and Wright, 1857). Latham himself argued the opposite – that the Indo-European languages were of Scandinavian origin. Cf. H. F. Augstein, 'Aspects of Philology and Racial Theory in Nineteenth-Century Celtism: The Case of James Cowles Prichard', *Journal of European Studies* 28:4 (1998): 355–71.

33   Matthew Arnold still felt it necessary to set straight any misconceptions that the Celtic languages were 'Un-Aryan' in his essay in 1867, 'On the Study of Celtic Literature', in *Lectures and Essays in Criticism*, ed. R. H. Super (Ann Arbor: University of Michigan Press, 1962) 299.

34   John Mackinnon Robertson, *The Saxon and the Celt. A Study in Sociology* (London: University Press, 1897).

35   C. Carter Blake, review of *The Life of Robert Knox, the Anatomist*, by Henry Lonsdale, *Journal of Anthropology* 1:3 (1871): 337. When Knox really is thinking biologically, as in *A Manual of Artistic Anatomy*, he in fact suggests that the races of Europe are to some degree mixed: 'The brain may now be examined, either from above downwards or from below upwards.... Place the brain upon its base as situated in the body, and remove as much as possible the membranes from its convexity. This displays the *convolutions*. In the mixed races of Europe these convolutions are not symmetrical, but they probably are so in the Bosjesman (yellow-skinned African race), and even in the negro. It is possible that the same remark may apply to many pure races of men whether white or black, but it certainly does not apply to the now existing European family of men, which, to a certain extent, is a mixed race.' *A Manual of Human Anatomy: Descriptive, Practical and General* (London: Henry Renshaw, 1853) 537.

36   Howard D. Weinbrot, *Britannia's Issue: The Rise of British Literature from Dryden to Ossian* (Cambridge: Cambridge University Press, 1993).

37   Malcolm Chapman, *The Celts: The Construction of a Myth* (Basingstoke: Macmillan, 1992); Simon James, *The Atlantic Celts: Ancient People or Modern Invention?* (London: British Museum Press, 1999).

38   See Eric Hobsbawm and Terence Ranger, eds, *The Invention of Tradition* (Cambridge: Cambridge University Press, 1983).

39   Thomas Price, *An Essay on the Physiognomy and Physiology of the Present Inhabitants of Britain, with Reference to their Origin, as Goths and Celts: Together with Remarks on the Physiognomical Characteristics of Ireland, and Some of the Neighbouring Continental Nations* (London: Rodwell, 1829) 1–2. Further references will be given in the text.

40   John Beddoe, *Memories of Eighty Years* (Bristol: Arrowsmith, 1910) 247–8.

41   Robert Knox, 'History of the Celtic Race continued', *The Medical Times* 19 (1848–9) 49.

42   George Ellis, *Irish Ethnology Socially and Politically Considered: Embracing a General Outline of the Celtic and Saxon Races: with Practical Inferences* (Dublin: Hoges and Smith, 1852) v.

43   Ibid., 2–3.

44   Thomas Babington Macaulay, 'Minute on Indian Education', *Speeches by Lord Macaulay, with his Minute on Indian Education* (London: Oxford University Press, 1935).

45   'Dr Knox on the Races of Men', *Medical Times* 17:455 (17 June 1848): 114.

46   *The Times*, 7 October 1852: 5.

47   Henry Lonsdale, *A Sketch of the Life and Writing of Robert Knox* (London: Macmillan, 1870) 366.

48   Robert Knox, 'New Theory of Race: Celt *v.* Saxon', *The Lancet* 2 (1857): 218–19.

49   John M'Elheran, 'On the General Development of the Human Frame in an Ethnological Point of View', *New York Journal of Medicine* 2:1 n.s. (1857): 30–50. I have used this spelling of M'Elheran's name; he also appears as McElheran. M'Elheran received a licentiateship from the Edinburgh Royal College of Surgeons in 1845. The licentiateship 'was initially a means for examining country surgeons, but very often it was used as a cheaper method of acquiring a basic medical qualification for those who could not afford to do so at Edinburgh University' (information from Steven Kerr, Assistant Librarian, Royal College of Surgeons of Edinburgh).

50   John M'Elheran, *Celt and Saxon: Address to the British Association on the Ethnology of England . . . Letters to the "Times" and other journals, on the races of Celt and Saxon . . . To which are added the reply of the "Times," and the comments of the leading British and Irish Journals* (Belfast: Read, 1852).

51   John M'Elheran, *The Condition of Women and Children Among the Celtic, Gothic, and Other Nations* (Boston: Patrick Donahoe, 1858) 8.

52   M'Elheran, *The Condition of Women*, 318, 26.

53   *The Times*, 7 October 1852: 4.

54   *The Times*, 7 October 1852: 4–5.

55   Richard Tuthill Massy, *Analytical Ethnology: The Mixed Tribes in Great Britain and Ireland, and the Political, Physical and Metaphysical Blunderings on the Celt and Saxon Exposed* (London: Balliere, 1855; repr. 1858). Further references will be cited in the text. Records of the British Census of 1861 indicate that Tuthill Massy was born in Ireland.

56   *Medical Times* 19 (1848–9): 232–3, 285–6.

57   Tuthill Massy, *Analytical Ethnology*, 145.

58   Samuel George Morton, *Crania Americana; or, A Comparative View of the Skulls of Various Aboriginal Nations of North and South America: To which is prefixed an Essay on the Varieties of the Human Species* (London: Simpkin, Marshall, 1839);

Joseph Bernard Davis and John Thurnam, *Crania Britannica: Delineations and Descriptions of the Skulls of the Aboriginal and Early Inhabitants of the British Isles: With Notices of their Other Remains*, vol. 1 (London: Printed for Subscribers, 1856–65) 238. The review of *Crania Britannica* in the *Anthropological Review* 6:20 (1868): 52–5 argued that its scholarship was already out of date. Cf. John Beddoe, 'On the Stature of the Older Races of England, as Estimated from the Long Bones', *Journal of the Anthropological Institute of Great Britain and Ireland* 17 (1888): 202–10.

59 John Beddoe, *The Races of Britain: A Contribution to the Anthropology of Western Europe* (Bristol: Arrowsmith, 1885) 297.

60 Daniel Mackintosh, 'Comparative Anthropology of England and Wales', *Anthropological Review* 4:12 (1866): 2. Further references will be given in the text.

61 Ibid., 3–8. Though not citing him by name, we can see the degree to which Edwards' theory of hybridity had become generally accepted by this time from Mackintosh's statement affirming the endurance of types even after some inter-blending or crossing of races: 'Among men there would appear to be types which have become sufficiently hardened to resist amalgamation, and even in England many phenomena would seem to indicate that hybridity is followed by extinction or reversion to the original. In some parts, where interblending has occurred to a great extent, we still find distinct types identifiable with those which may be classified in remote and comparatively unmixed districts; and very frequently two or more types may be seen in the same family. In many cases, typical amalgamation does not apparently take place at all, but the children of two parents of distinct types follow or 'favour' the one or other parent, or occasionally some ancestor more or less remote' (p. 7).

62 Ibid., 8. The first Welsh type is represented in Mackintosh's figures 1–4, the second by 7–9, the third by 10 and 11, and the fourth by 15.

63 See, for example, Thomas Wright, *The Celt, the Roman, and the Saxon: A History of the Early Inhabitants of Britain, Down to the Conversion of the Anglo-Saxons to Christianity, Illustrated by the Ancient Remains* (London: Arthur Hall, Virtue, 1852); Pike, *The English and Their Origin*.

64 William Z. Ripley, *The Races of Europe: A Sociological Study* (London: Kegan Paul, Trench, 1900); H. J. Fleure, *The Races of England and Wales; A Survey of Recent Research* (London: Benn Bros, 1923).

65 Beddoe, *The Races of Britain*, 5.

66 Grant Allen, 'Are We Englishmen?' *Fortnightly Review* 34 n.s. (1880): 485. Cf. William Greenslade and Terence Rodgers, *Grant Allen: Literature and Cultural Politics at the Fin-de-Siècle* (Aldershot: Ashgate, 2005).

67 H. H. Risley and E. A. Gait, *Census of India, 1901*, 3 vols (Calcutta: Superintendent of Government Printing, 1903).

68   See James Urry, 'Englishmen, Celts and Iberians: The Ethnographic Survey of the United Kingdom 1892–1899', in *Functionalism Historicized: Essays in British Social Anthropology*, ed. George W. Stocking, Jr. (Madison: University of Wisconsin Press, 1984) 97.

69   T. Rice Holmes, *Ancient Britain and the Invasions of Julius Caesar*. Second impression containing corrections by the author (London: Oxford University Press, 1936) 458.

Chapter 5   Matthew Arnold's Critique of 'Englishism'

1   Matthew Arnold, 'On the Study of Celtic Literature', in *Lectures and Essays in Criticism*, ed. R. H. Super (Ann Arbor: University of Michigan Press, 1962). Further references will be cited in the text.

2   Emerson, *English Traits*, 27–8.

3   Emerson, 'Fate' (1860), cited in Philip L. Nicoloff, *Emerson on Race and History: An Examination of 'English Traits'* (New York: Columbia University Press, 1961) 143.

4   Robert Chambers, *Vestiges of the Natural History of Creation* (London: John Churchill, 1844).

5   Samuel Taylor Coleridge, *On the Constitution of Church and State, According to the Idea of Each*, ed. J. Colmer (London: Routledge and Kegan Paul, 1976). Cf. R. J. Smith, *The Gothic Bequest: Medieval Institutions in British Thought, 1688–1863* (Cambridge: Cambridge University Press, 1987) 153–6.

6   Emerson, *English Traits*, 156.

7   *The Times*, 4 September 1865: 8.

8   Donald MacKay, *Flight from Famine: The Coming of the Irish to Canada* (Toronto: McClelland and Stewart, 1992); Hereward Senior, *The Fenians and Canada* (Toronto: Macmillan, 1978), *The Last Invasion of Canada: The Fenian Raids, 1866–1870* (Toronto: Dundern, 1991).

9   'Transported Fenians,' *The Times*, 22 April 1868: 5. The ship included John Boyle O'Reilly, who eventually escaped to the US in 1869 and then masterminded the dramatic Fenian escape from Fremantle prison in 1876.

10   Emile Burnouf, *La Science des religions* (Paris: Maisonneuve, 1872).

11   Thomas Wright, *The Celt, the Roman, and the Saxon: A History of the Early Inhabitants of Britain, Down to the Conversion of the Anglo-Saxons to Christianity, Illustrated by the Ancient Remains* (London: Arthur Hall, Virtue, 1852).

12   Ernest Renan, *The Poetry of the Celtic Races, and Other Studies*, trans. W. G. Hutchison (1854, London: Scott, 1896).

13   J. W. Jackson, 'Iran and Turan', *Anthropological Review* 6:21 (1868): 125.

14 'The raceless and nationless chaos of the late Roman Empire was a pernicious and fatal condition, a sin against nature. Only one ray of light shone over that degenerate world. It came from the north.' Houston Stewart Chamberlain, *The Foundations of the Nineteenth Century*, trans. John Lees (London: John Lane, Bodley Head, 1911) vol. 1, 320; the exact phrase 'raceless chaos' comes at vol. 1, 527.

15 F. W. Farrar, 'Race in Legislation and Political Economy,' *Anthropological Review* 4:13 (1866): 129, 125.

16 Frederic E. Faverty, *Matthew Arnold, the Ethnologist* (Evanston: Northwestern University Press, 1951) 33, 35.

17 *The Times*, 28 December 1866: 6.

18 Luke Owen Pike, *The English and Their Origin: A Prologue to Authentic English History* (London: Longmans, Green, 1866). According to the genetic archaeologist Bryan Sykes, it was, in the end, Pike who got it right: 'Overall, the genetic structure of [the population of] the Isles is stubbornly Celtic' (*Blood of the Isles*, 287).

19 Thomas Nicholas, *The Pedigree of the English People: An Argument, Historical and Scientific, on the Formation and Growth of the Nation; tracing race-admixture in Britain from the earliest times, with especial reference to the incorporation of the Celtic aborigines* (London: Longmans, Green, Reader, 1868); 'The Origin of the English: Pike *v.* Nicholas', *Anthropological Review* 7:26 (1869): 279–306; 8:28 (1870): 69–85; John Beddoe, *Memories of Eighty Years* (Bristol: Arrowsmith, 1910) 205–13.

20 Pike, *The English and Their Origin*, 6.

21 Ibid., 10; Georges Pouchet, *The Plurality of the Human Race*, trans. H. J. C. Beavan (London: Published for the Anthropological Society, by Longman, Green, Longman and Roberts, 1864).

22 Pierre Paul Broca, *On the Phenomena of Hybridity in the Genus Homo* (1860), trans. and ed. C. Carter Blake (London: Published for the Anthropological Society, by Longman, Green, Longman and Roberts, 1864) x, 16–24.

23 Broca, *On the Phenomena of Hybridity*, 22. Broca had developed the full critique of Knox, establishing the hybridity of the French, in his 'Mémoire sur l'Ethnologie de la France', in *Mémoires de la société anthropologie de Paris* 1 (1860) 1–57.

24 Herbert Spencer, 'The Comparative Psychology of Man', *Mind* 1:1 (1876): 13; Rudyard Kipling, 'England and the English', in *A Book of Words* (London: Macmillan, 1928) 180.

25 Pike, *The English and Their Origin*, 246.

26 Nicholas, *The Pedigree of the English People*, v, vii.

27 G. M. Trevelyan, *The Mingling of the Races, being Book One of 'History of England'* (London: Longmans, Green, 1934).

28 Matthew Arnold, *Culture and Anarchy, with Friendship's Garland and Some Literary Essays*, ed. R. H. Super (Ann Arbor: University of Michigan Press, 1965) 163–75. For a detailed analysis of *Culture and Anarchy* from an ethnographic perspective, see Young, *Colonial Desire*, 55–62.

29 See, for example, John Wilson, *A Lecture on the Israelitish Origin of the Anglo-Saxons* (London: Hatchard, 1864); Rev. Robert Douglas, *God and Greater Britain: The British Race from the Twentieth Century B.C. to the Twentieth Century A.D.* (London: James Nisbet, 1902). For a comprehensive history of the British Israelites in this period, see Eric Michael Reisenauer, *British-Israel: Racial Identity in Imperial Britain, 1870–1920*, dissertation, University of Chicago, 1997.

30 Nicholas, *The Pedigree of the English People*, 525–6, 529; J. W. Jackson, 'The Race Question in Ireland', *Anthropological Review* 7:24 (1869): 75.

31 *The Times*, 6 September 1866: 5.

32 *The Times*, 8 September 1866: 8.

33 Arnold, 'Celtic Literature', 392–3.

34 C. Carter Blake, 'On the Historical Anthropology of Western Europe', *Anthropological Review* 4:13 (1866) 159.

35 *The Times*, 25 January 1847: 4.

36 *The Times*, 27 September 1857: 6.

37 Anon., 'The Teuto-Celtic and Slavo-Sarmatian Races', *Anthropological Review* 4:12 (1866): 64.

38 J. W. Jackson, *Ethnology and Phrenology as an Aid to the Historian* (London: Trübner, 1863).

39 Coleridge, *On the Constitution of Church and State*, 24, 31.

40 Coleridge, 'Manuscript Fragment on the Catholic Question', 1821, in *On the Constitution of Church and State*, 227; *On the Constitution of Church and State*, 85.

41 Thomas Arnold, *Principles of Church Reform*, 3rd edn (London: Fellowes, 1833) iii–iv. Further references will be cited in the text.

42 Tod E. Jones, *The Broad Church: A Biography of a Movement* (Lanham, MD: Lexington Books, 2003).

43 Allen J. Frantzen, 'Bede and Bawdy Bale', in *Anglo-Saxonism and the Construction of Social Identity*, ed. Allen J. Frantzen and John D. Niles (Gainesville: University Press of Florida, 1997) 30.

44 John Wolffe, *God and Greater Britain: Religion and National Life in Britain and Ireland 1843–1945* (London: Routledge, 1994) 187.

45 Ibid., 162–75.

46 Frances E. Kingsley, ed., *Charles Kingsley, His Letters and Memories of his Life* (London: Macmillan, 1904) 264. Charles Kingsley, 'The Roman and the Teuton: A Series of Lectures delivered before the University of Cambridge', new edn with preface, by Prof. F. Max Müller, *The Works of Charles Kingsley* vol. 10 (London: Macmillan, 1880–5).

47 On the role of law, see Robert Colls, *The Identity of England* (Oxford: Oxford University Press, 2002) 13–33; Diane Kirkby and Catharine Coleborne, eds, *Law, History, Colonialism: The Reach of Empire* (Manchester: Manchester University Press, 2001).

48 Kingsley, 'The Roman and the Teuton', 114–15.

49 Ibid., 214, 102.

50 Roger Smith, 'European Nationality, Race, and Commonwealth in the Writings of Sir Francis Palgrave, 1788–1861', in *Medieval Europeans*, ed. Alfred P. Smyth (Basingstoke: Macmillan, 1998) 233.

51 Emerson, *English Traits*, 39.

52 Kingsley, *Charles Kingsley*, 352.

53 James A. Murrray, ed., *A New English Dictionary on Historical Principles: Founded Mainly on the Materials Collected by the Philological Society* (Oxford: Clarendon Press, 1888–1928).

54 Richard Chenevix Trench, *On Some Deficiencies in Our English Dictionaries*, 2nd edn (London: John W. Parker, 1860) 6.

55 John Willinsky, *Empire of Words: The Reign of the OED* (Princeton: Princeton University Press, 1994).

56 In addition to those cited at the end of chapter 4, see, for example, W. C. Mackenzie, *The Races of Ireland and Scotland* (Paisley: Alexander Gardner, 1916).

57 'The British Race-Types of To-day,' *The Times*, 11 October 1887: 13; 25 October 1887: 4.

58 William Cunningham, *Alien Immigrants to England* (London: Swan, 1897) 260, 270.

59 George Eliot, *Impressions of Theophrastus Such. Essays and Leaves from a Notebook* (Edinburgh: William Blackwood, n.d.) 186.

Chapter 6   'A Vaster England': The Anglo-Saxon

1 Anon., 'Knox on the Saxon Race', *Anthropological Review* 6:22 (1868): 257–8.

2 'Knox on the Saxon Race', 260; William Maccall, 'The Fabulous Anglo-Saxon', *National Reformer* 7:8 n.s (1866): 122–4.

3 Matthew Arnold, 'On the Study of Celtic Literature', in *Lectures and Essays in Criticism*, ed. R. H. Super (Ann Arbor: University of Michigan Press, 1962) 395. J. R. Marriott's *The Making of England: An Introductory Lecture* (Oxford: Holywell Press, 1901) offers a useful contemporary view of the end of the Saxonist era in English historiography.

4 Sidney Whitman, *Teuton Studies* (London: Chapman and Hall, 1895).

5 Kingsley, *Westward Ho!*, in *The Works of Charles Kingsley* vol. 6 (London: Macmillan, 1880–5) 591.

6 Sir Francis Palgrave, *The Collected Historical Works of Sir Francis Palgrave* (Cambridge: Cambridge University Press, 1919) vol. 4, 167.

7 Daniel Mackintosh, 'Comparative Anthropology of England and Wales', *Anthropological Review* 4:12 (1866): 17.

8 *The Times*, 12 July 1848: 5.

9 This contrasts with Baucom's *Out of Place*, where the English are identified with England.

10 The only British user of 'Anglo-Saxon' with reference to people cited by OED in this period is the General, and liberal politician, Thomas Perronet Thompson.

11 *The Times*, 29 May 1840: 5.

12 For example, *The Times*, 20 October 1842: 5: 'Lord Durham . . . ascribed Canadian evils to the existence of a bitter conflict of races. . . . The Anglo-Saxon race, according to him, was fated to rule, – the French to wane and recede before it.' On Mexico and the Republic of Texas, see, for example, *The Times*, 18 May 1842: 5.

13 *The Times*, 27 May 1844: 4.

14 *The Times*, 7 October 1852: 5. Compare *The* Times, 2 December 1848: 5, cited in chapter 3.

15 Later versions of *The Anglo-Saxon* include W. T. Stead's *Review of Reviews* (1890–1936), which was supported by Cecil Rhodes, and *The Anglo-Saxon Review* (1899–1901), edited by Lady Randolph Spencer Churchill.

16 James Orton, *The Proverbialist and Poet* (Philadelphia: E. H. Butler, 1851).

17 'Prospectus', *Anglo-Saxon Magazine* 1 (1849): 3–11.

18 *Anglo-Saxon Magazine* 1 (1849): 9–10.

19 Thomas Nicholas, *The Pedigree of the English People: An Argument, Historical and Scientific, on the Formation and Growth of the Nation; tracing race-admixture in Britain from the earliest times, with especial reference to the incorporation of the Celtic aborigines* (London: Longmans, Green, Reader, 1868) 554.

20 Benjamin Disraeli, 'Speech at the Crystal Palace', 24 June 1872, reprinted in C. C. Eldridge, *Disraeli and the Rise of a New Imperialism* (Cardiff: University of Wales Press, 1996) 88.

21 Catherine Hall, *Civilizing Subjects: Metropole and Colony in the English Imagination 1830–1867* (Chicago: University of Chicago Press, 2002).

22 Edward Wakefield, *A View of the Art of Colonization* (London: John W. Parker, 1849); Eric Richards, *Britannia's Children: Emigration from England, Scotland, Wales and Ireland since 1600* (London: Hambledon and London, 2004); Carl Bridge and Kent Fedorowich, *The British World: Diaspora, Culture and Identity* (London: Frank Cass, 2003).

23 By 1844, the United States was receiving 60 per cent of British emigrants. See Richards, *Britannia's Children*, 122.

24 The total number during the classic period of emigration (1815–1930) has been estimated at 18,700,000 (ibid., 6).

25 *The Times*, 3 June 1847: 4.

26 *The Times*, 14 June 1847: 4.

27 Richard Gott, 'Little Englanders', in *Patriotism: The Making and Unmaking of British National Identity*, ed. Raphael Samuel, vol. 1 (London: Routledge, 1989) 90–102.

28 George Lamming, *In the Castle of My Skin* (1953; Harlow: Longman, 1986) 29.

29 Goldwin Smith, *The Empire: A Series of Letters Published in 'The Daily News' 1862, 1863* (Oxford: John Henry and James Parker, 1863) viii.

30 Ibid., 6.

31 Ibid., 8, 9, 35.

32 *Spectator*, 22 April 1871: 467, cited in OED.

Chapter 7   'England Round the World'

1 F. Max Müller, *Lectures on the Science of Language: delivered at the Royal Institution of Great Britain in April, May, & June 1861* (London: Longmans, Green, 1861). Charles Wentworth Dilke, *Greater Britain: A Record of Travel in English-Speaking Countries* (1868; 8th edn, London: Macmillan, 1888) 273. Further references will generally be cited in the text.

2 Niall Fergusson, *Empire: How Britain Made the Modern World* (London: Allen Lane, 2003).

3 James L. Bryce, *The Races of the Old World: A Manual of Ethnology* (1863; London: John Murray, 1869) 308.

4 Robert Knox, *The Races of Men: A Philosophical Enquiry into the Influence of Race over the Destinies of Nations, with Supplementary Chapters* (London: H. Renshaw, 1862).

5 Knox, *The Races of Men*, 72–3.

6 R. G. Latham, *Man and His Migrations* (London: John Van Voorst, 1851) 41–4.

7 Henry Lonsdale, *A Sketch of the Life and Writing of Robert Knox* (London: Macmillan, 1870) 378.

8 Dilke, *Greater Britain*, 217–18.

9 Charles Lyell, *Principles of Geology: Being an Attempt to Explain the Former Changes of the Earth's Surface, by Reference to Causes Now in Operation* (London: John Murray, 1833) vol. 3, 31.

10 Lyell, *Principles of Geology*, 3rd edn (London: John Murray, 1834) vol. 3, 89–90.

11 Dilke, *Greater Britain*, 217. Similarly, though he does not advocate empire in its imperialist sense, he makes it clear at the same time that he sees no moral issues involved in terms of imperial annexation – Dilke calmly discusses the question of whether it would be worth annexing China and Japan – only economic ones.

12 James Cowles Prichard, *The Natural History of Man; Comprising Inquiries into the Modifying Influence of Physical and Moral Agencies on the Different Tribes of the Human Families* (London: Baillière, 1843) 19. Ironically, in view of Farrar's remarks cited earlier, this was exactly parallel to the contemporary definition in Mexico of the *mestizo* as the new *rasa cosmica* by Vasconcelos and others. See Robert J. C. Young, 'Gilberto Freyre and the Lusotropical Atlantic', in *Terras e gentes. Ano 2000 ANAIS*, Proceedings of the VII congresso Abralic (Associação Brasileira de Literatura Comparada, Universidade Federal da Bahia, Brazil), reprinted in *Unisa Latin American Report* 22:1–2 (2006): 5–21. Following Prichard, John Crawfurd continued to argue that all races were intra-fertile; however, he still adhered to Edwards' thesis of reversion to type after a few generations, so his work did not really offer any significant alternative to the Edwards thesis. John Crawfurd, 'On the Classification of the Races of Man', *Transactions of the Ethnological Society of London* 1 (1861): 354–78.

13 Ibid, 530, 551, 542, 530. In general, Dilke is quite sympathetic to the Indians, and complains at the British treatment of them – that though they may be fellow-subjects of the English 'they are in practice not yet treated as our fellow-men'. Ibid., 552. The bulk of J. S. Mill's enthusiastic letter to Dilke, written after reading *Greater Britain* in 1869, concerns his discussion of India (Mill, *Collected Works*, vol. 17, 1559–63).

14 Eleanor Bulley, *Great Britain for Little Britons* (London: Wells, Gardner, 1881; 6th edn by 1904), which bears a dedication 'to all English-speaking children'. See Velma Bourgeois Richmond, 'Historical Novels to Teach Anglo-Saxon-ism', in in *Literary Appropriations of the Anglo-Saxons from the Thirteenth to the Twentieth Century*, ed. Donald Scragg and Carole Weinberg (Cambridge: Cambridge University Press, 2000) 175.

15 C. A. Middleton Smith (1879–1951) was also the author of *The British in China and Far Eastern Trade* (London: Constable, 1920).

16 Madame de Staël, *An Extraordinary Woman: Selected Writings of Germaine de Staël*, trans. Vivian Folkenflik (New York: Columbia University Press, 1987) 376.

17 Eric Richards, *Britannia's Children: Emigration from England, Scotland, Wales and Ireland since 1600* (London: Hambledon and London, 2004) 175; Karl Marx

and Friedrich Engels, *Manifesto of the Communist Party* (1848; Moscow: Progress Publishers, 1952) 46.

18 J. A. Mangan, ed., *The Cultural Bond: Sport, Empire, Society* (London: Frank Cass, 1992).

19 Henry M. Field, *History of the Atlantic Telegraph* (New York: Charles Scribner, 1866) 364; Anon., *The Atlantic Telegraph: Its History* (London: Bacon 1866).

20 John Ruskin, 'Inaugural Lecture', in *The Works of John Ruskin*, ed. E. T. Cook and Alexander Wedderburn (London: George Allen, 1903–12) vol. 20, 41–3.

21 Cecil Rhodes, *The Last Will and Testament of Cecil Rhodes* (London: 'Review of Reviews' Office, 1902) 58.

22 Rhodes, *Last Will and Testament*, 125; Felix Gross, *Rhodes of Africa* (London: Cassell, 1956) 160–1.

23 *The Rhodes Trust* (Oxford: Rhodes House, 1996).

24 Rhodes, *Last Will and Testament*, 59.

25 Ibid, 102.

26 J. R. Seeley, *The Expansion of England. Two Courses of Lectures* (1883; London: Macmillan, 1897). Further references will be cited in the text. Karl Radek, 'Address, Second Session Sept. 2, 1920', *The Communist International in Lenin's Time. To See the Dawn. Baku, 1920 – First Congress of the Peoples of the East*, ed. John Riddell (New York: Pathfinder Press, 1993) 90–1.

27 John Kendle, *Federal Britain: A History* (London: Routledge, 1997).

28 Edward A. Freeman, *History of Federal Government from the Foundation of the Achaian League to the Disruption of the United States*, vol. 1: *General Introduction, History of the Greek Federations* (London: Macmillan, 1863).

29 Edward A. Freeman, *Greater Greece and Greater Britain, and, George Washington, The Expander of England. Two Lectures* (London: Macmillan, 1886) 90–1. Cf. C. P. Lucas, *Greater Rome amd Greater Britain* (Oxford: Clarendon Press, 1912).

30 Christopher Hutton, 'Race and Language: Ties of "Blood and Speech", Fictive Identity and Empire in the Writings of Henry Maine and Edward Freeman', *Interventions: International Journal of Postcolonial Studies* 2:1 (2000): 64–8.

31 J. A. Froude, *Oceana, or England and Her Colonies* (London: Longmans, Green, 1886) 12. Further references will be cited in the text. On Froude's imperialism, see Thomas W. Thompson, *James Anthony Froude on Nation and Empire: A Study in Victorian Racialism* (New York: Garland, 1987).

32 Both Carlyle and Froude compared the Irish to monkeys before Kingsley. 'The inhabitants', Froude remarked in 1841, describing the road from Bantry to Killarney, 'seemed more like tribes of squalid apes than human beings'. See 'A Tour in Ireland', in Waldo Hilary Dunn, *James Anthony Froude, A Biography* (Oxford: Clarendon Press, 1961) vol. 1, 69. Indeed, it may well have been

Froude who suggested the idea to Kingsley – they were travelling together when Kingsley sent his ubiquitously quoted comment in a letter to Froude's sister in July 1860.

33 J. A. Froude, *The English in the West Indies, or the Bow of Ulysses* (1887; London: London, Longmans, Green, 1909) 43.

34 J. A. Froude, *Two Lectures on South Africa, Delivered before the Philosophical Institute, Edinburgh Jan 6 & 9, 1880* (London: Longmans, Green, 1880) 13.

35 J. A. Froude, 'England and Her Colonies', in *Short Studies on Great Subjects*, 2nd ser. (New York: Scribner, 1871) 158–9.

36 For a modern historical delineation, see David Cannadine, *Ornamentalism: How the British Saw Their Empire* (London: Allen Lane, 2001).

37 J. A. Froude, 'A Fortnight in Kerry. Part I', in *Short Studies on Great Subjects*, 2nd ser., 178.

38 John Mackinnon Robertson, *The Saxon and the Celt. A Study in Sociology* (London: University Press, 1897) 294.

39 Froude, 'A Tour in Ireland', vol. 1, 70.

40 Froude, 'England and Her Colonies', 152.

41 Ibid., 150.

42 Roger Scruton, *England: An Elegy* (London: Chatto and Windus, 2000) 32.

43 Froude, *Oceana*, 84–5, 86, 88, 92–3, 103, 105, 112–13, 156, 188.

44 Ford Madox Hueffer [Ford], *England and the English. An Interpretation* (New York: McLure, Phillips, 1907) 254.

45 J. A. Froude, *The English in the West Indies*. Cf. Simon Gikandi, *Maps of Englishness: Writing Identity in the Culture of Colonialism* (New York: Columbia University Press) 84–118.

46 Ibid., 2–4.

47 John R. Dos Passos, *The Anglo-Saxon Century and the Unification of the English-Speaking People* (New York: G. P. Putnam's sons, 1903); Stuart Anderson, *Race and Rapprochement: Anglo-Saxonism and Anglo-American Relations, 1895–1904* (London: Associated University Presses, 1981); Paul A. Kramer, 'Empires, Exceptions and Anglo-Saxons: Race and Rule Between the British and United States Empires, 1880–1920', *Journal of American History* 88:4 (2002): 1315–53.

48 Emerson, *English Traits*, 20.

49 See, for example, Rosinka Chaudhuri, *Gentlemen Poets in Colonial Bengal: Emergent Nationalism and the Orientalist Project* (Calcutta: Seagull Books, 2002); Daniel Coleman, *White Civility: The Literary Project of English Canada* (Toronto: University of Toronto Press, 2006); Andrew Hassam, *Through Australian Eyes: Colonial Perceptions of Imperial Britain* (Carlton South: Melbourne University Press, 2000); Roslyn Russell, *Literary Links: Celebrating the Literary Relationship Between Australia and Britain* (Sydney: Allen and Unwin, 1997).

With the exception of India, all parts of the Empire treated in H. E. Marshall's *Our Empire Story* (London: T. C. & E. C. Jack, 1908) are illustrated with verses written by local authors.

50 Douglas B. Sladen, ed., *Australian Ballads and Rhymes: Poems Inspired by Life and Scenery in Australia and New Zealand* (London: Walter Scott, 1888) v–vi.

51 Goldwin Smith, *The Schism in the Anglo-Saxon Race: An Address Delivered before the Canadian Club of New York* (New York: American News, 1887).

52 Gauri Viswanathan, *Masks of Conquest: Literary Study and British Rule in India* (London: Faber, 1990).

53 Carlyle, *On Heroes and Hero Worship, and The Heroic in History* (1841), in *Sartor Resartus. Lectures on Heroes. Chartism. Past and Present* (London: Chapman and Hall, 1888) 269–70.

54 Krystyna Kujawińska and John M. Mercer, *The Globalization of Shakespeare in the Nineteenth Century* (Lewiston, NY: Edwin Mellen Press, 2003); Kim C. Sturgess, *Shakespeare and the American Nation* (Cambridge: Cambridge University Press, 2004).

55 Patrick F. McDevitt, *May the Best Man Win: Sport, Masculinity, and Nationalism in Great Britain and the Empire, 1880–1935* (New York: Palgrave, 2004).

56 Rudyard Kipling, *Rudyard Kipling's Verse. Definitive Edition* (London: Hodder and Stoughton, 1949) 221.

Chapter 8   Englishness: England and Nowhere

1 J. R. Seeley, *The Expansion of England. Two Courses of Lectures* (1883; London: Macmillan, 1897) 86.

2 Arthur Conan Doyle, *The White Company* (London: Smith Elder, 1891). Cf. H. Clive Barnard, ed., *The Expansion of the Anglo-Saxon Nations: A Short History of the British Empire and the United States* (London: A. & C. Black, 1920).

3 Domestic English nationalism, such as it was, is best analysed by Krishnan Kumar, *The Making of English National Identity* (Cambridge: Cambridge University Press, 2003).

4 J. H. Curle, *The Shadow-Show* (London: Methuen, 1912) 105.

5 T. S. Eliot, *Notes Towards A Definition of Culture* (London: Faber and Faber, 1948) 53.

6 John Barrell, *English Literature in History 1730–80: An Equal, Wide Survey* (London: Hutchinson, 1983) 207.

7 Houston Stewart Chamberlain, *Die Grundlagen des neunzehnten Jahrhunderts*, 2 vols (Munich: F. Bruckmann, 1899).

8　See Paul B. Rich, *Race and Empire in British Politics* (Cambridge: Cambridge University Press, 1996); Niall Ferguson, *Empire: How Britain Made the Modern World* (London: Allen Lane, 2003) 240 ff.

9　M. Ollivier, ed., *The Colonial and Imperial Conferences from 1887 to 1939* (Ottawa : E. Cloutier, 1954).

10　Paul B. Rich, *Race and Empire in British Politics* (New York: Cambridge University Press, 1986) 69.

11　www.anglosphereinstitute.com.

12　Winston S. Churchill, *History of the English-Speaking Peoples*, 4 vols (London: Cassell, 1951–6).

13　Jack Lindsay, *England, My England: A Pageant of the English People* (London: Fore Publications, 1939) 3.

14　Perry Anderson, 'Components of the National Culture', in Alexander Cockburn and Robin Blackburn, eds, *Student Power* (London: Penguin, 1969) 269–76.

15　T. S. Eliot, *Little Gidding* (London: Faber and Faber, 1942) 9.

16　Nirad Chaudhuri, *Autobiography of an Unknown Indian* (New York: Macmillan, 1951) 99. Chaudhuri recorded his experiences of his first visit to England, at the age of 57, in *A Passage to England* (London: Macmillan, 1959).

17　Ford Madox Hueffer [Ford], *England and the English* (New York: McLure, Phillips, 1907) 318.

Index